PETER DORMER

the new ceramics
trends+traditions

REVISED EDITION

with 261 illustrations, 95 in colour

THAMES AND HUDSON

Illustration Acknowledgments

Numerals indicate Plate Numbers unless otherwise specified
Agnalt, Terje 104; Crafts Council, London 11, 16, 18, 42, 46, 52, 61, 77, 156–7;
Crafts Magazine 139; Cripps, David p. 193, p. 195 (right); 1, 19, 33, 37, 76, 78, 93,
114, 155, 178, 183, 207, 213, 220; Dean Powell, Andrew 69–70; Dobbie, Ian 18, 42,
52, 77; Ficdencks, Roger 105; Frisse, Courtney 111, 133 (Everson Museum of Art);
Garth Clark Gallery, New York 36, 38, 39, 54–5, 69–70, 73, 116, 120, 124, 126, 137,
140, 143, 147, 152, 161–2, 181–2, 188; Gerritsen, Rene 210–11; Grummer, Frans
203; Hancock, Grant 98; Helen Drutt Gallery, Philadelphia 7, 24–6, 57–8, 67–8,
82–5, 101, 107–9, 134, 148–50; Hill, Tim 27, 56, 117, 122, 142, 177; Katz, Louis 205;
Knispel, Andreas 145; Kreitzer, Caryn/Archon 209; Myers, Steve 54–5, 148–50;
Nixon, Martin 176; Patterson, Darryl/Archon p. 199; Renwick Gallery, Washington
D.C. 59, 127, 179, 192; Rose, Bruce 143; Schnebeli, Heini 167; Schopplein, Joe 36,
199–201; Stedelijk Museum, Amsterdam 10, 64–6, 71–2, 118–19, 166; Stillings,
Jamey 9, 57–8; Storey, John 97; Tate Gallery, London p. 117 (right); Teigens
Fotoatelier 144; Tosch, Randall 7; University of Iowa Museum of Art 7, 14, 53; Van
den Kruis, Peer p. 195 (left); 206, 208, 212, 214–16, 221; Victoria and Albert
Museum, London p. 114 (left and right), p. 117 (left), p. 121 (left); Ward, David
86–9, 103; Webster, Eric 11; Wilson, Bengt 193; Wright, Roger 22, 32;
Württembergisches Landesmuseum, Stuttgart 3, 8, 123

*British Library Cataloguing-in-Publication Data
A catalogue record for this book is available from the British Library*

ISBN 0-500-27775-3

Printed and bound in Singapore

CONTENTS

INTRODUCTION Alison Britton   7

1 THE NEW ROLE OF THE POTTER   11
The Contemporary Pot   12
The American Century   19
Familiar Forms   24

2 POTTERY FORM   31
Matter over Mind   33
The Studio Pot   35
Neurological Findings   37
Mind over Matter   40
Bridging Disciplines   47

3 THE PAINTED POT   113
Decorated versus Decorative   120
High Art, Low Art   123

4 UNFAMILIAR FORMS   193
The Sculptural Ambitions of Potters   194

Biographies   217
Galleries and Museums   226
Exhibitions   228
Publications   230
Index   231

EDITORIAL ADVISERS

Alison Britton
British potter and writer on the applied arts

Garth Clark
American writer and ceramics historian,
director and owner of the Garth Clark Gallery, Los Angeles
and the Garth Clark Gallery, New York

Helen Williams English Drutt
Owner and director of the Helen Drutt Gallery, Philadelphia

Peder Rasmussen
Danish ceramist

Special acknowledgments

I wish to thank the following people and organizations for their considerable help:
Patrick Johnson, Italian-based critic; Annemie Verbeek-Boissevain, owner and director of
the Galerie De Witte Voet, Amsterdam; Professor Fredrik Wildhagen, design historian,
National College of Art and Design, Oslo; David Williams and his staff at the Crafts
Board of the Australia Council; Barbara Perry, Curator of Ceramics, Everson Museum of
Art, Syracuse, New York; the University of Iowa Museum of Art; Joan Mannheimer; staff
of the Renwick Gallery, the Smithsonian Institution, Washington, D.C; the Stedelijk
Museum, Amsterdam; Dr E. Klinge, Hetjens Museum, Düsseldorf; Hans-Ulrich Roller and
Heribert Meurer of the Württembergisches Landesmuseum, Stuttgart; *Crafts Magazine*,
and the Crafts Council of England and Wales. Notwithstanding the inestimable
guidance given by these individuals and my editorial advisers, the responsibility for the
final choice of material rests with me.

INTRODUCTION
Alison Britton

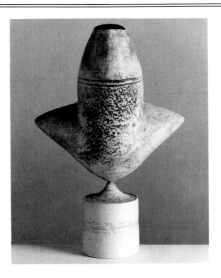

Form. Hans Coper. Stoneware.
h. 16cm. UK, 1972

There is prose and there is poetry. In pottery there seems to remain a possibility for providing both, sometimes in the same object. Pottery can be about design or about art, and occasionally both. Pots succeed because they move the spirit, like art, or because they exactly fill a requirement, like design. That one discipline can straddle both areas with dual emphasis is distinctive.

Being a potter is absurd in modern times. As Hans Coper wrote in 1969: 'Practising a craft with ambiguous reference to purpose and function one has occasion to face absurdity. More than anything, somewhat like a demented piano-tuner, one is trying to approximate a phantom pitch.' In part the irrelevance of the role is blanketed by the fact that people do seem to keep on wanting pots, to use and to look at. Some of this desire is romantic: handmade things are 'nicer', more virtuous, than industrially made things – they are unique, marked by the erring human hand, more particular. Then there is the prestige of having something that cost more than mere utility required, and ultimately there is investment in 'good' names and rocketing values. Pots are easy to live with and don't need explaining; they are more accessible to many people – conceptually, financially and in scale – than contemporary fine art.

The bulk of pottery throughout history has been down-to-earth, necessary stuff, descriptive of past eating habits and past rituals, and essential, because of its capacity to survive, to archaeologists and to social historians. This gives it a strong position in our sense of culture and history. But clay is an extraordinary substance: very plastic and malleable, it can also be poured as a liquid or carved and scraped in a dry state, and finally, it is very durable and hard when fired. This versatility has been exploited in the imitation of other materials and other things for centuries, and since the beginning clay has been used to make things beyond the needs of daily life, for entertainment. You could say that as a material it is prone to metaphor, and practical objects have been formed in some disguise or other for ages. There must have been humour in a Greek scent bottle being shaped like a foot in a leather sandle, and wit in drinking out of a ceramic animal horn rather than a real one. Clay has been used for toys as well as oil lamps, and chandeliers as well as urinals. Both daily life and fantasy/luxury have been served by pottery from earliest times, which leaves little room for some of the recent outrage at departures during the last decades from the purist dominance of the Anglo-Oriental school in studio pottery, where beauty exists only in utility. Just as early in this century some of those hostile to abstraction would have you believe that previously painting and sculpture had *always* been about faithful presentation and the values of the Renaissance, so in this generation some critics would have it that pottery of worth has *always* been simple, natural, primarily functional, and wheel-made.

Most pots have indeed been round and shiny and upright, and with good reason. (Rapidly constructed on a wheel, easy to clean and stack). But there have always been some pieces, constructed in the same spirit perhaps, but for some reason elevated above the batch as more vigorous, or full of life or poise or beauty, that have been destined to an ornamental rather than a useful life. With that as an acceptable fact, it is not surprising that other pots should follow that did not spring up with an overt function in their maker's mind, but with the intention only to decorate. There have been some revealing examples in the course of history – Hispano-Moresque dishes, elaborately painted with lustres on tin glaze in the 14th century, were exported to Italy and thought to be far too beautiful to be plates; they were stuck into the walls of churches. The dish/wall-plaque dual role is very well established, even without the cement, through Palissy and Thomas Toft in the 16th and 17th centuries to Picasso and Miró in our own. Were the Della Robbias making gigantic plates in sections? A well-trodden path of pots made for looking at allows also for pots to be constructed in elaborate rather than economic ways, and allows them then to be made off the wheel, and in all manner of eccentric shapes. And just as a dish can also be a painting hung on the wall, or propped on a shelf, it follows that a pot can be a painting that travels round an entire object, smoothly in the case of a circular or spherical pot, and with interruptions and related planes in the case of a slab-built or angular pot.

The fact that pots are three-dimensional has misled people into making claims for modern not-so-useful pots being sculpture, when the more essential connections are with painting. However elaborate or unusual a pot is in its form, the degree to which its existence depends on 'containing', actual or suggested, and on the expression of one particular material, disqualifies it from the broad concerns of sculpture. The American painter George Woodman, in an article called 'Ceramic Decoration and the Concept of Ceramics as a Decorative Art', discussed the relationship of pots to both painting and sculpture. 'In the undecorated pot, all there is to see is a contour or silhouette; it has no particular identity except at its edges.' This at once separates vessel ceramics from sculpture. And he goes on: 'A sensibility to the organization of surfaces in relation to their contours is not really the province of construction and space, but of the visual organization of fields' (*American Ceramics*, 1982). With pottery there is a separate concern for the surface, and what occurs on the surface is crucial to a sense of completion.

And what does a Modern Pot look like? Tendencies that I have been most aware of, and been a part of, in the 1970s and 80s, could be generalized like this: many potters are handbuilding rather than throwing, even when they are making regular curvaceous forms. The consistent silhouette of the round upright and shiny traditional pot has been interrupted – pots are demanding to be approached from different viewpoints because of asymmetry or flattening or complex multiple forms. Pots can lie down as well as stand up. Pots may have a clear sense of position, a stance, an obvious front side and back side perhaps, or variable ways of resting on a surface, offering different moods. The anthropomorphism of neck, belly and shoulder that is an established part of the language of pottery is not lost, though the figure may not be vertical. Colour and pattern are complicated and important, and surfaces are often dry or matt rather than glossy, as changing planes are masked by high sheen. Colour and pattern may be incorporated in the making process at an early stage, and sometimes glaze is done away with altogether. There is contrast and discord rather than harmony and a blending in with nature. Pots are often descriptive of a jangled urban life rather than serene rurality. Stimulus comes from far and wide and not just from the traditions of pottery. Techniques are elaborate and varied.

Does this represent an end, or a beginning? There is something to be gained from a comparison with Mannerism, which followed the Renaissance. Mannerism has been perceived either as the decadent petering out of a great creative surge, or as an important initiation of a heightened self-awareness in art, with the central concept of the work of art as 'absolute', as an enduring virtuoso performance. The term derives from the Italian word *maniera*, meaning style. In the 17th century it was always used positively, and did not include the negative aspect of 'stylization' or stereotyping. Mannerists also had the concept of 'difficulty' as a high aim; virtue lay in the conquest of difficulty. Mannerist works of art are complex rather than economic, and consciously refer to art itself: as John Shearman has written, 'it was common for Mannerist artists to adapt artistic forms or compositional devices, originally invented with expressive function and to use them in a non-functional way, capriciously' (*Mannerism*, 1967.) Shearman also observes: 'The capacity of artists to manipulate for their own ends forms invented in a different spirit is one of the facts of life that helps to explain how Mannerism grew out of the earlier Renaissance.' This self-consciousness is what brought me to the analogy: the Leach school was the Renaissance – Leach was not solely responsible for the eruption of Studio Pottery early this century but he was a tremendous catalyst both practically and theoretically – and my generation have consumed this energy and are now posed on top of it like Mannerists, reversing the normal relationship of form and content.

I have written about self-consciousness before (and I do not use the word derogatorily), primarily in *The Maker's Eye* catalogue. (Crafts Council, London, 1982). 'Function, or an idea of a possible function, is crucial, but is just one ingredient in the final presence of the object, and not its only motivation. . . . A "modern" novel (after Proust and Joyce) is both made of, and about, language. Some objects are similarly self-referential, that is, they perform a function, and at the same time are drawing attention to what their own rules are about. In some way such objects stand back and describe, or represent, themselves as well as being. In the analogy with the novel "function" stands for "story" as the central content'. I went on to suggest that these objects can be seen as another link in the traditional chain of 'practical objects in disguise'. The function of the Greek scent bottle is not impaired by the caprice of the foot disguise, a Martin Brothers Bird Jar is dominated by its decorative disguise but it is still a jar. In these new pots a jug can also be a representation of a jug without losing the function. The input of still-life painting into this way of thinking is considerable, clearly demonstrated in the work of the British ceramists Andrew Lord and Elizabeth Fritsch, in very different ways, she by flattening forms into two and a half dimensions, and he by a Cubist reconstruction of the way an object is defined by the light falling on it.

The critic and historian Philip Rawson is one of those who are dismayed by recent developments. 'The creator's proper job is to lead the spectator's attention to dwell in a space which is not that of the common world . . . Not all sexy silhouettes give good central presence and imply strong volumes. What matters is the way the pot surface and the volumes which it promotes move positively and generously towards you at its focal place to give a valid sense of "being there". So chillingly often we are nowadays given pots that retreat, flattening themselves and huddling back into diagrams.' I would argue that pots such as I have described are not huddling into diagrams but gliding towards paintings, which is not cowardice but a selfconscious (and Mannerist) bravura. They are playing with the gap between the expectation of use and the actuality of contemplation, and such gaps can be entertaining, and 'transporting', in the way that Rawson requires, out of the common world.

Some potters are dealing first of all with formal ideas and a kind of commentary, and others are dealing first of all with practicalities. For those who enjoy ambiguity there are all the things in the middle with a double presence, prose and poetry, that intrigue most.

1

THE NEW ROLE OF
THE POTTER

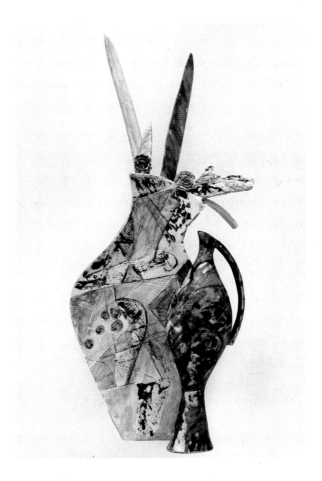

Jugs. Sue John. Stoneware. h.45cm. UK, 1982

The Contemporary Pot

Studio pottery is currently more exuberant, more experimental and sometimes more anarchic than ever before. At the same time, it is also conservative and a guarantor of decorative tradition. The tension between these extremes, together with the diversity of work along the way, give contemporary ceramics its special flavour and interest. Ceramics, as an applied or decorative art, is also valued more highly today than it has been for many years. This change in interest has come about in part because the decorative arts and decoration generally have been rehabilitated by society's tastemakers – designers, architects and critics. Yet there is another reason. Since the last World War the applied arts, and ceramics in particular, have become more attractive to the ordinary householder. Ceramics has become a popular art form – expressive, domestic in scale, familiar in form, but often with sufficient variety to engage the mind as well the eye. To call studio pottery a populist art form is not to imply that everyone should or could practise it, but to indicate that the best and most innovative of pottery's modern practitioners keep faith with pottery's domestic roots.

The development of and interest in studio ceramics will gather pace during the rest of the 1980s because the diversity of object that is now being provided parallels the new diversity in the design of other consumer objects – a diversity made possible by the extreme flexibility of new technology.

A glance through the pictures in this book reveals that the emphasis rests heavily upon the ceramic vessel – in all its variety. On the whole, I believe that ceramics is about pots and that ceramic sculpture should usually be considered alongside other sculpture. Sculpture, broadly speaking, is concerned with a much wider metaphorical and conceptual range than is normally expected of or possible in pottery. Pottery is judged by a number of criteria – but metaphorical and conceptual content need not be among them. My general (though not total) exclusion of sculpture is based on the practical assumption that it is sounder to compare like with like. Modern pottery is, in any case, rich and surprising enough to merit its own discussion.

Modern handmade pottery falls broadly into two categories: production pottery, in which a potter makes batches of useful domestic wares for sale; and studio pottery, objects made on a one-off basis as a form of art. The status of this pottery art is one of the subjects of this book, but increasingly the two categories are becoming blurred as the century progresses.

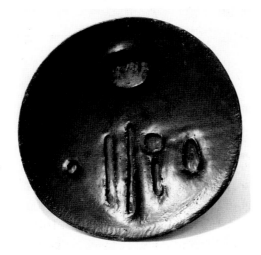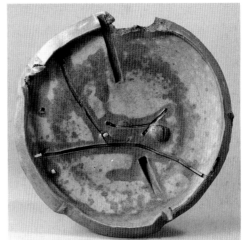

Left, Dish. Ruth Duckworth. Stoneware. d.29cm. UK, 1962

Right, Untitled. Peter Voulkos. Stoneware. d.45cm. USA, 1980

The emergence of modern studio pottery dates from the 19th century in Europe because, like handcraft in general, it was a way of opposing the tendencies of industrialization. John Ruskin and William Morris tried very hard, as did Viollet-le-Duc in France, to revitalize interest in the craftsman. The variety of arts and crafts movements and ideas that engaged France, England, Germany and the USA in the early 20th century became focused for a while on one institution – the Bauhaus. Everyone knows that the Bauhaus became Europe's most important art school, initiating ideas which shaped the style of architecture, industrial and graphic design, but it also, by default, influenced the design world's attitudes towards the crafts.

The craft element in the Bauhaus philosophy was at first a part of the core of the art school's curriculum, but craft was downgraded when the Bauhaus moved from Weimar to Dessau in 1925 and Gropius redefined his aims. Gillian Naylor's study, *The Bauhaus Reassessed* (1985), explains how the workshops became 'laboratories', and worksmanship became a means of prototyping for the machine. Educationally, handwork was seen more as a way of sensitizing designers to materials than as an end itself. It is interesting that the ceramics workshops established in Weimar were not moved to Dessau, though elsewhere the idea of craft as an end in itself persisted, despite the way in which the crafts were shunted off by the art and design world into a small kingdom of their own.

Nevertheless, within its own territory pottery is not always parochial. By tradition it has been an activity in which imitation of styles taken from other applied arts or other countries has been rife. The art historian and artist, Philip Rawson, says in his seminal book *Ceramics* (1971) that during the 18th century European ceramic shapes, such as coffee pots, together with similar items made in China and Japan for the European market, accurately reflect changes of fashion in silver tableware. And a characteristic of the modern studio potter in the last two decades has been an ability to use art or design for craft ends. At the same time, among the studio potters in particular, there has been a growing spirit of internationalism.

Between the World Wars a number of potters emigrated from Continental Europe to the United States and Britain. Finnish-born Maija Grotell emigrated to the United States after studying at the School of Industrial Art in Helsinki and doing postgraduate work there with the Belgian-born Alfred William Finch – one of Europe's most important pioneers in studio pottery. She had a major impact in the USA and among her pupils featured in this book is the ceramist Richard DeVore. Frans and Marguerite Wildenhain, graduates of the Weimar Bauhaus, came to the USA from Germany in 1939, Gertrude and Otto Natzler from Vienna in 1938. Ruth Duckworth, perhaps one of the most influential of modern potters, was born in Germany, emigrated to Britain shortly before the Second World War, and in 1964 went to Chicago; in Britain she had helped to make English potters aware of sculptural possibilities in clay. And, lastly, two potters of crucial importance to the development of British pottery – Hans Coper (Germany) and Lucie Rie (Austria) – were both refugees from Nazism.

The influence of these émigrés since 1945 has been profound. However, this has also been a period of dominance in pottery by the USA, which has resulted in a division between English-speaking countries (together with those where English is widely spoken) and the rest of the Western world. Since the early 1970s there has been an exchange of ideas through books, magazines and lecture tours on a circuit which includes North America, Great Britain, Australia, Scandinavia and Holland. Meanwhile, France, for example, while it has produced such 197, 198 outstanding ceramists as Claude Varlan and Claude Champy, has not been to a large extent p. 24 internationally involved in the development of contemporary craft pottery. By contrast, it has generated some of the most interesting fine art using clay as a medium – the painter Edouard Pignon, for instance, has created several large tiled monuments. Indeed, France has continued the tradition of accepting that its painters and sculptors will make forays into the applied arts – a flexibility that is seldom found in the Anglo-American art world. Thus Tamara Preaud and Serge Gauthier's book *Ceramics of the Twentieth Century* (1982) shows us tile pieces by Matisse and ceramic sketches by Raoul Dufy for garden works. By comparison West Germany has maintained a consistently high standard, but unlike the experimental attitude seen in much of the American pottery world, here the work is restrained, with the excitement resting not in form, but in the glazing. Among a number of very good West German potters are Karl and 121, 151 Ursula Scheid, Antje Brüggemann-Breckwoldt and Renate and Hans Heckmann. East German 123, 173 work tends to be more radical again – seen, for example, in the expressionist pots of Karl Fulle. 174, p. 15

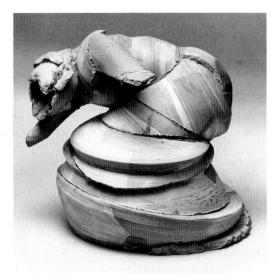

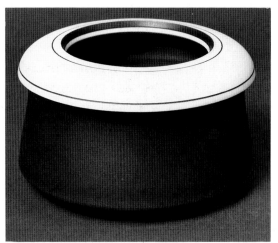

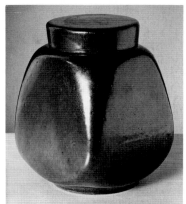

Above, Figure. Karl Fulle. Stoneware. h. 40 cm. East Germany, 1985

Above right, Bowl. Ursula Scheid. Porcelain. d. 15 cm. West Germany, 1985

Right, Jar. Liebfriede Bernstiel. Stoneware. 18 cm. West Germany, 1985

Certain countries, such as Britain or Australia, have tended to respond like sponges to outside influences – unlike West Germany and France, which have gone their own way. Britain, for example, swallowed Oriental influences between the two World Wars and especially in the late 1940s and early 1950s. This was followed in turn by a marked Scandinavian input and a dose of Americanization. Today, Britain and Australia together are demonstrating a rampant pluralism and eclecticism. As things have turned out, both countries have gained immeasurably by being open to different influences and new ideas. In Britain – which continues to occupy an important place in the development of 20th-century studio pottery – the range currently includes the refined craftsmanship of David Leach's Anglo-Orientalism, Elizabeth Fritsch's beautifully painted vessels and Wally Keeler's perverse, almost medieval, salt-glazed functional pottery.

p. 33; 33
136, 155
27, 56

One can identify certain national characteristics. Ceramics in Holland owes little to a craft ideology and much more to design, whereas in Britain pottery, especially functional pottery, is frequently nostalgic or, at the very least, borrowing from the past. Scandinavian pottery exhibits the colour range and proportion in its decoration that one finds in Scandinavian architecture and textiles. And American potters, irrespective of whether they are making 'art' or teapots, are frequently inclined to make it big and to make it in a rough but very sound, workmanlike way. Obviously, these are generalizations, but they should not be surprising since, as an applied art, to some extent pottery is bound to reflect a culture's dominant aesthetic. For a quick, but instructive, reference, look at the work of Geert Lap (Holland), Jane Hamlyn or Richard Slee (UK), Ingrid Mortensen (Norway) and Kenneth Ferguson (USA). Finally, by way of further confirmation of national characteristics look also at Matteo Thun's work in Italy: utterly confident design, post-modernist, challenging and chic – Italian from top to bottom. As for the pluralism of Australia – we have only to take note of what Dr Peter Emmett has to say in the catalogue to the 1984 'Mayfair Ceramic Award', in which he identifies all the following contemporary references: Japanese folk art; Oribe; Sodeisha; Islam; pre-Columbian; Art Deco; contemporary painting; primitive art; and textiles.

13, 60
122, 163–4
67, 124
43–4, 47–8

Generalizations apart, contemporary craft pottery owes much of its current practice and theory to two men – Bernard Leach (UK) and Peter Voulkos (USA) – though this is not to say that they are necessarily the best (or the only) innovators, or even the most original potters of their respective generations. Certainly Leach (1887–1979) was the most important figure in handmade pottery in the 1940s and 1950s; Germany, France, Denmark and the USA, as well as Britain and other countries, felt his impact at different points. Leach did not invent studio pottery, but he was able to formulate a philosophy justifying what he did, and it was so persuasive, so rich in its appeal to puritan aesthetics, that it captured the craft pottery movement's imagination. One publication did the trick – A Potter's Book, published in 1940.

Leach began his ceramics in Japan, where he lived from 1909 to c.1920. On his return to England he set up a pottery in St Ives, Cornwall. A Potter's Book begins with an opening essay called 'Towards A Standard', in which the following judgment is typical: 'The upshot of the argument is that a pot in order to be good should be a genuine expression of life. It implies sincerity on the part of the potter and truth in the conception and execution of the work.' The rest of the book is full of prescriptive recipes for making good, honest pots and lays down an approach which later endorsed several generations of plain, crinkly, brown pots wearing their humility on their surface.

Eventually, humility as a style went out of fashion – and for many potters it never was in fashion, because it was a style that cut them off from the modern world and its art. A Potter's Book tries to repudiate the effect that modern art and design had had on the crafts and design

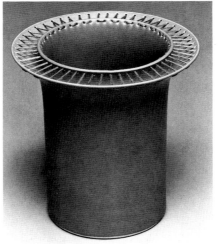

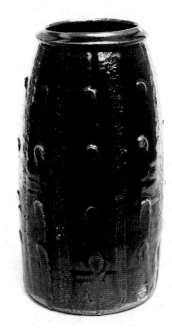

Jar. Barbara Nanning. Stoneware, textile. h. 30 cm. Holland, 1985

Incised jar. Bernard Leach. Stoneware. h. 30 cm. UK, 1972

throughout the 1920s and 1930s. Leach wrote: 'Thence has arisen the affirmation of the mechanical age in art – functionalism. This, through let us say, Picasso, le Corbusier and Gropius of the Bauhaus, is having its effect on all crafts. A movement which, however based by its initiators on a new and dynamic concept of three-dimensional form, tends amongst those who attempt to carry the idea into industry to an over-intellectual effort to discover norms of orderliness and utility. Such a process limits the enjoyment of work to the designer, and overlooks the irregular and irrational element in all fine activity, including the making of pottery.'

Oliver Watson, of the Victoria and Albert Museum, London, has stressed that Leach was not the only pioneer and that he did not singlehandedly rescue craft pottery from oblivion or re-invent the tradition. Watson cites William de Morgan (1839–1917), the Martin Brothers (the last of whom died in 1923), and William Staite Murray (1881–1962) as all-important, and says: 'Leach did not receive outstanding critical success in the 1920s and 1930s (indeed he was going steadily bankrupt) but was seen by the critics and the public alike as another, if rather eccentric potter.' Moreover, Leach's interests in Korean, Japanese and Chinese ceramics, as well as his appreciation of the Oriental approach to process and material, were shared by fellow potters.

All true, no doubt, but the *Realpolitik* of the pottery world is no different from any other – one person has a louder voice than another. The important question is whether he was really an important influence, a person who shaped the direction of studio pottery. There is only one answer – yes.

Leach had some extremely successful lectures in the USA in 1950 and 1953, though by no means all those who heard him were converted. William Daley (USA) recalls the irritation created by Leach telling Americans that they needed a taproot for their pottery and suggesting that they look to the past. As Daley says, the American potters' taproot was in the present, in contemporary painting and sculpture.

The USA is vastly important to the development of modern pottery. It gained from the European émigrés, and it was also influenced by Zen. The American-based ceramics historian, Garth Clark, describes the position in the early 1950s as follows: 'The dominant influence was the impact of Japanese pottery and the Zen Buddhist theories that accompanied it. On the West Coast in particular, the artists were sympathetic to Oriental philosophy, and a popular interest in Zen was growing under the leadership of scholars such as Alan Watts in San Francisco. The Zen concept of beauty appealed to the American potter for a number of reasons. In the wares of the tea ceremony, they saw new forms of expression in the subtle asymmetry, the simplicity, and the often random, abstract decoration. The earlier works of Japan inspired as well, particularly prehistoric Jomon pottery with its architectonic structure, curiously weighted proportions, and tension between surface and form.' According to Clark, the first contact that American potters had with Oriental philosophy was through Leach's *A Potter's Book*. Then followed the 1950 coast-to-coast lecture tour and its successor in 1953, when Leach was accompanied by the potter Shoji Hamada and by Soetsu Yanagi, founder of the Mingei craft movement and Director of the National Folk Museum of Japan.

Peter Voulkos was much influenced by the East, but he also became interested in ceramics by p. 13, p. 23 36 Miró, Chagall, Léger, Fontana and Picasso. Voulkos, it seems, was a voracious devourer of information about European pottery, Greek pottery and the East, as well as contemporary American sculpture and painting, which had itself been informed by influences as diverse as Russian Constructivism and German Expressionism. Voulkos became the man who acted as a conduit between pottery and fine art, although not even he was able to bring pottery into the avant-garde. Pottery has trailed, in America as elsewhere, behind developments in fine art, except possibly in the matter of decoration, where it might be said that certain potters – Betty Woodman, for example (but not Voulkos) – kept the torch of decoration alight during the matt-grey days of modernism, minimalism and conceptualism. Nevertheless, applied art's role is not that of trail-blazer, but of something equally important and sometimes underrated; for our ornamental and functional artefacts are expressions of our individuality and day-to-day values.

The American Century

When a country's economy is doing well, then usually its whole culture is doing well: for often the confidence and energy which comes from business and trading success spreads rapidly through the arts, universities and publishing and through the technical, scientific and educational communities.

It is a commonplace observation that after the Second World War America emerged with immense wealth and power. Yet what needs emphasizing, especially in a book which deals with craft and the special intelligence which is to do with making, is just how successful the American economy became at producing objects. Its success was based on practicality – Americans made their money with their hands and with their machines. They did not philosophize or speculate, they did. A single set of statistics about manufacturing in wartime America is revealing: at the beginning of the Second World War, it took 196 days to build a Liberty ship; this was soon cut to 27 days and by 1943 America turned out one Liberty ship every 18.3 hours.

Such energy was almost bound to have its effect on art. Serge Guilbaut, an art historian at the University of British Columbia, published a book in 1983 entitled *How New York Stole the Idea of Modern Art*. Guilbaut argues that there was a determination in the American wartime government to prepare for peace and that much attention was given to the broader role, both at home and abroad, of American culture. Art can be used to create good will and provide a generally agreeable, long-term condition for trade. Art also has, in the broadest sense, an important role in making a contribution to national identity.

Guilbaut quotes the critic Clifton Fadiman in a wartime radio discussion in 1941: 'We are through as a pioneer nation; we are now ready to develop as a civilisation'; and, 'I think the enjoyment and appreciation of art is one means of insuring the kind of psychological unity we are after, and that it is important in national defense.'

The art that was to spearhead this Americanization was not in any sense 'traditional' – the key was innovation, innovation and yet more innovation. A letter to the *New York Times*, unearthed by Guilbaut, appealed to the entrepreneurial instincts of the American artist: 'Now is the time to experiment. You've complained for years about the Frenchmen's stealing the American market, well things are on the up and up. Galleries need fresh talent, new ideas.

Money can be heard crinkling throughout the land. And all you have to do, boys and girls, is get a new approach, do some delving for a change – God knows you've had time to rest.'

The rest is history – Jackson Pollock, Mark Rothko, Robert Motherwell . . . and on to the present day.

The drive was not to replace Europe's pre-war eminence in aesthetics – or rather Paris's eminence – by replicating European art. The drive was to make America, New York, the centre of aesthetics through American art. Always a few years behind, ceramics caught the same enthusiasm. Evidence for this is found in Rose Slivka's article 'The New Ceramic Presence' in *Craft Horizons* in 1961, which reads for the first part like a piece of cultural propaganda for the USA.

With the voice of a citizen of the most powerful country in the world, Slivka wrote: 'America was a philosophic product of the age of reason and the economic spawn of the industrial revolution . . . we have become the most developed national intelligence in satisfying functional needs for the mass (in a massive country).' She then praised 'the speed, strength and violence of the machine'. Such optimism – grounded in the material security of the American economy, with home and foreign markets assured – is understandable.

Significantly, Slivka associated the concept of freedom, derived from economic, industrial and capitalist strength, with freedom from European cultural mores and freedom of gesture in contemporary pottery. First, she declared that America had been too involved with practical matters to cultivate the idea of beauty. At the same time, she argued that the classical beauty of harmony and balance is West European and not appropriate for America. American culture centred on innovation and improvisation – and perhaps Slivka had in mind the pioneers who could make do with whatever came to hand and build roughly but soundly anything from houses to barns to carts, a talent for practicality which has passed from generation to generation. She revered such painters as Jackson Pollock and Mark Rothko and Yves Kline for establishing an American aesthetic; and in her article she slipped in, through the back door, the connection between Pollock and pottery, with an over-simplified but partly justifiable claim: 'Pottery, of course, has always served as a vehicle for painting.'

And it was not only American painting (which, as she observes in passing, had by 1960 permeated all the arts abroad) but also American sculpture which communicated to American pottery 'its own sense of release from the tyranny of traditional tools and materials, a search for new ways of treating materials and for new forms to express new ideas.' Finally (her article is quite exhausting to read, since one has to keep scaling mountainous adjectives), Slivka draws our attention to 'freedom' – 'The freedom of the American potter to experiment, to risk, to make mistakes freely on a creative and quantitative level that is proportionately unequalled anywhere.' So, who says pottery cannot be ideological? The concept of freedom, whether it was entrepreneurial in the capitalist sense, or whether it involved pioneering in technology, or was expressed in the right to have your own gun or leave your own mark, found expression in gestural art and gestural pottery.

The year of Slivka's article – 1961 – is interesting in the light of Garth Clark's history of the period, in which he sees the 1950s as the decade of liberation for American pottery, thereby allowing, in the 1960s, the 'American ceramist to establish an artistic beach head for the medium'.

With hindsight, it may seem that some of the territory captured by the American ceramist is hardly inspiring. The West Coast produced funk ceramics by a number of people, of whom
119 Robert Arneson was the leader and the most talented. Funk ceramics was like a less intellectual version of Pop art, although – like Pop art – it used the imagery of a materialist, affluent society. However, whereas the masters of Pop art had style and irony – Claes Oldenburg and Andy Warhol are examples – funk ceramics was, by and large, clumsy, the visual counterpart of a bar-room joke between a pair of cowhands. An example of funk wit is the *Black Camera* by Fred Bauer, in which the camera lens is metamorphosed into a penis. Among American ceramists, there also emerged, partly through funk figuration, a great interest in and deftness for making figurative and narrative objects of great verisimilitude. Clay can be pressed into any form; it is a good medium for pursuing *trompe-l'oeil*. But these developments remain, with few exceptions, too literal and too skill-orientated (see, for one of the exceptions, the illustration of Richard
66 Shaw's work). On the whole, once you have admired the craftsmanship, that is an end of the matter.

The Leach tradition continued and a contemporary vessel movement emerged in the 1960s at Alfred University, New York State. Nevertheless, running parallel with funk, and with clay as the vehicle for verisimilitude, was abstract sculpture in clay and pottery/sculpture installations. Funk, verisimilitude, abstraction and installation all came together in 1982 when the influential Whitney Museum of American Art in New York put on an exhibition of six American ceramists under the title *Ceramic Sculpture*. It was a summary of twenty years of American 'art' ceramics. Featured were Peter Voulkos and John Mason showing abstract, volumetric sculptures; Kenneth Price exhibiting a remarkable collection of works around the theme of the cup, together with installations such as *Happy's Curios: Town Unit 1*, which consisted of glazed earthenware and a wood cabinet; Robert Arneson with figurative self-portrait works such as
118 *Fragment of Western Civilization*; David Gilhooly, a funk ceramist with an obsession with frogs; and Richard Shaw, showing both verisimilitude assemblages in clay such as *House of Cards with Two Volumes* and playful stick figures such as *Figure on a Palette*.

'Ceramic Sculpture' was an important exhibition conceived on a doubtful premise – trying to present ceramic sculpture as a coherent category of its own. Of the artists in the show, Peter

Voulkos was misrepresented, since essentially his work is to do with pottery. Of course Voulkos, like John Mason, produces competent sculptural objects, but neither is a major sculptor, and Voulkos's great contribution has been to the pottery tradition.

The ceramics world in the USA has been caught up, more than in any other country, by an apparent need to give pottery status by claiming for it the categories of either painting or sculpture. It as though ceramics is trying to get out of the exile to which it has been confined by the forces of modernism, the Bauhaus, the Museum of Modern Art, New York, and the art market. All kinds of ambitious people are involved – critics and curators, as well as artists, seem to wish to disavow the links with pottery. And yet there is no need for this: a potter of the calibre of Voulkos elevates pottery through pottery.

Peter Voulkos was born in 1924. A graduate in painting from Montana State University, with an MA in Ceramics from the California College of Arts and Crafts, he was invited in 1954 to set up a ceramics department at Otis Art Institute in Los Angeles. There he worked with a sculptor, Rudy Autio – whom he had first met at the Archie Bray Foundation, Montana, and whose importance in ceramics – Garth Clark believes – has yet to be credited.

Voulkos is a gifted craftsman – and an expressive one. The Everson Museum in Syracuse has a large earthenware covered bowl made by him in 1951: a superb piece of throwing. His talent for clay is undisputed. Various people – students and colleagues – who have worked with him (in 1959 he went to Berkeley to start a ceramics department there) have given frequent and generous accounts of his ability. Billy Al Bengston, who gave up ceramics some years ago to work as a painter, said: 'We stood in awe and admiration of Voulkos's extraordinary capacity to handle clay. He was also technically superior to anyone at that time [the 1950s] and probably still is today [1966].' Voulkos pushed ceramics well away from functional, utilitarian work and in a sense walloped the vessel into asymmetrical, primeval 'statements'. For a while he 36 concentrated on sculpture, but has persisted in making clay works, and since the 1970s has produced a series of plates which are punctured with holes, blistered with pellets of porcelain, and ribbed and strapped across the surface. He tends to remain within shouting distance of the vessel. There is generally a familiarity about the form which gives a Voulkos ceramic work more cogency and validity than his sculptures. In recent years, perhaps, he has become caught in a rut, a victim of his own myth, or at least a victim of that greater myth about freedom and the American potter which others have generated.

This is using the term 'myth' in the spirit of the artist Judy Chicago when she remarked: 'A species makes myths that correspond to its needs and allow it to act on the needs that are momentarily paramount.' The myth concerning Peter Voulkos involves the assumption that here we have a man who produces brilliant clay works by not caring, by whamming the clay this way and that, without knowledge of tradition, without deliberate, even academic reference to

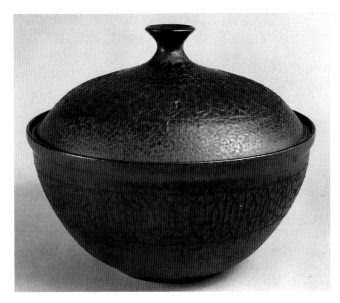

Covered bowl. Peter Voulkos. Earthenware.
h.29cm. USA, 1951

the past. This is the myth of the freebooter which is so misleading to younger potters and to outsiders. For, quite apart from the testimony of Voulkos' own work (which in later years is perhaps an erratic testimony), and apart from the bouquets presented to him by people such as Kenneth Price and Billy Al Bengston, it is clear that Voulkos is steeped in the history of his craft as well as its technique. It might be attractive to students to think of pottery as being possible simply by letting it all hang loose, but Voulkos does not demonstrate this. None the less, commentators on his work, as well as on the man himself, have created an image of the ceramist and his craft that is careless, gutsy and mindlessly defiant. To an extent, this has been part of the anti-aesthetic, anti-European myth, but not everyone is convinced.

It may be that the link between Voulkos and Abstract Expressionism has been overplayed. One thing should be noted: even allowing for the fact that Voulkos had developed his experimental expressionistic approach in the mid-1950s, this still puts ceramics, even at its most daring, several years behind developments in painting.

Although Slivka's article in *Craft Horizons* was liberally illustrated with Voulkos's works and other new ceramic presences (including John Mason and Henry Takemoto), quite a few readers wondered what on earth was going on. One of them wrote in to say: 'As of late, I have noticed that more and more space has been devoted to what I call sick art, that is, those ceramics and objects that do not express anything beautiful or nice. Is it that the art and artist in America have gone sour?' The correspondent gave his own position away very clearly by saying that he was an importer of art and furniture from Scandinavia.

Familiar Forms

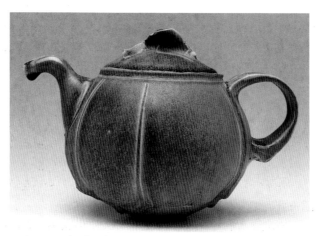

Teapot. Claude Champy. Stoneware. d. 17 cm. France, 1985

We should always come back to the thought that pottery is a domestic art of familiar forms. Its main function at this stage of the 20th century is delight, diversion, sanctuary, self-expression. Though a modern pot may seem 'traditional' in its appearance, it is the product of a modern idea and a modern ideology. Few potters make pots out of necessity and even fewer people in modern industrial societies buy craft pots from necessity. Both the production and purchase of such pots are accounted for by specifically 20th-century reasons. Among the most important of these reasons is self-expression. It is, nevertheless, expression on a scale and of an intimacy that relates it most closely to the individual viewer and owner, and his or her ordinary experiences of day-to-day life. At the same time, the clay vessel is also an artefact which coincides with a characteristic 20th-century need (especially American need) for the individual to become a maker, and to leave his or her signature or gesture for someone else to see. These gestures, whether in the form of Abstract Expressionist painting or the clay vessel, tend to have a sensuous, physical 'meaning'.

Some thoughts on pottery's strength through familiarity of form, although he does not use that expression, are provided by Philip Rawson in *Ceramics*. Rawson makes the simple but pertinent point that food has played a vital part in endowing pots with their special symbolic qualities. And this fact leads to others, such as the extreme importance of tactile qualities in pottery. You cannot use pottery without touching it, and touch – experience of the particularities of surface, as well as generalities of form – is part of the familiarity of pottery. This touching is no mere caress or cautious reassurance that the thing in front of you does exist. Often when you handle a contemporary studio pot you can get some sense of how the thing was made: modern potters often leave their working gestures in the clay. (Many contemporary potters believe that pottery, like sculpture, can – and perhaps ought – to involve the maker's whole body, as well as the mind.)

In this sense the claywork that has been produced by Robert Turner, Jerry Rothman, Graham Marks, Betty Woodman and Ruth Duckworth – to name just five contemporary, but very different Americans – is all part of clay's deepest traditions of expression through volume, malleability and surface. It is an attitude about pottery which is the very opposite of the impetus bringing industrial ceramic wares into existence. Industrial ware cannot leave the traces of its maker in its form; it becomes always a perfect example of a designer's concept. The handmade form emerges from intelligent intuition, the industrial ware is analytical.

Similarly, the reason why designers of intellectual chic, such as the Italian Ettore Sottsass and his Memphis group, take such pains to keep all craft expression and ideology out of their ceramics is because they want to express analysis and ideas. The expressive possibilities of handcraft are to be avoided, since they might lead the observer (and toucher) of Memphis wares away from Sottsass's concepts. Moreover, one aspect of the individual handmade artefact is that the record, the story of its making, and the demonstration of its maker's gestures are open to the observer and the user. If you can see and feel how a thing is made, you may also identify imperfections, and imperfections set people off interpreting and making analogies about the work for themselves. Perhaps a designer, as a purveyor of ideas, would not want to give others the licence to see things he has not seen himself. The craft or art maker may be more generous – although this is conjecture and the reality is demonstrably not so clear cut or so sentimental. (Indeed, Memphis ceramics is in the hands of a craftsman – Alessio Sarri. It is his knowledge and the craft-based workshop which produces the wares that make Memphis pottery possible.)

Expression, especially self-expression, takes a variety of forms. For some potters, above all those making quasi-traditional wares, it takes the form of a very determined and almost ritualistic ordering of their entire lives – in which expression is not merely in the pots themselves but in the detail of daily existence. Such potters are viewed in some circles romantically, in others as unnecessarily escapist. Their sincerity, however, is not doubted. One of Australia's best known salt-glaze potters, Janet Mansfield, a producer of functional ware in quasi-Japanese idiom, has written: 'I was first drawn to clay for practical reasons. I wanted to make things and I wanted these objects to be useful and add quality to everyday living. Even more I needed to create a personal expression that had meaning, that I hoped would have integrity and could aspire to some beauty. . . . I am happiest when I am making pots and can be content for weeks at a time alone concentrating on my work.'

Or take, for example, this extract from an exhibition leaflet accompanying the work of one Britain's best quasi-traditional potters, Richard Batterham: 'The rhythm of nature at large is reflected in his way of life, as he works without modern appliances that make potting "easy". For throwing, drying and glazing he has to watch the seasons; the vast workshop is sparsely heated.' The leaflet goes on to remark that Batterham's decision to live this way during the second half of the 20th century is of special significance: 'In this era of industrialisation, his philosophy, his style of living and the work born from this, quietly tell us of one mind, of one body, of one individual achieving a rather colossal goal.'

There are potters who, on greeting one another, are less likely to ask what kind of work the other does than what sort of kiln he or she is building. Not all craftsmen share such obsessions. The Norwegian potter Arne Åse uses a computer-controlled electric kiln with gas-fired 144–5 reduction. All Åse has to do is press a few buttons and retire to think. He is sceptical about the way people in pottery try to lose themselves in the labour of their craft. He believes that skill and the development of craft knowledge are essential, but he does not accept that one should place too much emphasis on the labour.

Making pottery can be an activity involving a lot of routine labour which some craftsmen find attractive. We might reflect on other activities offering a similar pattern of repetition and predictability – cooking, gardening, painting a door, or driving an automobile are useful comparisons. You know how to do the thing, and what the result should look like; and you know what the criteria are for success or failure. The result is work that is the opposite to innovation, experiment and speculation; it is labour that is escapist or consoling. Escapism through predictable labour is one of the reasons why some kinds of craft are popular.

There is a mystique about the process of doing something by hand which is all part of the attraction of crafted pottery for the layperson. This mystique of the 'handmade' is both a strength and the achilles heel of much craft pottery. The strength is clear: the very notion of someone choosing to make wares by hand implies a special kind of care, thoughtfulness and integrity. Service from one human being to another is at the heart of contemporary attachment to, and sentiment for, 'craft'. The term 'craft' at least suggests more care than seems possible with machine or robot-produced objects.

The achilles heel is less apparent to an untutored audience. It is easy enough to wear 'handmade' as a badge – it is possible to wham something together crudely, with more ignorance than skill, so that the thing looks obviously handwrought. People are taken in by this look, believing it to be what a crafted pot ought to be.

The ideology of handmade wares is also based, to an extent, on a false assumption – the assumption that making a thing by hand is in fact a better act of service, a better (in all senses of the word) way of making objects. Yet the majority of objects on which we rely day-to-day to provide safe and predictable service are not built by hand but, increasingly, by dedicated, computer-controlled lathes; the recent history of aircraft manufacture, for example, is a history of removing the human craftsman from as much of the building process as possible.

Nevertheless, it is, of course, that very deskilling, that removal of the hand and expression from all kinds of day-to-day artefacts, that has increased the value of the applied arts to those who make them. And it is the demonstration of individual expression that makes the modern applied arts attractive to those who buy them. Thus a concept of self – being one's self, expressing one's self, exploring the mind (and the body) of one's self – is central to contemporary ceramics, regardless of whether it is functional or not.

John Gill, a ceramist now teaching at Alfred University, New York, has spoken about the 'modern sentimental attachment to clay' – by which he means the squidginess of the stuff, its plasticity, its malleability, its mudpieness, with all the implications and suggestions of self-absorbed, childhood concentration in play.

One confronts the notion that a great part of clay's appeal is therapeutic. If so, it is not difficult to speculate about the overt attractiveness of the medium and the craft in the early postwar years in Europe and in America. Is it just a coincidence that there was a dramatic increase in people, especially men, taking to clay (and the plastic arts generally)? Did this flourishing reflect an intense need, after a brutal and long war, for individuals to make and create for themselves? Some sharp observers of the American scene, such as Helen Drutt, who runs one of the USA's most respected and influential applied arts galleries, believe that to be the case.

Moreover, the sentimental, playful (and sexual?) attachment to clay is communicated to the purchaser of the works, as well as being felt by the maker. There is no doubt that the attractions of one of Betty Woodman's 'pillow pitchers', or Kenneth Ferguson's idiosyncratic and tumescent teapots, are grounded in simple biological instincts; they are nice to hold and to play with.

American potters, reflecting the general contemporary obsession with self, are convinced that when they pot they explore themselves. Thus Jill Bonovitz (USA) states: 'I am striving to take the traditional form of the vessel and imbue it with my evolving consciousness of my inner self. I am presenting the vessel with a relaxed yet suspenseful attitude.' Although this guileless statement would be greeted with scepticism in European circles, many ceramists would recognize the notion that the vessel can be uncoupled from its attendant history of function to be presented for contemplation only.

The history of contemporary pottery is a history of the pot as a vehicle for expression. And yet 'function' has been at the heart of the discussion as to what form the pot should take. The pro-functionalists and the anti-functionalists have slogged it out in a fight as to whether or not modern ceramics is a 'craft', or whether it is 'art'. Among the gladiators has been Rose Slivka, and in the euphoric article mentioned earlier, she said: 'We are accustomed to our functional problems being solved efficiently and economically by mechanical means. Yet we are acutely aware of our particular need for the handicrafts today to satisfy esthetic and psychological urgencies.' Was this a clear call to potters of all kinds – including those who make objects for use? Not a bit of it. Slivka swept aside the concept of 'use' so that a new kind of potter could take centre stage: 'The painter-potter, therefore, engages in a challenge of function as a formal and objective determinant, he subjects design to the plastic dynamics of interacting form and colour . . . and even avoids immediate functional associations – the value by which machine-made products are defined – a value which can impede free sensory discovery of the object just as its limitations can impede his creative act. And so the value of use becomes a secondary or even arbitrary attribute.'

This is all very well, but it is somewhat rarefied. Stylistic developments, developments in the role of 'function' versus 'art', are tied to economics. Potters, in common with artists, are not fools: usually they make what they can sell, or at least ensure that they can sell something – perhaps their skill and time as teachers. The fact that America and Europe enjoyed economic growth after the Second World War helped to create the right conditions for potters to go out on a limb and express themselves as artist-craftspeople.

Handcraft pottery transformed itself into 'art-craft'. In so doing, it was responding to market forces. Handcraft domestic ware was long ago pushed, with handcraft processes generally, to the economic and social periphery. To continue to work as a producer of clay vessels in the post-Second World War years one needed an appropriate strategy. This new angle did not, of course, suddenly strike everyone at once; it evolved and emerged haphazardly and incoherently. Some roots may certainly be traced back to influential figures, such as Leach and Voulkos. They took the pot and put it into the art or applied art category, where value comes essentially through the apparent aesthetic merits of the work. The economic status of the handcrafted studio pot and handcrafted functional pottery depends upon the degree to which both are perceived as art. The concept or title of 'art' is worth money simply because people believe that it is worth paying extra for art.

The handcraft domestic pot is also conceived of as an item which will materially thicken the experience of day-to-day domestic life – this is its added value, the reason for paying extra for it and the element that makes domestic pottery economically viable. Pottery had no alternative but to become 'art' because 'art' brings in money. This is not cynicism, merely an observation of the way things are: market forces and practicality will keep domestic pottery low in price relative to studio pottery, but high relative to factory ware.

Rose Slivka correctly heralded the development of one kind of ceramic 'art', but we have not, in the last two decades, witnessed any lessening of interest in making, or demand for, pots which look as though they have a use. Thus Michael Cardew, an English historicist potter (and Bernard Leach's first pupil), was able to write in 1981: 'The argument still goes on about the difference between craft and art. But since we must have definitions, I personally would suggest as an interim working one that the essence of a craft (as opposed to an art) is that it is useful.' What had particularly pleased Cardew was an American poll in which the twelve most popular living potters and ceramists included five makers of useful pots, five 'artists in clay' and two borderline cases.

In fact one way and another function has remained either as an actual or as a metaphorical component of the majority of contemporary ceramic work. It is not hard to see why. For whilst it may be the case that the potter as individual creator is satisfying his or her own creative and psychological needs, as well as encouraging the public to satisfy its own creativity vicariously through purchasing the work, it is undoubtedly a strength of the pottery or the vessel 'tradition' that lay people can recognize the form, understand it and judge its worth more easily than they can the abstract artefacts of painting or sculpture.

This is not to say that laypeople enjoy everything they recognize; sometimes they are outraged. Nevertheless, it is significant that several of the postwar ceramists who might be said to have expanded the range of ceramics have remained attached to the idea of 'function'. References to jugs, bowls, plates and to the historical precedents of clay pots in the home, or clay vessels in ceremonial and ritualistic settings, provide the modern potter with a vocabulary, one which the audience can understand. Ceramists as different as Babs Haenen (Holland), George Timock (USA) and Kenneth Price (USA) illustrate the role of the familiar form as an expressive object. Kenneth Price, talking about the series of non-functional 'cups' he has produced over the years, explained: 'With them the functional side can be metaphorical. You can refer to a kind of vernacular of the cup, the cup as a motif or something – it doesn't have to be functional.'

To a great extent, all handmade pottery uses function as a metaphor. Michael Cardew's quality as a craftsman is not in dispute, but was there an element of self-deception in his assumption that the essence of his work was its usefulness? Cider flagons and harvest jugs are hardly in demand for their function; instead, they are nice forms with pleasant overtones of the pastoral idyll. Such wares are as metaphorical in their association with history as Ken Price's cups appear to be with ritual.

Ritual in the domestic sense, however, may have its part to play in the genuinely functional handmade pottery. Helen Drutt owns some cups and saucers produced by Betty Woodman which, because of their scalloped, flowing, undulating forms, are a joy to clasp in both hands and drink from. However, the cups are unstable in their saucers, a fault that raises an interesting question. Do we argue, as Garth Clark has argued, that the fault makes you more careful, makes you take time off to drink from the cups so that the activity becomes a little ritual of its own? Or are potters and critics deluding themselves, and indulging in superficial intellectual justification of what common sense should tell us is a mistake?

To an extent, and because the handmade pot exists first and foremost as a self-consciously expressive object, potters can, if they wish, have the argument all ways at once. Some of them do. Thus a not-infrequent cry of the quasi-traditionalist, at least in Britain, is that he or she is not involved with design but with feeling. Yet not uncommonly the same individuals will insist that true understanding of their wares is only possible through use. But there is no reason why expression, and the aesthetic of the handmade, and adequate design, should not coexist in the same object. One would not, after all, recommend making a person lame to make them pay more attention to the hitherto banal aspect of walking. Nevertheless, because the demand for handmade pottery is aesthetic, rather than utilitarian, people will put up with design faults. It is one of the odder aspects of making functionally irrelevant objects in the guise of utility that the maker can afford to be irresponsible about their performance so long as they look and feel as though they are handcrafted. And this willingness to sacrifice ease of use for style is noticeable even in attitudes to functionally necessary objects – very many clothes, cars and consumer durables of all kinds are bought because they look good, despite flaws in their performance.

Rose Slivka probably got it right when she placed function in a secondary role. But she underplayed the notion that function was a theme in modern pottery which made it popular and easy to understand, as well as providing subject matter for the potter. No one minds the modern potter improvising on his or her theme – as long as there is a melody we can all whistle along with.

2

POTTERY FORM

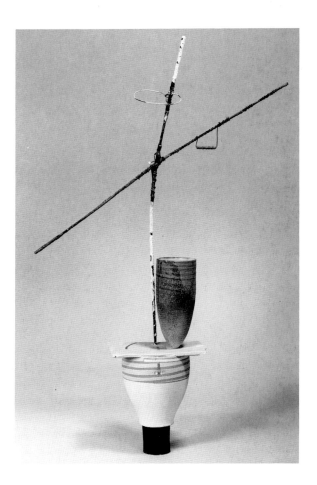

Untitled form. Thom Bohnert. Stoneware and wire. h.58cm. USA, 1984

Writers on ceramics usually divide the subject into form and decoration. In one sense this division is false – pottery is a synthesis of form and surface. One cannot, except artificially, separate the two in the case of a host of contemporary ceramists – Wayne Higby (USA), or Horst Kerstan (West Germany), or Hans and Renate Heckmann (West Germany), or Penny Kokkinos (Canada), or Arne Åse (Norway), or Peder Rasmussen (Denmark) among them. Yet to write about pottery, no less than painting or literature, we have sometimes to take things apart to see how the whole works, and this chapter therefore focuses on form. A further division of form into 'thrown' and 'constructed' is more obvious: they are two separate approaches. One, throwing, proceeds from intuition and a skill that has become second nature; the other, construction, requires a thinking closer to that of the sculptor's – measured, thought out, less instinctive.

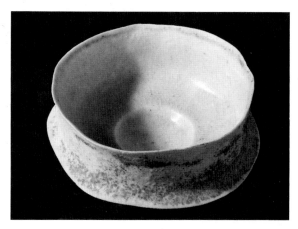

Pinched pot. Ruth Duckworth. Porcelain. d. 12 cm. UK, 1963

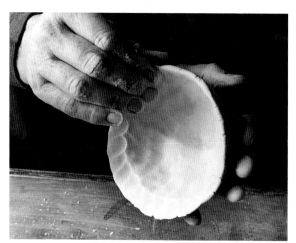

Pinch building. Mary Rogers. Porcelain. d. 10 cm. UK, 1981

Matter over Mind

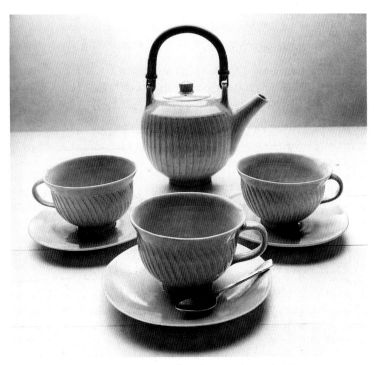

Teaset. David Leach. Porcelain. h.25cm (teapot). UK, 1976

Consider the following two descriptions of throwing – the first by the New Zealand-born potter, Bill Newland: 'Throwing is concerned with inner force – dynamic growth from the wheel, like a triangle on its apex or a crocus from its stem striking its way upwards. A good thrown pot is not one which hangs over its anklestraps or is prolapsed. After all, we learn to accept from the cradle that the fully ripe and expanded fruit is best, apples that look like prunes are rejected.' And then there is Daniel Rhodes, writing in his book *Pottery Form* (1976): 'Throwing is a unique process. . . . Thought need not intervene between the action of the fingers, the hands, the eyes, and the realization of the form. I do not mean to imply that throwing is an automatic or thoughtless process – thought may enter into the conceptualization of the form and later in its evaluation. But it is true that throwing, perhaps more than any other craft, is a direct, immediate expression.'

Newland's remarks about good pots not hanging over their anklestraps must not be read as asserting that all thrown pots have to swell up like pumpkins. There is, despite the basic unthinking skill of good throwing, room for manoeuvre. Some ceramists have used throwing as a basis for achieving a sense of volume without turning their vessels into bloated fruits. But generally such throwing is mediated by construction. Richard DeVore, for example, begins by throwing a small basin and then handbuilds – thus the throwing element is about 10 per cent of the work. DeVore's work implies volume and that is also due to his understanding of the way light falls on a pot and how shadow can be used as part of a pot's architecture.

Another piece of interesting thrown pottery is the round teapot by Wally Keeler (UK): the 56 round body of the pot is hard and tight, like a cannon ball, but it suggests energy, and the thrown spout and lid are each elements that you want to cup in your hands – Newland-style. Once again, however, Keeler has interfered with the intuitive approach to throwing; he has used the elements to make an assemblage, resulting in a pot that is a mixture of both analytical design thinking and intuitionist craft throwing. Unity is provided by the beautifully modulated salt-glaze surface – like the marks of a soft-ground etching.

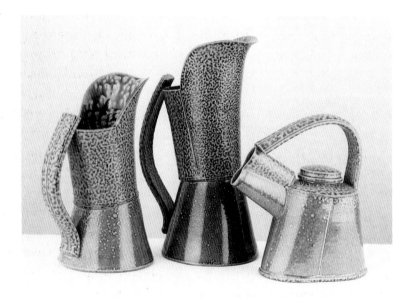

Two jugs and teapot. Wally Keeler. Salt-glazed stoneware. h.30 cm. UK, 1984

The Studio Pot

The majority of the pots shown and discussed in this book are the work of studio potters like DeVore and Keeler; they have chosen the activity for all kinds of aesthetic, sometimes philosophical reasons – they are products of art schools. Occasionally, one comes across potters who throw traditional forms and acquired their skill not from art school, but simply by apprenticing themselves to a family pottery. In Britain there are few such potteries, but in Italy several survive. One man, Luigi Gaudenzi, is continuing in a small pottery that has existed since 1730. He uses local clay and is a straightforward artisan potter with no ambitions towards 'art' or modern studio craft. He is, nevertheless, in love with his work. Typically, his work consists of harvest jugs, flagons and bowls: the forms are full, the handles join nicely to the bodies and only his glazes are, to my eyes, too hard – bouncing too much light off the form. All Gaudenzi's pots are functional.

However, the respected American studio potter, Wayne Higby, has put the case against function: 'the contemporary vessel must express the irreducible dynamics of pottery [which include pottery's history of function and utility], but remain outside the realm of function. When the possibility of use enters into the vessel equation, the pure formal essence of the pot is altered to accommodate practical considerations that inevitably restrict the artist's freedom. A pot that is neither a vessel nor a functional object will lack definitive presence and create confusion in the viewer's mind. Confusion is not the same as ambiguity.'

Developing Higby's comments with reference to two unconventional users of thrown vessels
34, 162 – Jerry Rothman and Robert Turner (both USA) – we can see that, of the two, Rothman is both more extravagant in his use of sculptural assemblage and interference with the thrown form and also nearer to the theme of function. Rothman proceeds through the simple technique of comparison and contrast – swelling thrown forms are juxtaposed with tough extruded or slab forms, and smooth with rough surfaces. He produces what Garth Clark has described as 'Bauhaus wolves in baroque clothing'. Clark finds Rothman's forms disturbing; I think they are funny and strong, if less adventurous than those of Wally Keeler.

54–5 Robert Turner, who manipulates his thrown forms whilst they are still wet, said in an interview in *American Ceramics* that getting a thrown form is the prelude to the next act. His work has a rawness about it, and it is not surprising that he should describe it all in terms of landscape. When Turner writes about what he is doing, he echoes the language of abstract sculptors of the

1960s, for whom the formal properties of how objects present themselves in space were the subject matter. He says of his pots, 'Their size is their reality', and speaks of his excitement at the way things exist 'powerfully in space', thereby describing a sentiment which many people feel in response to landscape (a sentiment more eloquently put by the English poet Charles Tomlinson, who described a mountain as a 'presence which does not present itself'). Both Rothman and Turner interfere with the thrown form because, for them, its vocabulary is too limited.

Thrown pottery falls into types, and individual examples of these types can usually be judged to fail or to succeed by clear criteria – this is all a matter of craft, not art. We are back to the business of knowing when a craft is done well or not – like washing a floor, you can see when it has been done badly. One of the most delightful of the many guides to this question is *Style in Pottery* by Arthur Lane, first published in 1948. Lane takes the reader-viewer through the various devices that a potter may employ to give his or her pot the right feeling of weight or volume: how, by the manipulation of the profile, and attention to the way the base of the pot operates or the way in which the eye is arrested by the rim or lip of the pot, the eyes are guided around and over the pot to suggest a perfect, harmonious thing. Of course, an aspect such as volume can be altered, through decoration as well as by changing the shape, but in essence what Lane gently demonstrates is the idea that pottery can succeed through the application of compositional recipes.

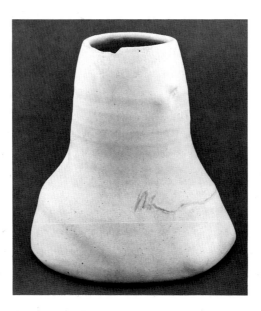

Shoreline. Robert Turner.
Porcelain. h.21cm.
USA, 1979

Neurological Findings

An American potter, Jack Troy, has related throwing on a wheel to research into the way the brain operates. Troy says that the potter proceeds by centering a blob of clay, opening the centre with thumb and fingers, thus giving a basic U-shape unless throwing a plate is intended. The inner wall of the form becomes the territory of the left hand, whilst the outer surface is governed by the right. Troy also points out that the left hand tends to pull the clay out from the axis of the wheel, whilst the right tends to push inwards.

He then introduces the findings of scientists who have researched into the workings of the human brain. It is well known that the human brain divides into two hemispheres – right and left. The left side controls the right hand, and the right side controls the left hand. Research confirms that in ninety per cent of right-handed human beings the brain's left hemisphere controls speech, and handles mathematical, analytical and rational thought. The right hemisphere of the brain deals with spatial relationships and image recognition, and handles intuition. So when a plate is thrown, the inner surface of the vessel (controlled by the left hand and the right hemisphere) is dominant; narrow cylinders result from the reverse combination. Thus the plate emerges from the potter's spatial and intuitive sense, and the cylinder results from the analytical sense. Deep bowls result from a complex interplay of both – which may be why those that are really satisfying, working well both inside and outside, are difficult to achieve. When one listens to potters discussing each others' pots, it is revealing that many of them are critical of the inside bottom of the bowl. It is here very often that even good thrown forms go wrong – the inner base of the bowl is described as 'unresolved', such irresolution being the result, perhaps, of an inadequate interplay between the analytical tendency of the left hemsiphere and the intuitive tendency of the right.

In *American Ceramics* Troy explained: 'I once heard the British potter Michael Cardew refer to the left hand as the "heart" hand in throwing, since it expands the clay wall from within, creating its sense of fullness and vitality. Cardew felt this was appropriate because the left arm is closer to the heart. This poetic connection makes sense in light of the hypothesis that our right hemispheres are the seat of spatial relationships. The left hand is most assertive in making bowls and voluminous, expansive enclosed forms. It is least assertive in making cylindrical shapes. The

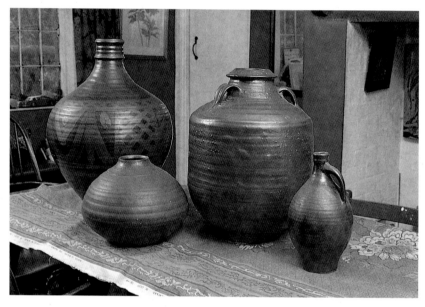

Thrown Pottery. William Newland. Earthenware. Max. h.75 cm. UK, forms developed 1950–90

more angular a form, the more it would appear to owe to the rational, mathematically oriented left lobe of the brain.'

If so, it follows that a potter's favourite form develops from a natural tendency peculiar to that individual's brain, whilst the viewer's preference for, say, a bowl rather than a cylinder might also reflect a similar innate disposition of his or her brain. Aesthetic judgment and preference thus become less a matter of intellect than an accident of biology. And yet it is also interesting to note in passing that in design-conscious societies such as Holland, where the De Stijl, design-orientated aesthetic predominates, analytical cylinders predominate – the work of Geert Lap or Jeroen Bechtold being examples.

In general, thrown pots are popular with lay people because, as Newland explained, the well-made, full-blown and above all wheel-thrown form appeals to the hands. There is no ambiguity about the appeal – the form is nice to hold; it invites you to trace its planes with your hands. Look, for example, at Val Cushing's work (USA), or that of Lisbet Daehlin (Norway) and Svend 15, 68 Bayer (UK). Even less mysterious is the appeal of watching someone at the wheel. Those who 18 cannot throw for themselves can almost sense the form growing quickly and rapidly in the hand. The response is probably sexual or, at any rate, connected ultimately with common biological responses. A potter throwing in China or Korea will throw a form intelligible not only to the hands of the potter living in New Jersey or South Australia, but also to those potters' non-potting neighbours. The appreciation of the thrown form (although not exclusively the thrown form) is basically non-intellectual.

Jack Troy's comments should not be taken as suggesting that being able to throw well is an easy skill to learn; probably very few people have the talent to throw superbly. But they do support the well-worn cliché of the contemporary potter that he or she is expressing self: as Troy himself points out, a thrown form is like a mind's imprint. His article confirms my belief that really good throwers are good throwers by birth and not tuition. And it also confirms the view that throwing pots is a non-intellectual activity. Consequently, if the potter is to do much more than generate what comes naturally to him, then the aspects of decoration or design or assemblage must assume an especial importance.

As we have seen with DeVore and Keeler, a number of the best throwers are not content to leave their work as simply well thrown. Pierre Bayle (France), for example, will go on to turn the pot and then to burnish it, or he will develop a bowl with handles, handles that are deliberately conceived of as abstract sculptural components, with the piece as a whole a combination of craft, art and design. Intuition and analytical thought have both contributed.

In the West, potters everywhere except Scandinavia and Holland (and to a small degree West Germany) are more interested in adding in 'art' to their craft than 'design'. That is to say, they prefer to alter their thrown forms to make them expressive of individuality, rather than to make 13, 60 them expressive as functional objects. Geert Lap produces work that is close to the perfection 46 of industrial design; Poul Jensen (Norway), whose work has a similar voice to that of Lap, has actually gone on to design for industrial production. One suspects that, on the whole, the contemporary potter fears function and fears design as too constricting. Keeler, like the Italian Memphis pottery discussed later on, proves these fears false.

Mind over Matter

Inevitably, the argument that thrown forms arise from intuitive skill, whilst constructed forms involve thought, is over simple. We have already seen that the thrown form is itself often just a starting point for a more complicated decorative or expressive object. Theoretically, as soon as thrown forms are developed in this way the maker is involved in decision-making that is to some extent analogous to the process of thought in sculpture or painting. In practice, by no means all constructed forms in clay result from conceptual thought because clay is an ideal medium for those who want to make arbitrary gestures and marks in it. Very often it is allowed to take control of the maker and is used as a free vehicle for intuitive expression.

Criticism and scepticism may be fit reactions to some of this work, but consider what is revealed by the work of the Dutch ceramist, Irene Vonck. Vonck rolls her wet clay into long 97, 130 sausages, places a sausage onto newspaper on the floor, and then quickly pulls the clay apart with her hands in rapid sweeping movements. She then places another sausage of clay alongside it, performing the same manoeuvre except that there is an overlap and join with the first piece of clay. With luck, wonderful baroque, leaf- or flower-like reliefs are created. These can be assembled into vessels or, as in the case of the wall construction she did for a post office in Wormerveer, Holland, form part of a big public applied artwork. The clay records the 131 movement of her hands, the colour heightens it. Vonck herself provides the best description of her work: 'Although I make the strokes – the clay has gone where it wants, unrestricted – it frays at the edges, curling around itself and tearing under the movement – this is so important and gives the work its strength. I have not laid my own will on the work – haven't cleaned it up, polished away any roughness, neatened any torn edges – but I accentuate what the clay has done itself – highlighting each crevice and profusion, each tear and bundle of clay. . . .'

In response to this, or other expressionistic clay work (the East German, Karl Fulle, is also an important figure), we have to ask: 'What are the criteria for success or failure?' It transpires that not everything is arbitrary: Vonck would normally abandon bad work herself. Success in her work depends on whether the forms contain sufficient vitality and demonstrate a fast, easy-flowing upward movement from base to top. If any of the forms within the piece appear stilted or clumsy, this movement is lost; and, as with all vessels whether thrown or constructed, what happens at the base is vital. A good Vonck piece leaps up with spontaneity, a bad Vonck looks

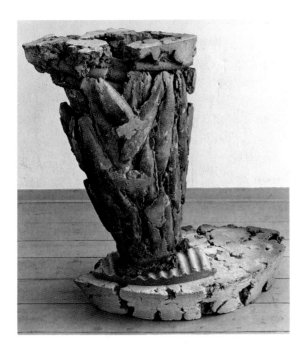

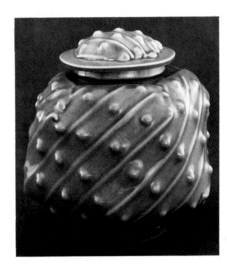

Left, Fish and Ships. Jos Verwiel. Stoneware. h.80 cm.
Holland, 1985

Above, Folded jar. Virginia Cartwright. Porcelain. h.19 cm.
USA, 1980

cut off clumsily at its base. This process is a little like watercolour painting; one blurted brush stroke can lose the whole piece.

The watercolour comparison applies more directly to one of the West's most important makers of clay vessels, Rudy Staffel (USA). He painted watercolours for a while many years ago and now, in his seventies, he is taking to it again. Staffel is a rarity in contemporary ceramics; as a result of experience and longevity, perhaps, his pots look like the product of both intuitive skill and thoughtful observation. He works fast at his porcelain vessels and he is a watercolourist in clay in the sense that, just as a good watercolourist uses the white grain of his paper to give him light and applies the minimum of paint, so to does Staffel strive to get light into his vessels and to use the minimum of clay. He creates vessels made up from straps and strips and sheets and blobs of clay that in some places let light shine through and in other block it out. Sometimes a strap of clay is used for reasons of composition, sometimes to support the side of the vessel. Frequently, the clay looks as though it has been pulled round in one single sweep, like a mark from a brush swung from the arm. Staffel handles the clay like a dancer.

In an important review of Staffel's solo show in Philadelphia in Spring 1985, Edward J. Sozanski of the *Philadelphia Inquirer* (11 April 1985) described the objects as follows: 'Surface fracturing is literal as well as metaphorical. Staffel's thrown forms are always asymmetrical; the projecting rim is usually pinched in at one point, or there may be one or more vertical ridges pressed into

24–6

the wall . . . if a fissure is made Staffel closes it with pinches of clay that look like butterfly sutures or dabs that resemble spot welds. . . . Staffel is frugal with special effects. In several pots, a thin sulphur wash applied sparingly before firing imparts a green tinge, but otherwise the pots are the colour of chalk.'

Staffel calls his vessels (although he is wary of the cliché) 'light gatherers'. They are sensitive, gentle objects and their importance rests in their fulfilment of one of pottery's most important contemporary roles: they are objects of domestic scale providing the individual with an opportunity for aesthetic consolation.

Another ceramist with an affinity with watercolour is the Englishman, Ewen Henderson. 93 Unlike Staffel, he does not literally use light in his pots, but he does convey an astonishing fluidity of colour and texture. This fluidity is often made just to 'hang in the air'. A characteristic Henderson pot is full of volume and the walls are so thin and friable, sometimes with the substance and feel of meringue, that one half expects them to blow away. Henderson can work with large pots three feet high and one and a half feet wide – they need to be embraced and held down, even though their dark colours and geologically striated patterns strongly suggest that they are earthbound anyway. Henderson works fast, pinching the clay and working with an unorthodox combination of porcelain and stoneware clays.

Not all constructors in clay work quickly. One practical consequence of constructing a form slowly, as opposed to throwing or making it quickly, is the time given to the ceramist to choose and compose what kind of images and symbols to build into the work. The most exciting and complicated decorative works tend to be constructed – the results can be seen in the achievements of, for example, Adrian Saxe (USA), Richard Slee (UK) and Kari Christensen (Norway) in the next chapter.

The rejection of the wheel is one way in which ceramists have been able to introduce new thought into pottery. Among the most important potters in this field in Europe have been the English women Alison Britton, Jacqui Poncelet and Carol McNicoll – although it must be said that Poncelet is now working as a sculptor.

Of the three, Alison Britton has been the clearest about why she builds asymmetrical, architectural pots rather than throwing vessels on the wheel. She says: 'The conventional 178, 183 thrown pot has absolute uniform symmetry in the vertical dimension and therefore its shape can be taken in from one viewpoint by its silhouette.' But Britton wants forms that surprise the spectator from different viewpoints. Much of her work in the 1970s consisted of handbuilt jugs – the spouts and handles, together with a disposition for asymmetrical planes, helped her make objects which got away from the predictability of round forms. Britton's more recent work is more abstract and vigorously painted. There are echoes of function, but that's all. It is important to know, however, that the shape and outcome of the pot are determined by the painting. She begins by rolling the clay into a sheet and then decorating the sheet with coloured slips (liquid clay). She uses the brush extensively and thinks about the marks she is making in terms of the patterns that are created. The outcome of the pot is shaped by this process because the pot is composed from the patterns on the sheet. Here is a mixture of the intuitive, the accidental and the thoughtful in a process which allows her time and scope for re-adjustment.

Jacqui Poncelet has gone even further; her most recent pieces – those that can still be claimed to belong to pottery – have entirely dispensed with function and references to function, and exist as allegorical, metaphorical objects, suggestive of sea creatures and the human figure. Some men have found them threatening.

86–90   Poncelet's work has contributed to the modern movement in ceramics. It does not spring from the same root as, say, American ceramics. For example, although ceramists such as Peter Voulkos and Robert Turner and Graham Marks are different from each other, they have an affinity of spirit. Each man has broken the limitations of the vessel to make new expressive forms, but each has done so in the American manner, which relishes the slurp or the squidginess of the clay – men are more sentimental about the stuff, perhaps, than women. Certainly there is very little about the clay form that is free in Poncelet's work. People often remark on the great transformation in her ceramics that occurred in the 1970s. She began with little white bone-china cups which wooed people by their exquisiteness; ten years later she was making rougher, tougher objects of a different order altogether and, it must be said, losing many fans in the process. Yet the tightness and control that is present in the bone-china cups is present in all her works, including the most recent; they are certainly not free or loose.

Another studio potter whose work shows a lot of control is Paula Winokur (USA). Winokur is especially interesting because for a while her ceramic objects have been non-functional, but recently she has begun to re-explore ceramics as a useful applied art. For example, she has produced for the Helen Drutt Gallery a porcelain fire surround which, with its small interior, cave-like crevasses and containers, contrasts themes of intimacy and domestic familiarity with emotions of secrecy. In many homes a fire surround and mantel shelf is, or was, a focal point, a place where things of special importance or domestic banality were put – a framed picture of a loved one, a box with bits of string and loose odds and ends, or a precious ornament. Winokur has made a surround which plays up this role to the point of becoming a commentary on it, though the surround is also functional – it can be commissioned for a job of work. Winokur has also, and this reflects some of her other work, managed to capture the sense of serenity and

81   stillness that is to be found in the still-life paintings of Giorgio Morandi. Other examples of her work are three-dimensional still-lifes; they are quiet, observant, reflective and feminine. This is emphatically not to use feminine as a simile for weak or retiring, but to indicate again the sense of control and care which quite frequently marks out art made by women.

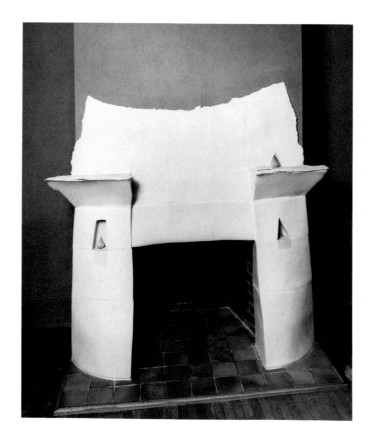

Is there a difference between the work which women and men ceramists produce – the one more careful, the other tending to build bigger, more robustly, more – sentimentally? Sometimes it may seem so, but there are exceptions to the rule: Betty Woodman (USA) is an extravagant potter, and an exception, and so too are Ruth Duckworth (UK/USA) and Beatrice de Germay (France). De Germay, like Poncelet, has moved from clay as applied art to (it might reasonably be argued) sculpture.

Other ceramists who have elevated the ceramic object to a new height of interest and aesthetic complexity without, it seems, falling into the trap of self-consciously trying to make art are William Daley, Graham Marks and Robert Hawkins.

To an extent, Daley's work has similarities with Alison Britton's: both ceramists construct planes which have the quality of taut sheets of muscle – planes that are not so much architectural as anatomical in the way they pull at one another and lightly bulge. Both ceramists pay as much attention to the interior as to the exterior of their pots and in both cases the relationship between line and plane is complicated and thought through as much like a three-

106–10

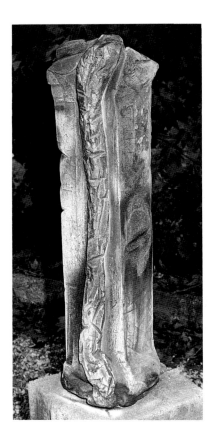

Opposite page
Fireplace Site II. Paula Winokur. Porcelain.
h. 1.61m. USA, 1985

This page
Clay sculpture. Beatrice de Germay. Earthenware.
h. 1.5m. France, 1982

dimensional abstract drawing as a solid form. The tactile sense is important in assessing Daley's work – you can feel the tension in the planes and the surface itself is finely textured but differentiated; it changes gently from place to place.

Daley has, however, experimented with surprising variations on his current theme. He likes animals and some years ago considered including some sort of animal – a reptile, perhaps – inside the pot, but the balance of imagery was all wrong. Daley's work is all about fine tensions – fine tensions between textures, between different planes and between the pot as a vessel and some other idea or object, such as a building or a landscape.

Critic Michael McTwigan, in an *American Craft* article, has said that Daley uses two kinds of edge – thin and sharp, or curled and folded. The importance of the edge in the composition of his work is described by McTwigan thus: 'For the lip of a vase, the rim of a bowl, is the tightrope on which our perceptions of the vessel must balance. It can be a kind of frame, delimiting a body (vase) or bounding a pictorial field (bowl).' What Daley is also exploiting, of course, is light and shade; he – and his wife Catherine, with whom he makes the vessels – is modelling with light and shade much as an architect or a constructor of monuments does. Sometimes, however, the geometry of a Daley piece is determined by the way the thing is being made – without a support here, or a ridge there, the wall of the vessel would give way.

Graham Marks's work is quite commonly referred to as sculpture, since the pieces are so large – they are among the most exciting clay works to come out of the modern movement in ceramics, partly because they play up, to an extraordinary degree, two of pottery's most important aspects: a sense of volume (the Newland principle, again) and the sense of touch. Even if you do not touch a Graham Marks work, the way in which he has constructed the surfaces offers a visual analogy of what it would feel like to touch it. There is also a sense of great mass, conveyed through analogy: for example, a number of the pieces look as though they have immensely thick walls crushing in on an interior space, but these walls are hollow. If the walls were not hollow, then the work would be difficult or impossible to fire without the clay exploding in the kiln. As it is, Marks has to build his kiln around the work, which is too big for conventional kilns.

Marks's works are intelligently thought out and their power comes, I believe, through their playing on basic human reactions. For example, his approach to the interiors of his works often introduces the idea of mystery – he may opt for a fissure and thereby suggest the element of risk, daring you, rather than inviting you, to put your hands in it. Other forms are more inviting, though sometimes the surfaces wriggle with suggested life – Marks can make his clay crawl and squirm in a cacophony of texture. All-in-all, Marks has made objects that are both familiar and alien. Michael McTwigan again has something enlightening to offer in *American Ceramics*: 'Coming closer we realise these are not wholes, but halves . . . will they reveal a vessel's inner volume, a melon's orange red flesh? Their easy resemblance to natural objects is misleading, and we are surprised when confronted by the irritating cores, which spiral to a terminus we can only guess at. Graham Marks reveals one mystery only to leave us at the door step of another.'

The development of the mysterious or the incongruous object in ceramics has been pursued by a number of constructivist potters including the Australian Robert Hawkins. But, unlike either Daley's or Marks's work, Robert Hawkins's *Cone Stand* takes its cue from the 20th century – scaled up, *Cone Stand* could be an image of the vast industrial debris that now litters much of the urban West. It is also suggestive of ritual – an object for a church or temple, perhaps, or an arcane tribal ceremony.

9, 57–8

99

Bridging Disciplines

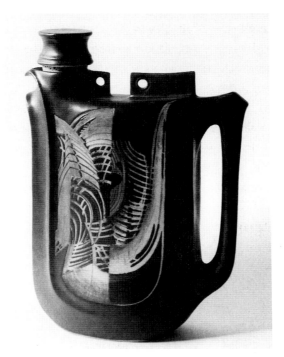

Coffee pot. Frank Steyaert. Stoneware. h. 30 cm. Belgium, 1984

Many ceramists, including some of those mentioned above, believe that – following the ideas pressed home by such critics as Rose Slivka – the ceramic-sculpture divide has been bridged. I do not. I believe that there is a distinction between an applied art such as pottery (whether it be functional or decorative) and fine art. It may be, of course, that there is much more decorative art shown in museums or sold in galleries and auction houses under the fine-art label than is usually admitted. The majority of sculpture and painting is imitative and repetitious, and appears to be no more (and no less) than decorative art or elaborate ornament. Nevertheless, the critical distinction between an applied art and a fine art has to do with the aim and purpose of the activity. For it seems that the role which fine art has striven to find for itself is the role of enlarging experience and adding to our understanding and knowledge. Very little visual art may be said to have done this, but more than enough this century has done so to make the argument stand up.

Applied art, such as pottery, is concerned with the embellishment of a given culture – in its ornament it can reflect society's values and aesthetic interests by borrowing from the discoveries of fine art, in the latter's role of mapping out the avant-garde.

In one instance, however, ceramics has been a part of the avant-garde – thanks to the Memphis design group in Italy. Eventually the ceramics produced under the Memphis flag will influence craft and studio ceramics generally, though by that time Memphis will be history. Memphis, the group of young architects and designers loosely associated around Ettore Sottsass, produced a big blast against modernism, borrowing stylistic devices from the fashions of the 1930s, 40s and 50s and combining them with 1980s decorative laminates. The furniture, glass and ceramics which emerged from this opposed at every turn and angle the modernist dictum inherited from the Bauhaus: function determines form. Some of the work was gross, some of it beautiful; often it was not especially well made. Yet always there were ideas.

Memphis has passed its first period of fame and acclaim, but in ceramics its founder members, such as architect/designer Matteo Thun, are continuing to develop work with the 43–4, 47–8 help of the designer-craftsman, Alessio Sarri, in Florence. People like Thun, Sarri, Michele de 28–31 Lucchi, Anna Gili and Andrea Nannetti and, of course, Sottsass himself, have injected modern ceramics with a new intelligence. Ceramics has always been an eclectic activity. Thun and the others have examined the dynamism of everything from Futurism and Constructivism to the streamlining of 1930s cocktail shakers and given the studio pot a new historicist larder to raid – 20th-century design. Above all, Italians have introduced intelligent humour into pottery.

Memphis apart, the modern constructors of clay objects have an uncomfortable burden to face up to: unlike the potter at the wheel, whose forms spring to hand by a combination (so it seems) of neurological inclination and physics, the constructor has always to make choices. Often such choices cannot be rationalized. Thus much modern ceramic work is in that sense arbitrary and has, finally, to be discarded, either by the maker or by future critics as the piece comes into focus. This is probably true of other activities in design and art. To date, the most successful constructors of clay objects have been those who keep close to pottery's recognizable forms; such forms provide potters like Staffel, or designers like Thun, with a theme. Hence the predominance of the vessel in this – and the next chapter – and the virtual absence of what could be called ceramic sculpture.

Opposite
1 Knitted bowl
  Carol McNicoll
  Constructed stoneware
  d.37cm
  UK, 1982

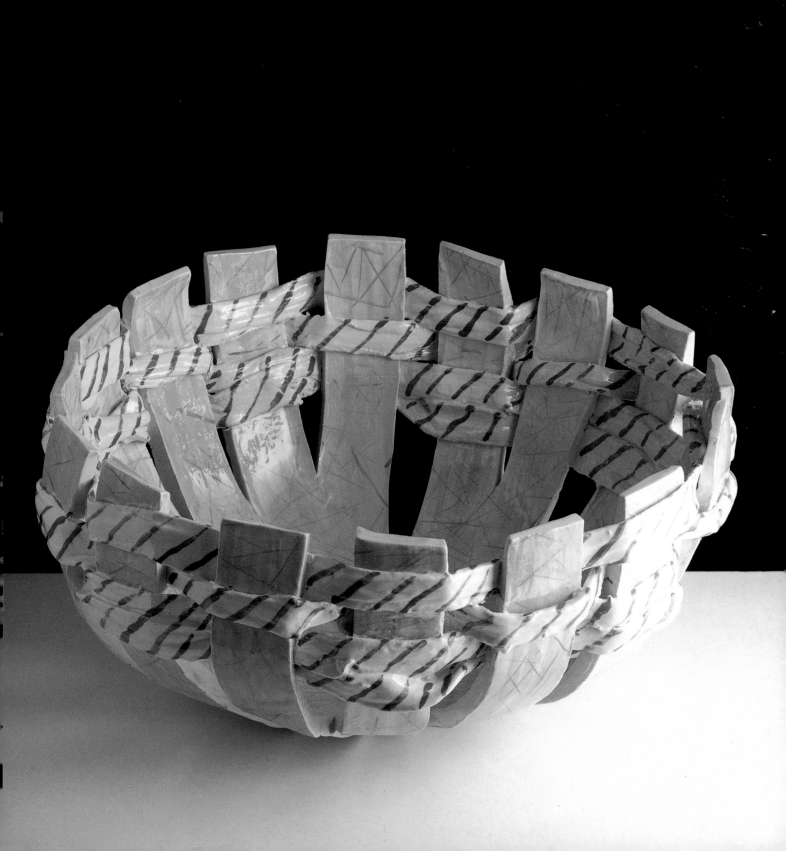

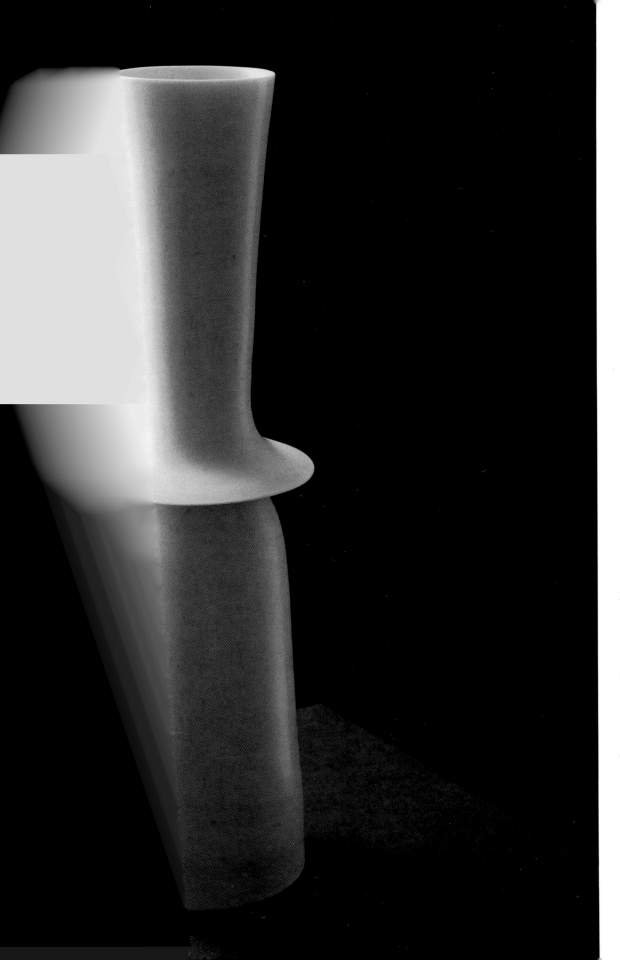

2 Vase
   Ben Oldenhof
   Porcelain
   h. 10 cm
   Holland, 1985

3 Vase
   Elisabeth Schaffer
   Stoneware
   h. 19.4 cm
   West Germany, 1980

4 Vessel
   Jeannie Mah
   Porcelain
   h. 30 cm
   Canada, 1985

5 Vessel
   Jeannie Mah
   Porcelain
   h. 30 cm
   Canada, 1985

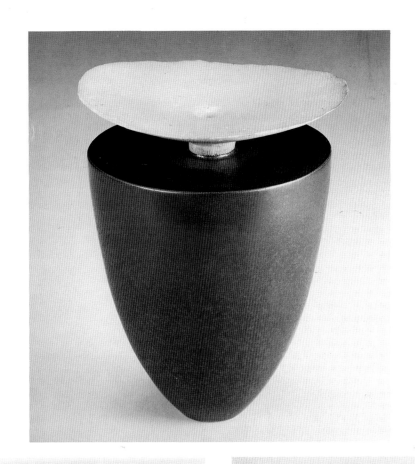

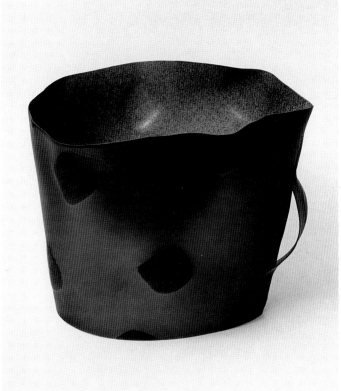

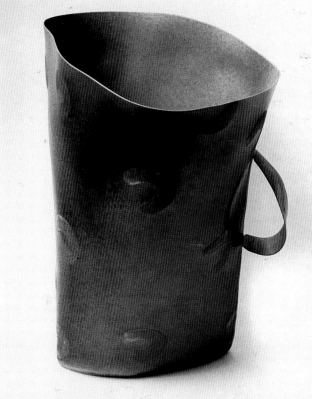

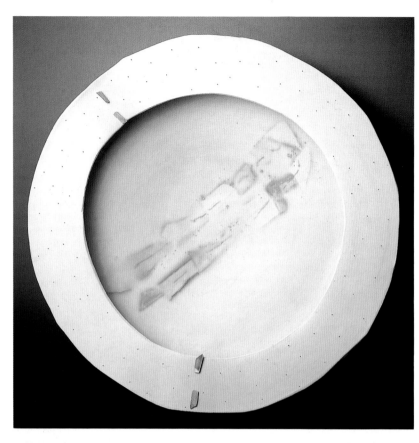

6 Plate
  Jill Bonovitz
  Terra sigillata
  d. 56 cm
  USA, 1985

7 Bowl
  Richard DeVore
  Wheel-thrown and altered
    stoneware
  d. 27 cm
  USA, 1977
  Collection of
    Joan Mannheimer

8 Jar
  Heidi Kippenberg
  Constructed stoneware
  h. 25 cm
  West Germany, 1980

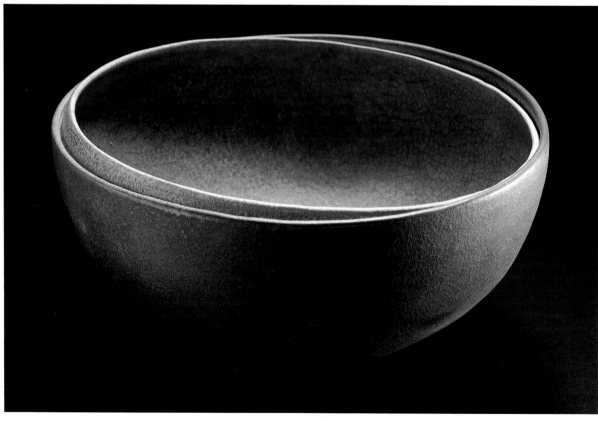

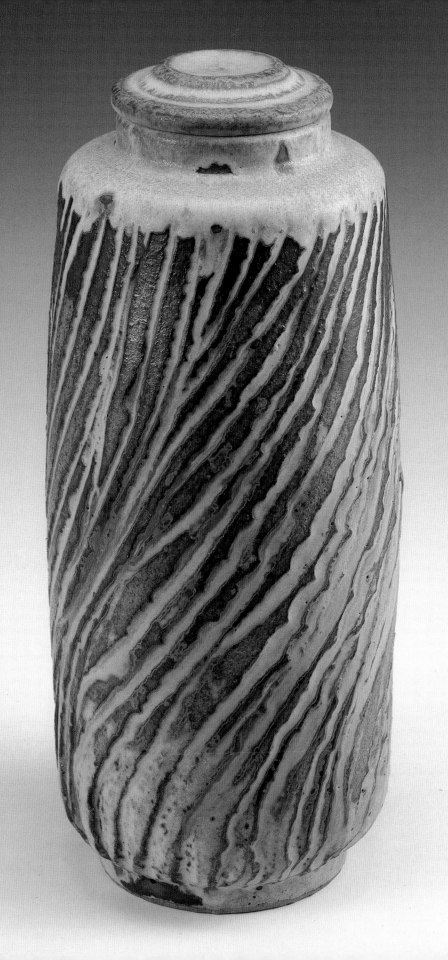

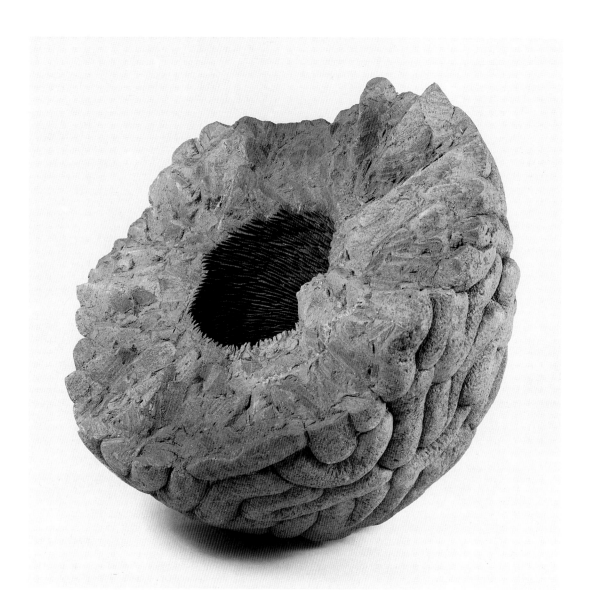

9 Untitled
  Graham Marks
  Constructed earthenware
  h.77cm
  USA, 1984

10 Untitled III
   Barry Flanagan
   Coiled earthenware
   h. 10 cm
   UK, 1980

11 Bowl
   Mary Rogers
   Coiled stoneware
   h. 20 cm
   UK, 1981

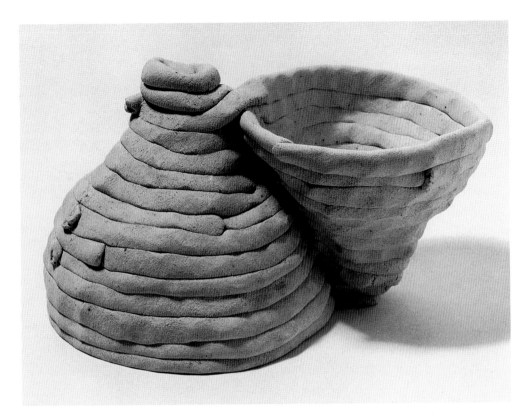

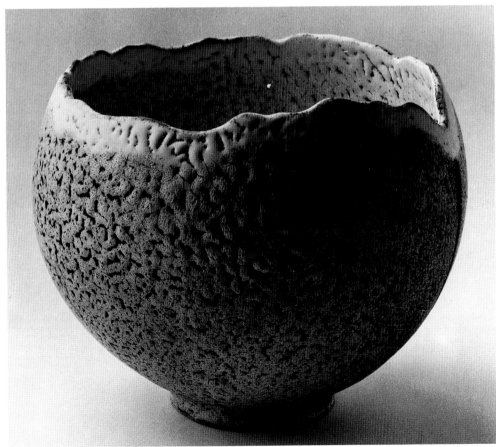

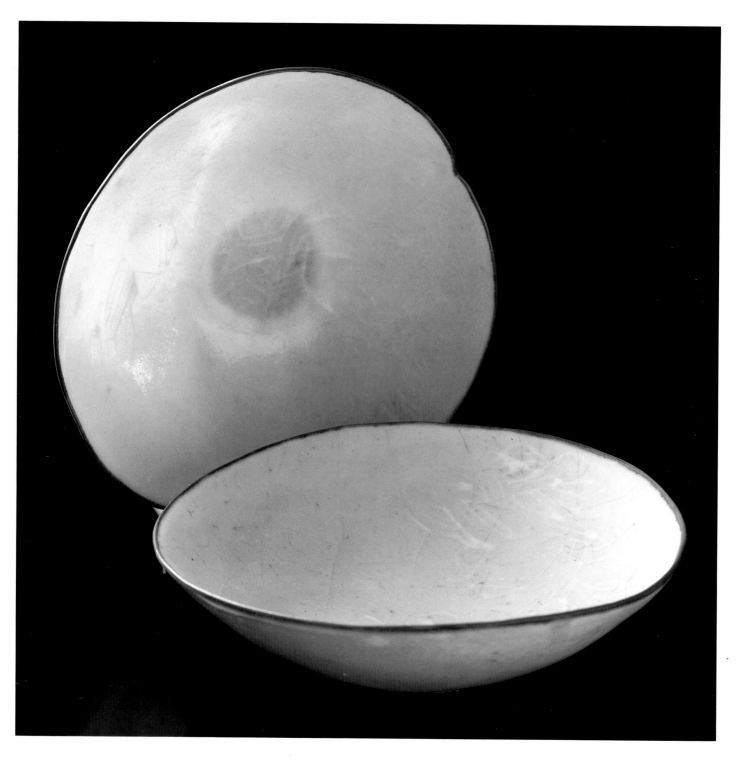

12 Bowls
    Kari Christensen
    High-fired porcelain,
      press moulded
    d. 14 cm
    Norway, 1976

13 Thrown form
    Geert Lap
    Stoneware
    d. 22.5 cm
    Holland, 1985

14 Expression no. 1
    Ron Nagle
    Earthenware
    h. 9 cm
    USA, 1978
    Collection of
      Joan Mannheimer

15 Cups
    Lisbet Daehlin
    Stoneware
    h. 8 cm
    Norway, 1985

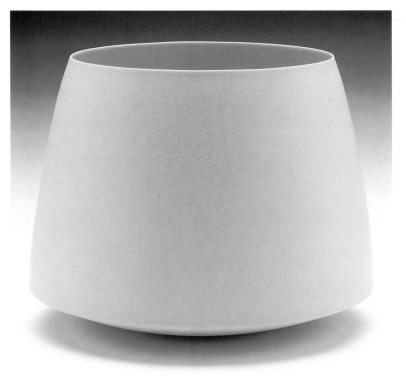

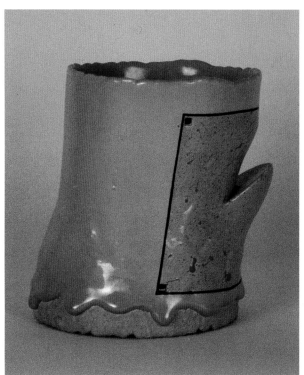

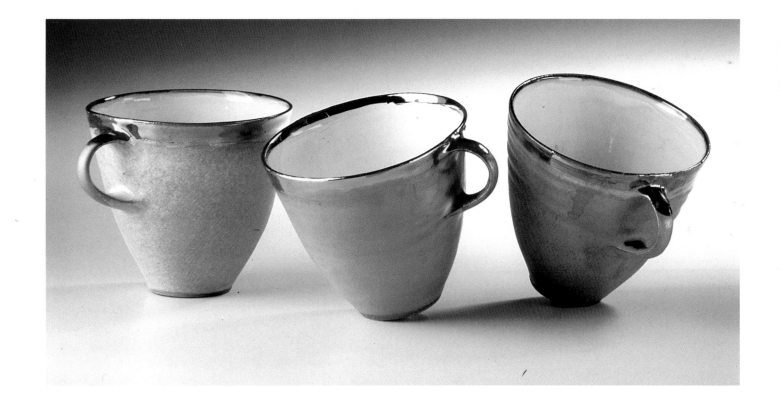

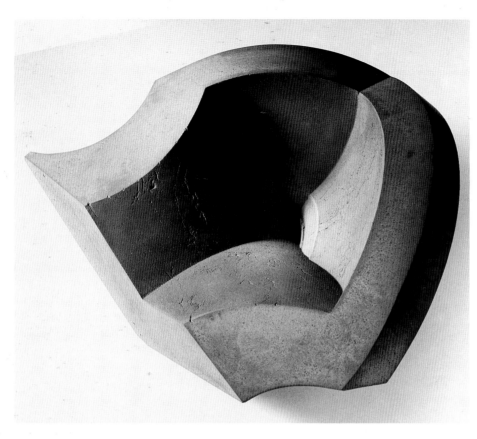

16 Baroque Interior piece No. 3
Martin Smith
Red earthenware, press moulded,
    machine-polished after firing
h. 16 cm
UK, 1982

17 Bowl
Richard DeVore
Wheel-thrown and altered stoneware
22 × 19 × 18 cm
USA, 1977
Collection of Joan Mannheimer

18 Pot for a tree
Svend Bayer
Wheel-thrown stoneware
h. 60 cm
UK, 1981

19 Jug
Mick Casson
Stoneware
h. 35 cm
UK, 1982

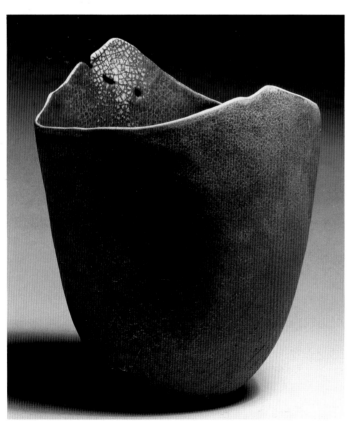

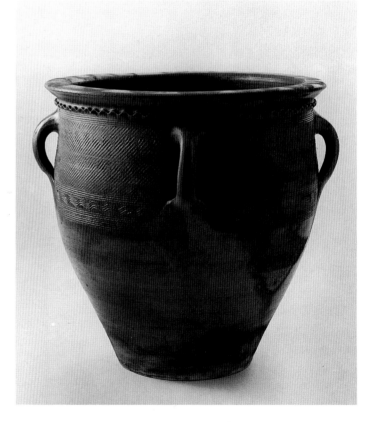

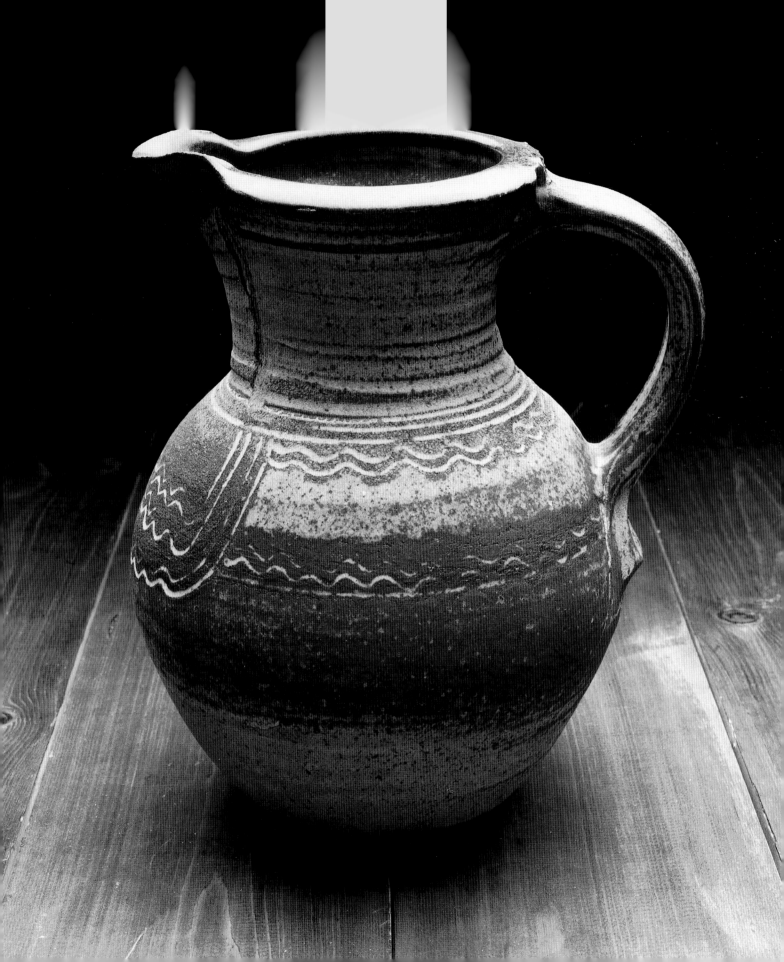

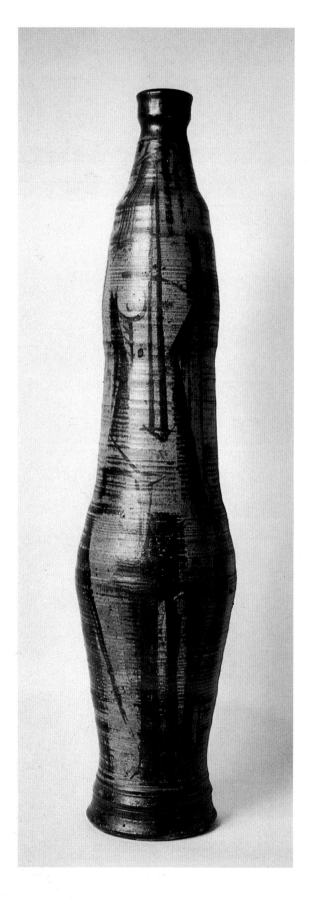

20 Salome
Robert Washington
Stoneware
h.56 cm
UK, 1986/7

21 & who the Pot . . .
Robert Washington
Stoneware
h.78 cm
UK, 1986

22 Vases
Jeroen Bechtold
Thrown stoneware
h. 17, 25, 34 cm
Holland, 1979–85

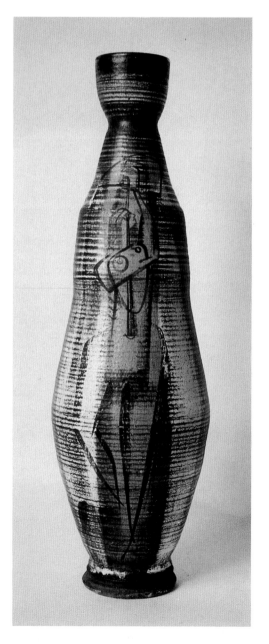

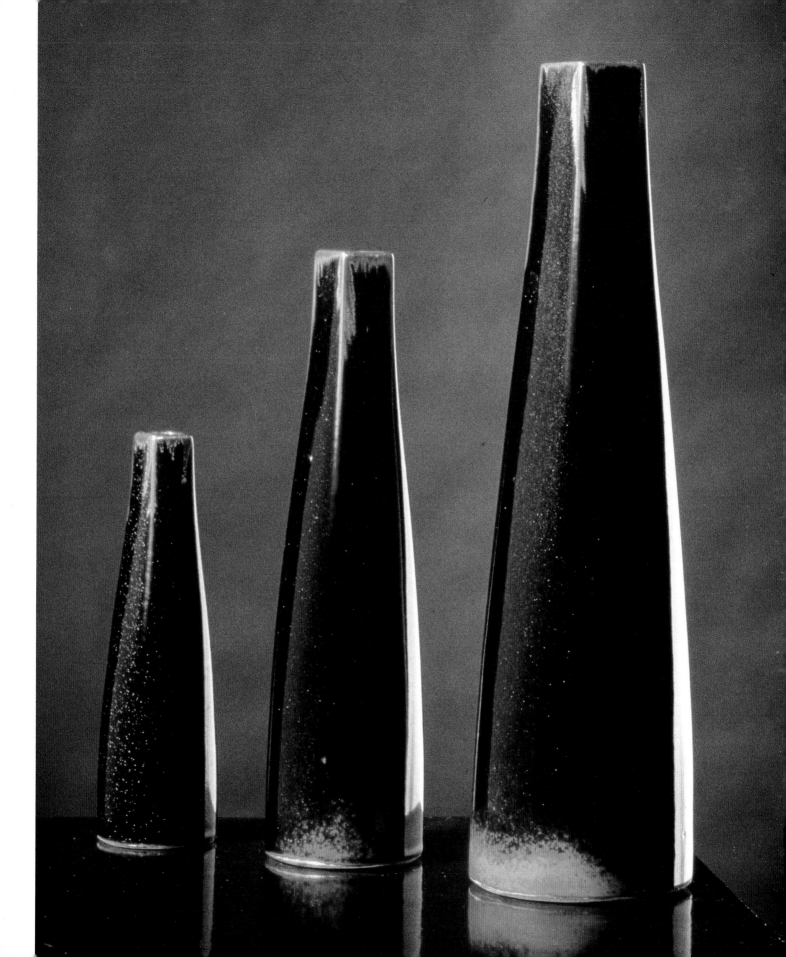

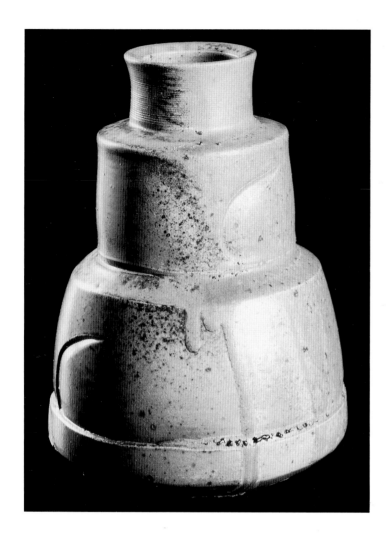

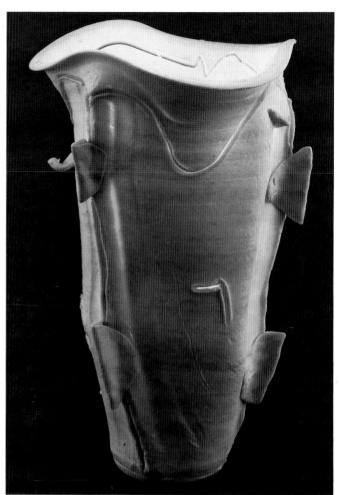

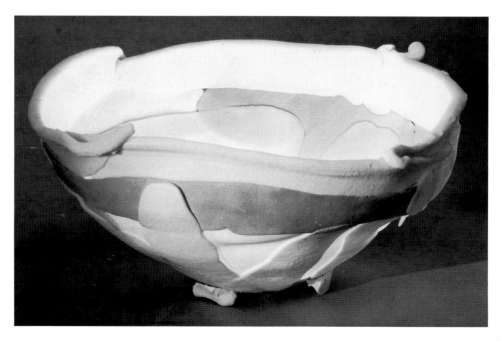

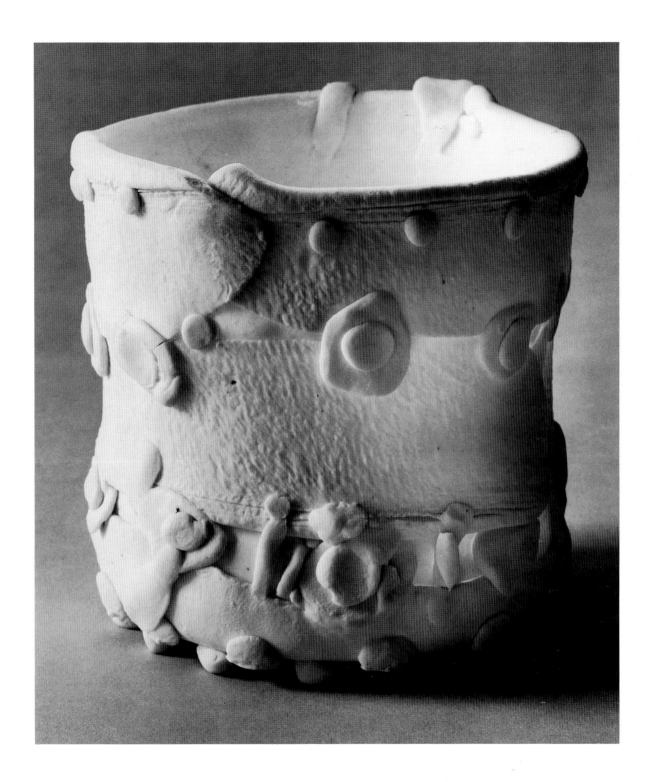

23 Vase
   Horst Kerstan
   Thrown and constructed
      stoneware
   h. 20 cm
   West Germany, 1985

24 Light Gatherer
   Rudy Staffel
   Thrown porcelain
   h. 25 cm
   USA, 1979

25 Light Gatherer
   Rudy Staffel
   Constructed porcelain
   h. 12 cm
   USA, 1979

26 Light Gatherer
   Rudy Staffel
   Constructed porcelain
   h. 15 cm
   USA, 1985

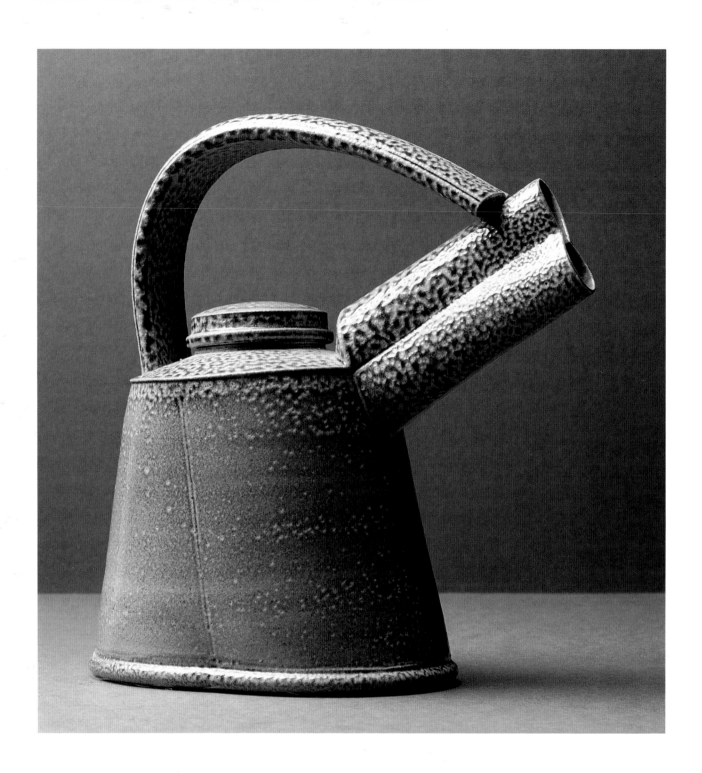

27 Teapot
Wally Keeler
Thrown stoneware, salt-glazed
h. 22 cm
UK, 1984

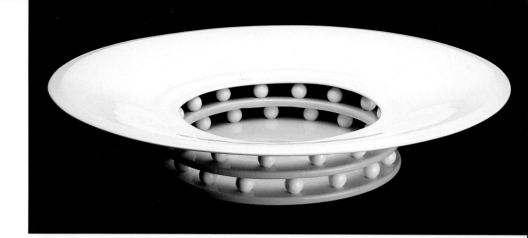

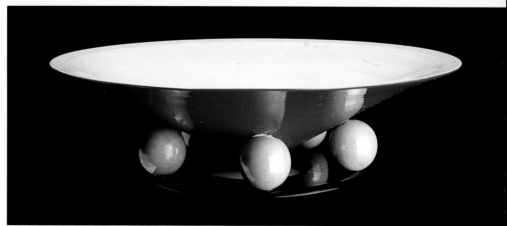

28 Mud Stars
   Alessio Sarri
   Stoneware
   d. 40 cm
   Italy, 1985

29 Mud Stars
   Alessio Sarri
   Stoneware
   d. 35 cm
   Italy, 1985

30 Mud Stars
   Alessio Sarri
   Stoneware
   d. 40 cm
   Italy, 1985

31 Mud Stars
   Alessio Sarri
   Stoneware
   d. 32 cm
   Italy, 1985

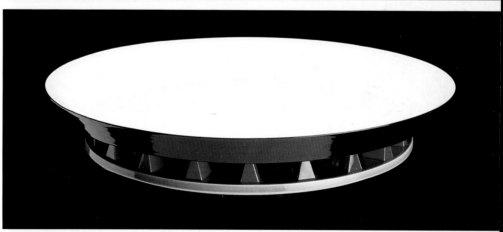

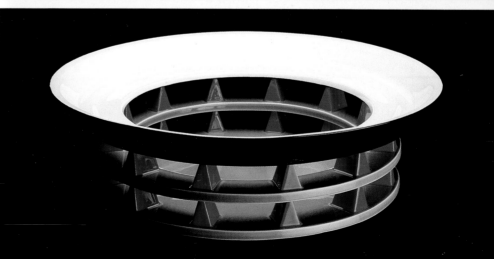

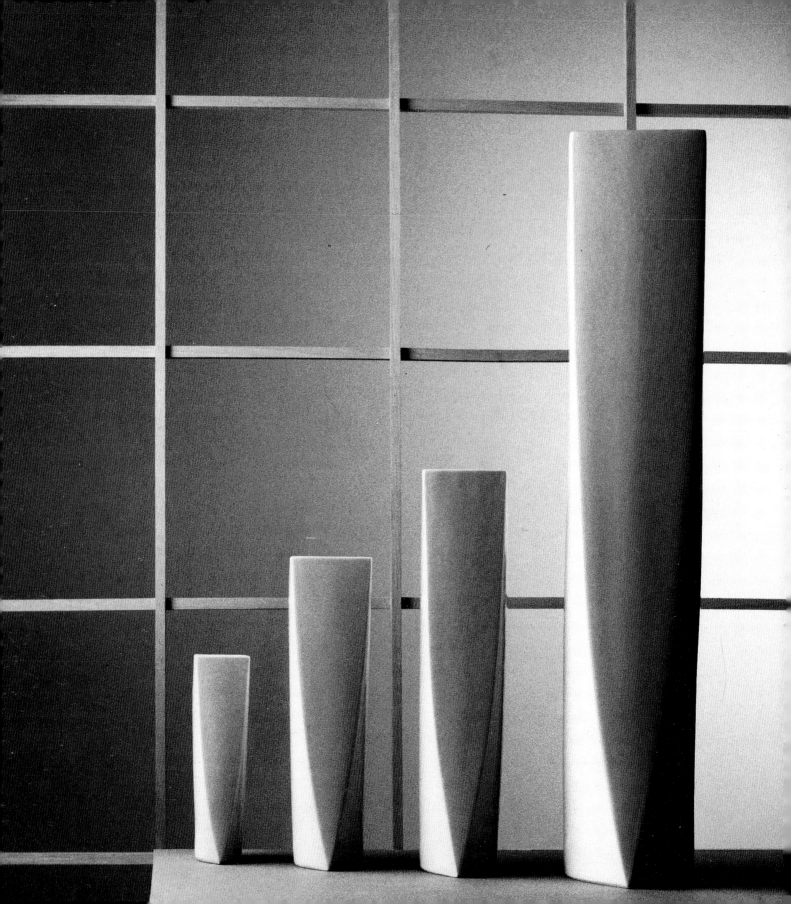

32 Vases
  Jeroen Bechtold
  Stoneware
  h. 13 cm, 19 cm, 24 cm, 43 cm
  Holland, 1983–85

33 Jar with triple-fracture rim
  Elizabeth Fritsch
  Constructed stoneware
  h. 14 cm
  UK, 1974

34 Ritual vessel
  Jerry Rothman
  Stoneware
  h. 55 cm
  USA, 1980

35 Twisted bottle with
    shattered vase
  James Lawton
  Stoneware
  h. 27 cm
  USA, 1984

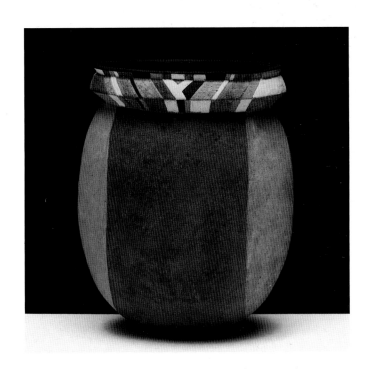

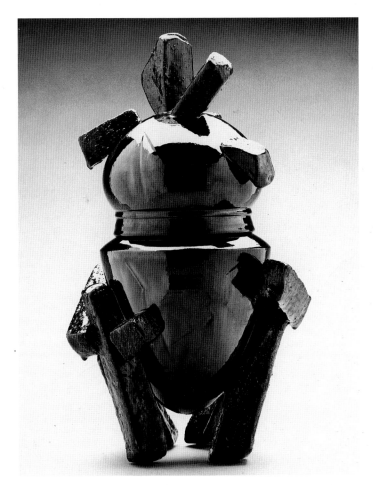

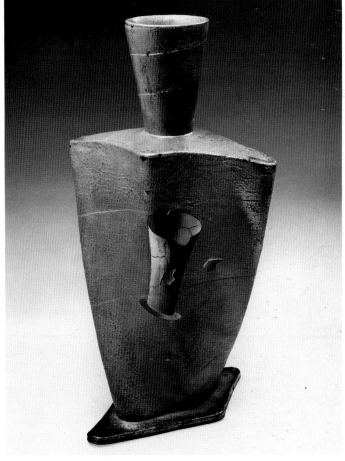

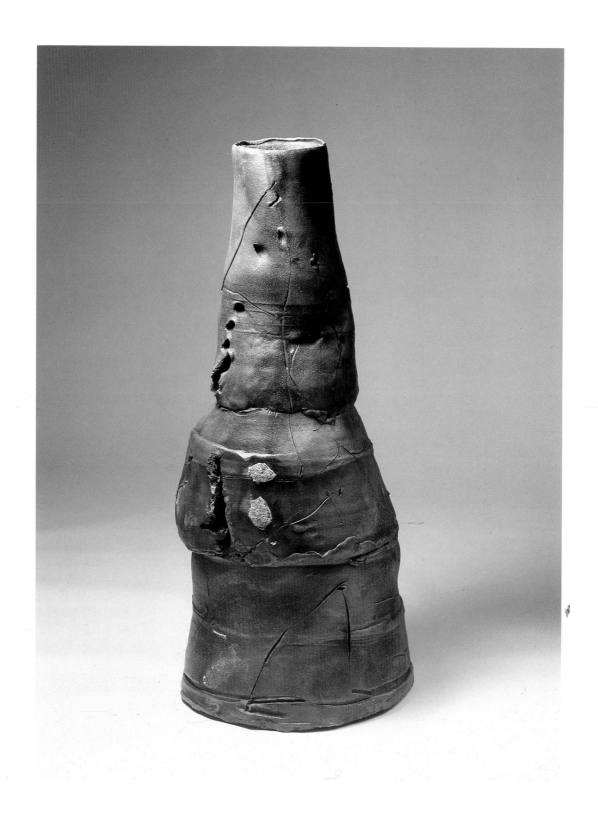

36 Large vase form
   Peter Voulkos
   Wood-fired stoneware
   h. 100 cm
   USA, 1981

37 Bottle
   Lucie Rie
   Stoneware
   h. 38 cm
   UK, 1979

38 Conjugation
   Elsa Rady
   Porcelain
   h. 27 cm
   USA, 1984

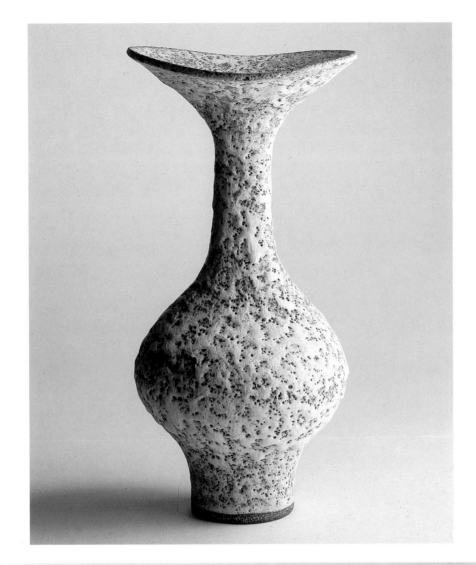

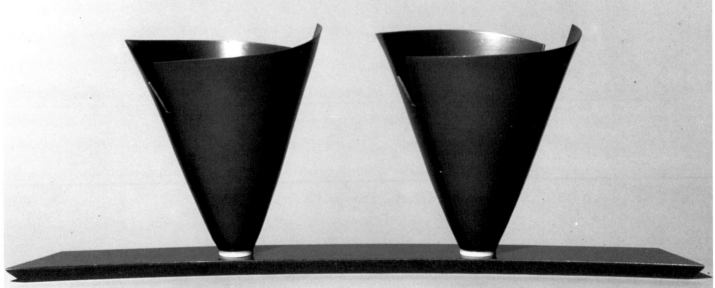

42 Teapots
   Jill Crowley
   Earthenware
   h. 12 cm
   UK, 1982

43 Teapots
   Matteo Thun
   Porcelain
   h. 25 cm
   Italy, 1983

44 Amphora
   Matteo Thun
   Porcelain
   h. 40 cm
   Italy, 1982

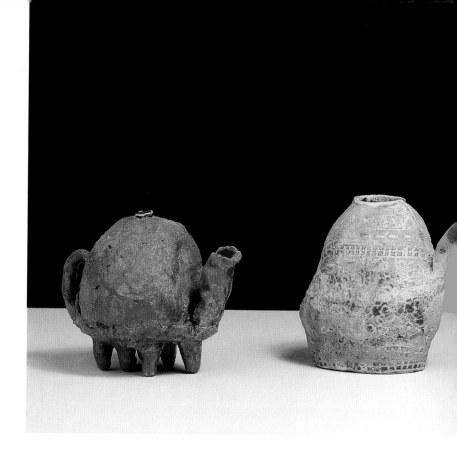

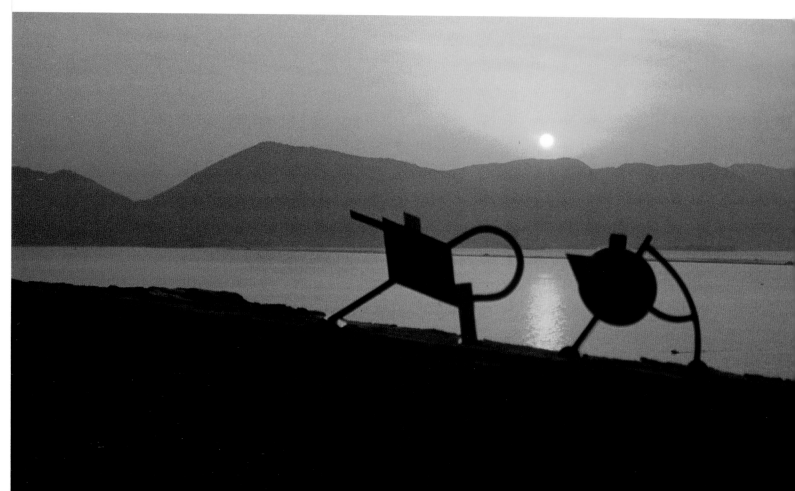

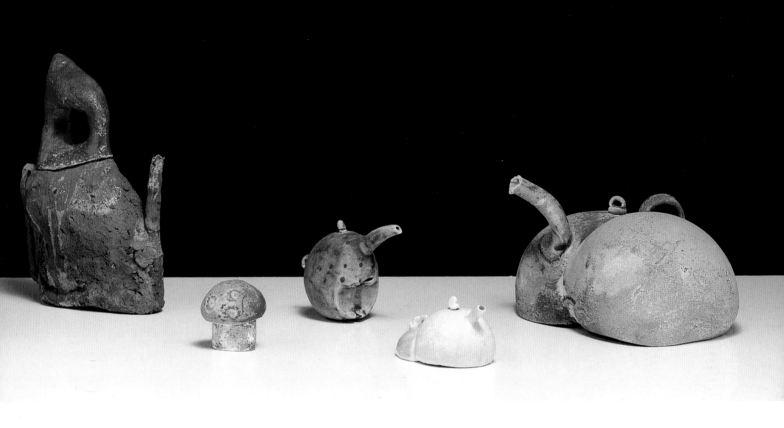

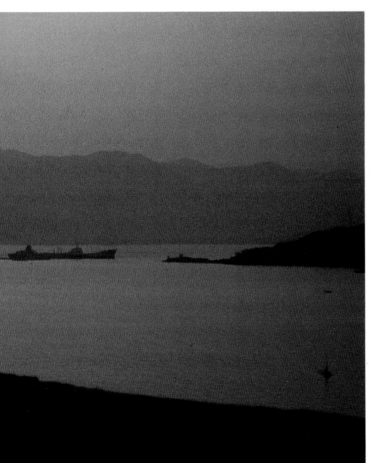

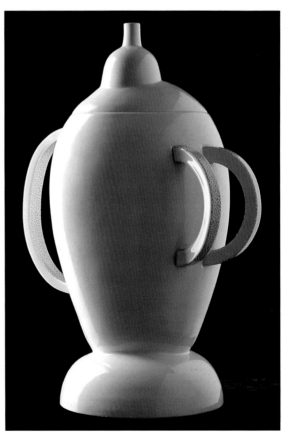

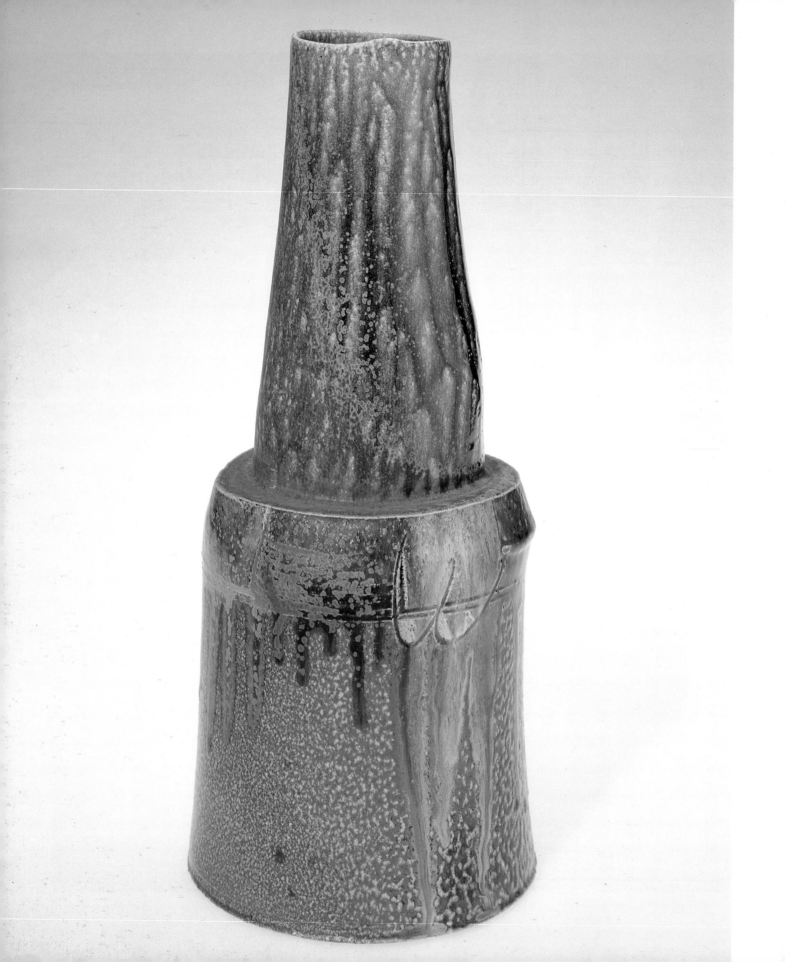

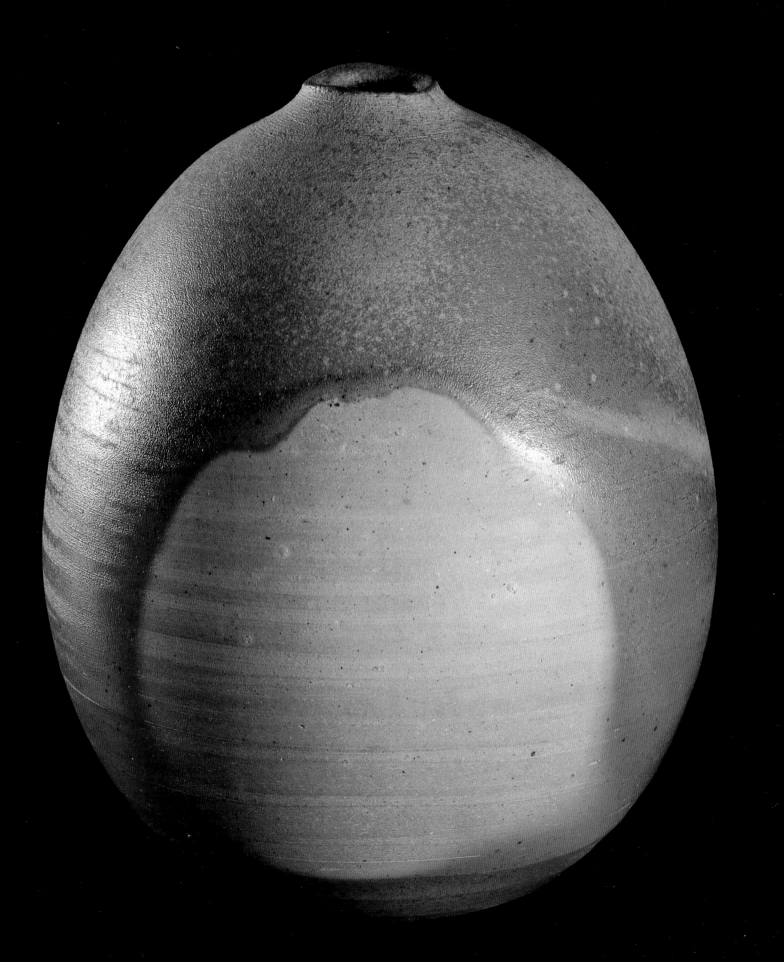

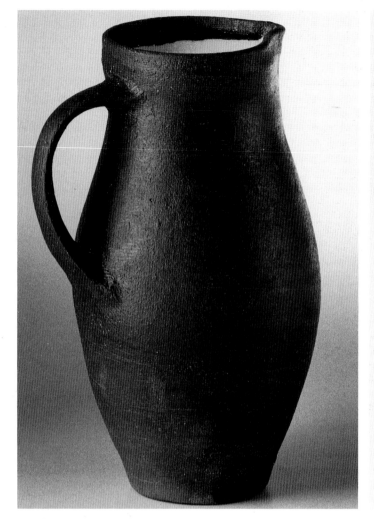

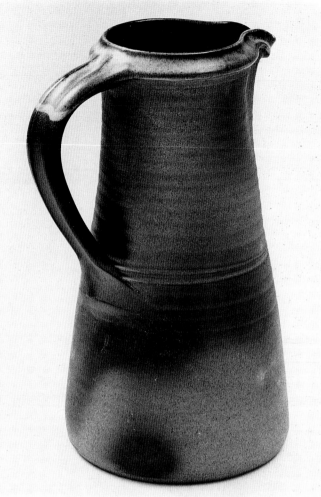

51 Jug
   Lisbet Daehlin
   Stoneware
   h. 22 cm
   Norway, 1985

52 Jug
   John Leach
   Stoneware
   h. 34 cm
   UK, 1981

53 4 Bag Vessel
   Stephen De Staebler
   Handbuilt stoneware
   h. 52 cm
   USA, 1979
   Collection of
       Joan Mannheimer

54 Oshogbo
   Robert Turner
   Stoneware
   h. 27.5 cm
   USA, 1982

55 Ashanti
   Robert Turner
   Stoneware
   h. 30 cm
   USA, 1982

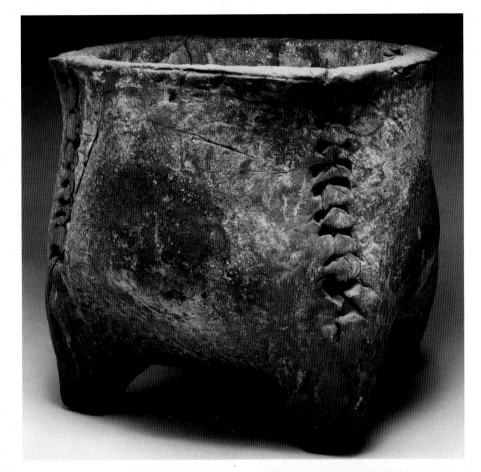

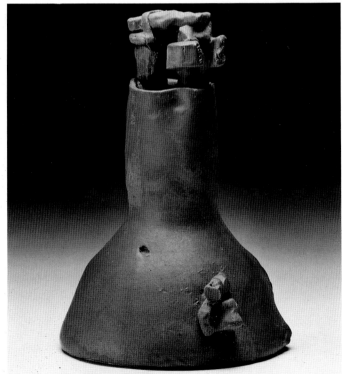

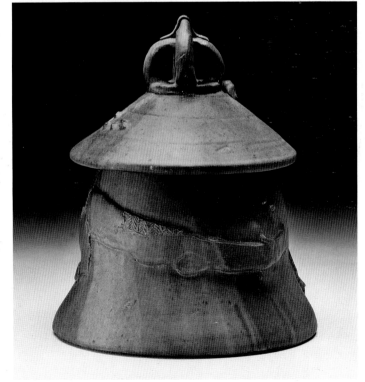

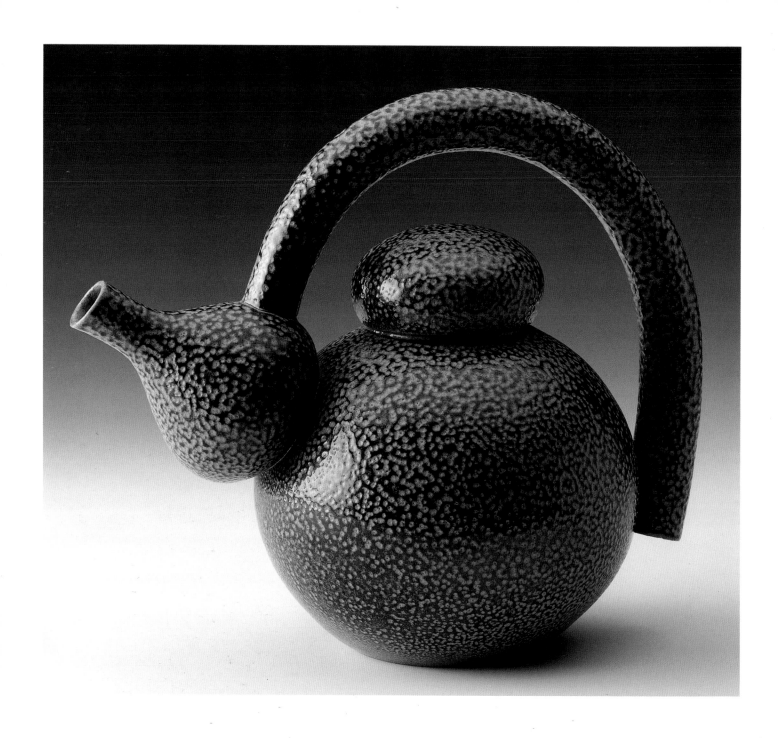

56 Teapot
   Wally Keeler
   Stoneware, salt-glazed
   h. 20 cm
   UK, 1983

57 Form
   Graham Marks
   Constructed earthenware
   h. 78 cm
   USA, 1984

58 Form
   Graham Marks
   Constructed earthenware
   h. 78 cm
   USA, 1984

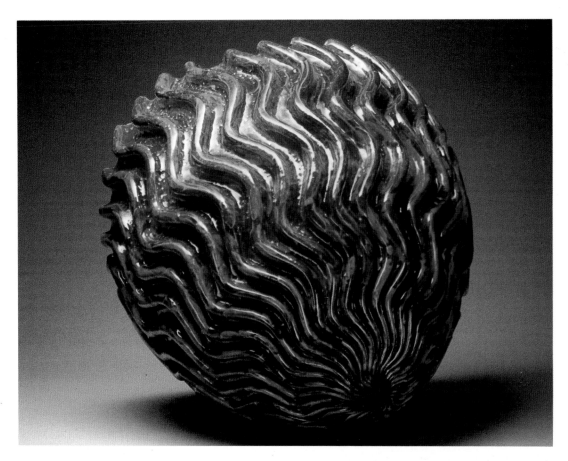

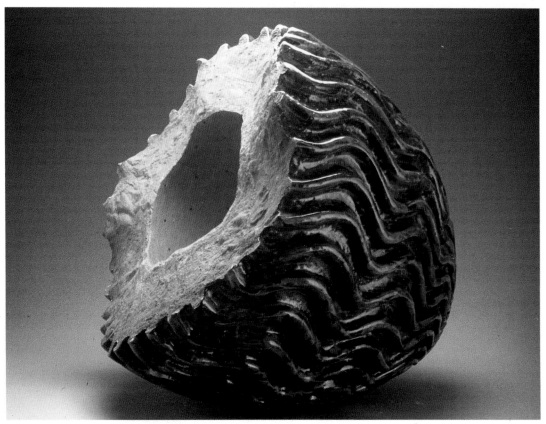

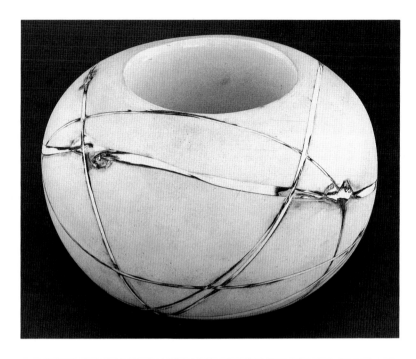

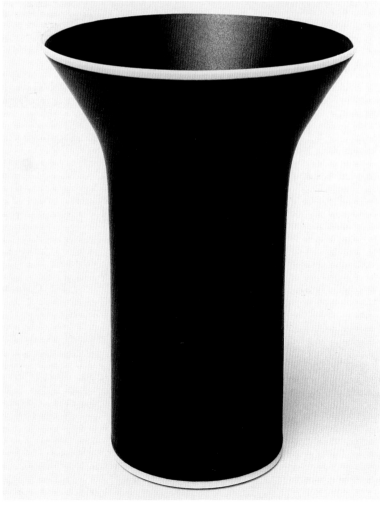

59 Large bowl
James Rothrock
Cast and assembled porcelain
h. 24.5 cm
USA, 1979

60 Vase
Geert Lap
Porcelain
h. 30 cm
Holland, 1985

61 Bowl
Mary Rogers
Stoneware, coil-built
h. 20 cm
UK, 1981

62 Bowl
Jennifer Lee
Stoneware, handbuilt
h. 28 cm
UK, 1985

63 Vessel
George P. Timock
Raku, handbuilt earthenware
h. 37 cm
USA, 1975
Collection of Joan Mannheimer

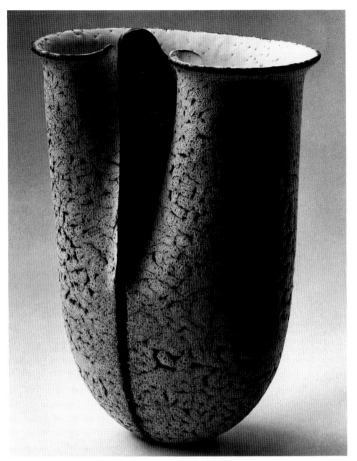

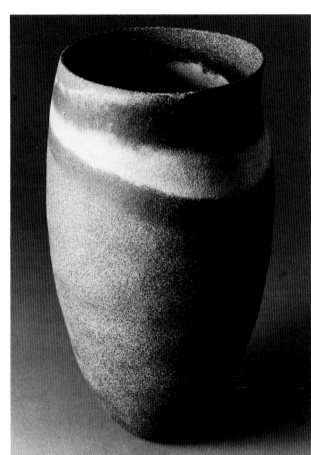

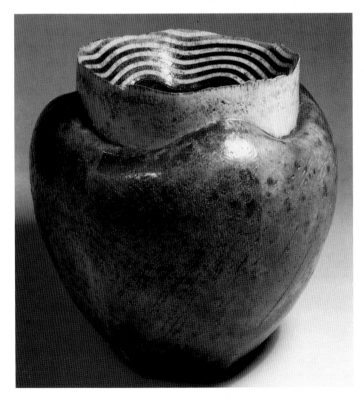

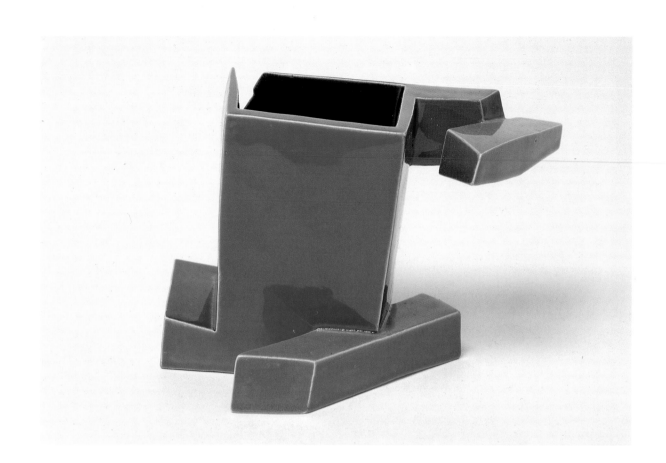

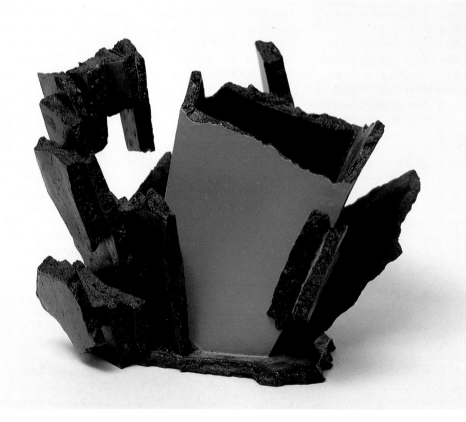

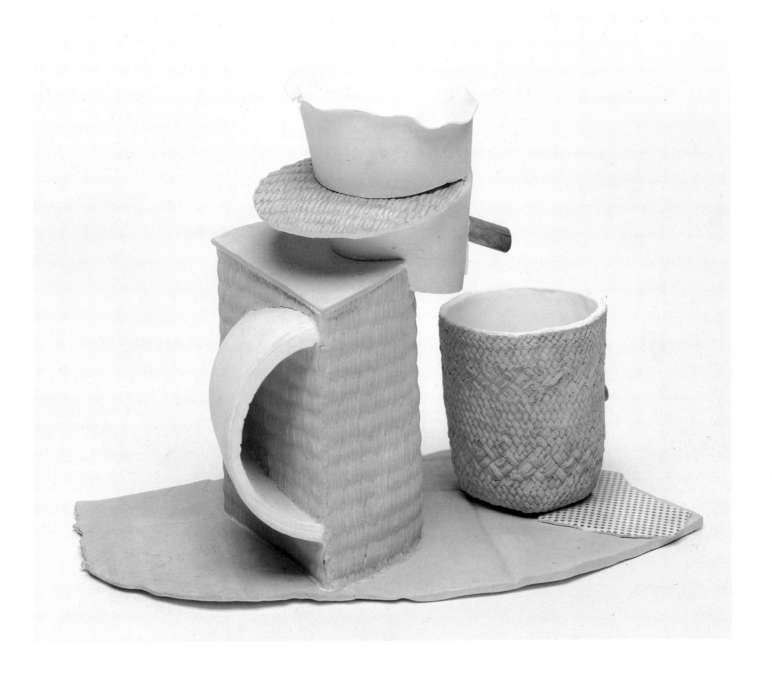

64 Untitled – architectural cup
Kenneth Price
Glazed earthenware
h. 9.5 cm
USA, 1973

65 Slate Cup
Kenneth Price
Earthenware
h. 12.5 cm
USA, 1972–77

66 Straining Machine Construction
Richard Shaw
Slip-cast porcelain
h. 43 cm
USA, 1976

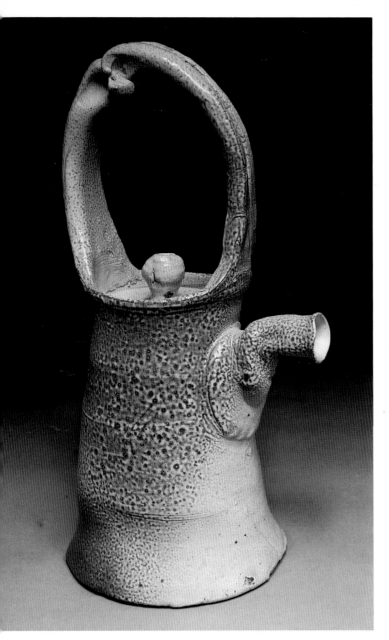

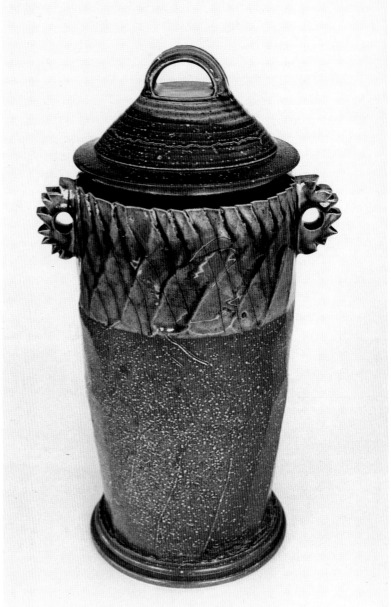

67 Teapot
   Kenneth Ferguson
   Salt-glazed porcelain
   h.40 cm
   USA, 1979

68 Storage jar
   Val Cushing
   White stoneware, salt-glazed
   h.41 cm
   USA, 1984

69 Teapot
   Chris Gustin
   Stoneware
   h.60 cm
   USA, 1984

70 Vase
   Chris Gustin
   Stoneware
   h.63 cm
   USA, 1984

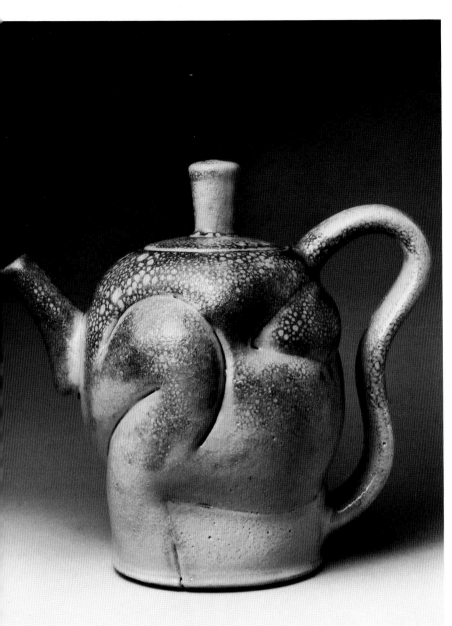

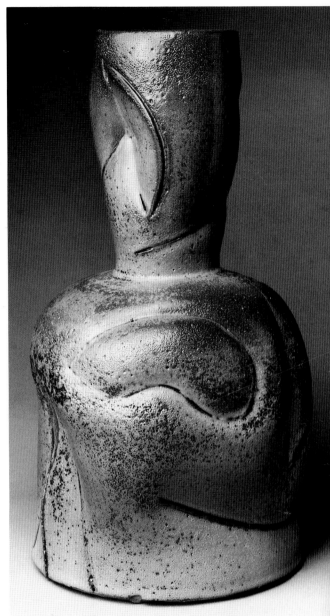

Overleaf
71 Untitled
   Ron Nagle
   Slip-cast earthenware
   h. 21 cm
   USA, 1974

72 Untitled
   Ron Nagle
   Slip-cast earthenware
   h. 6.5 cm
   USA, 1975

73 Icosidodecamerous End
      Cutting Bowl
   Adrian Saxe
   Porcelain with raku base
   h. 13 cm
   USA, 1982

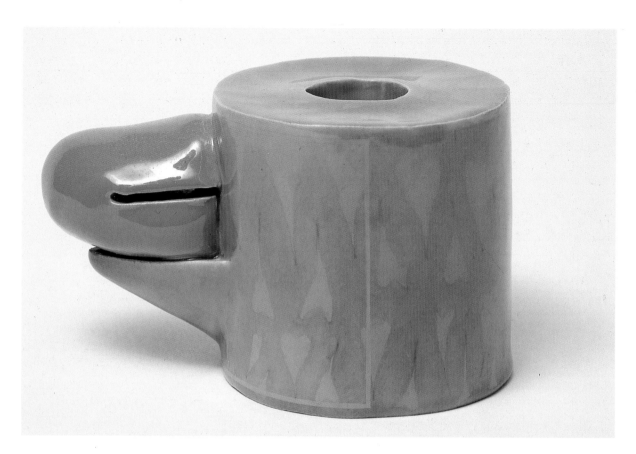

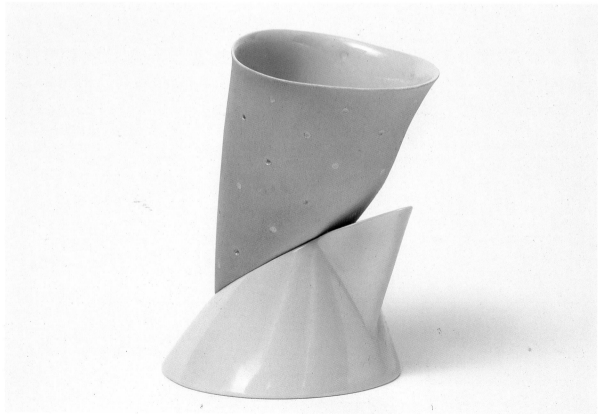

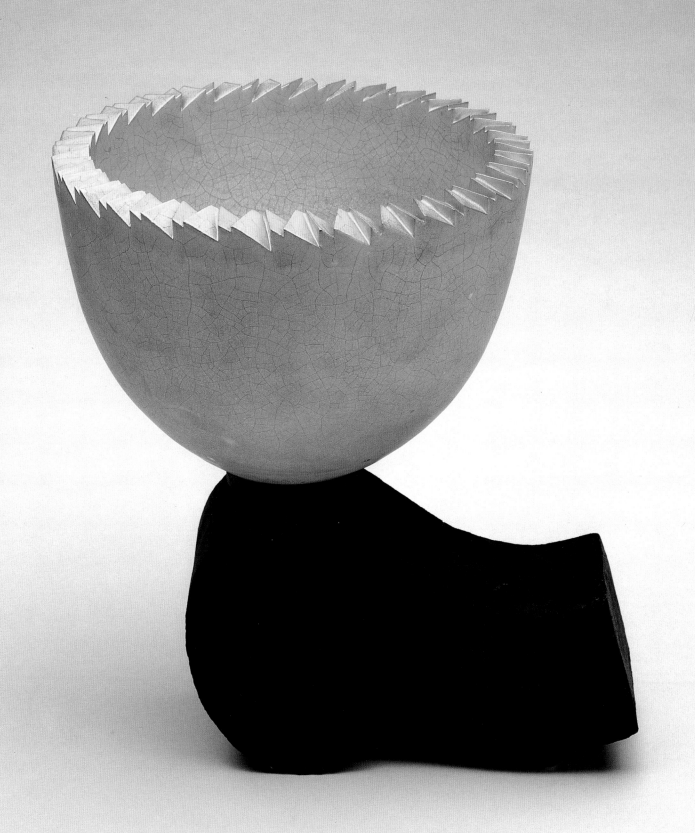

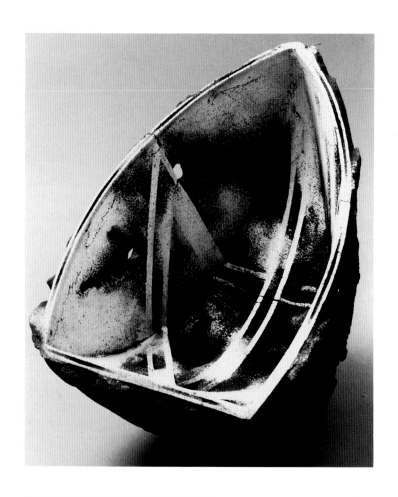

74 Vessel form
   Steve Heinemann
   Earthenware
   h. 30 cm
   Canada, 1984

75 Bowl
   Barbara Nanning
   Stoneware and textile
   h. 14 cm
   Holland, 1984

76 Bowl
   Lucie Rie
   Porcelain
   h. 9 cm
   UK, 1972

77 Winged bowl
   Colin Pearson
   Thrown porcelain
   h. 15.5 cm
   UK, 1980

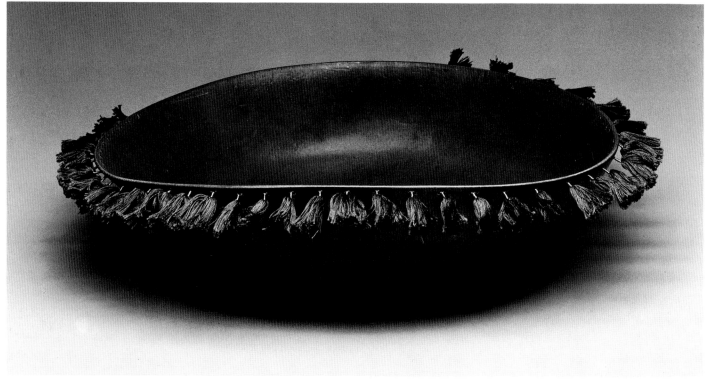

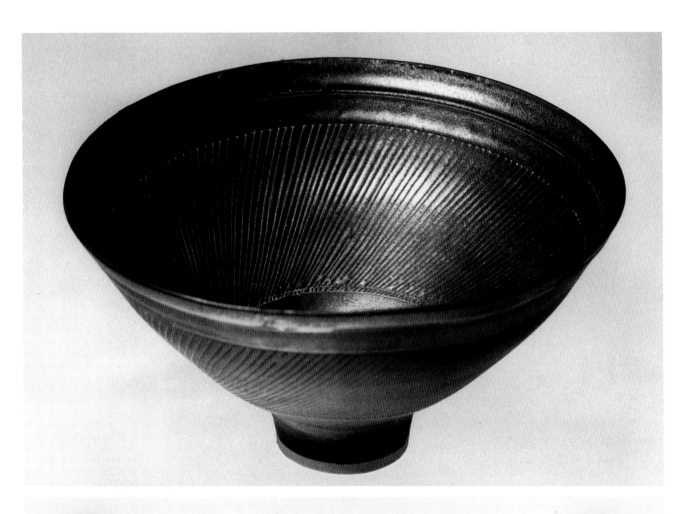

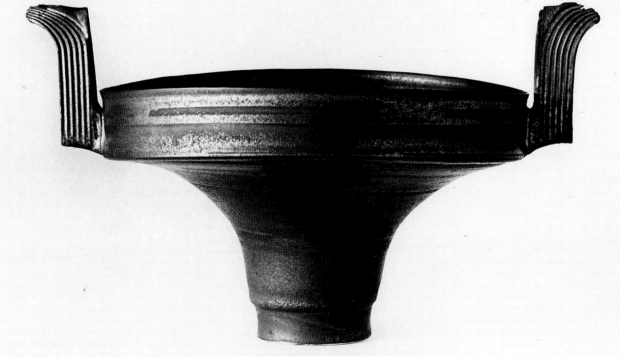

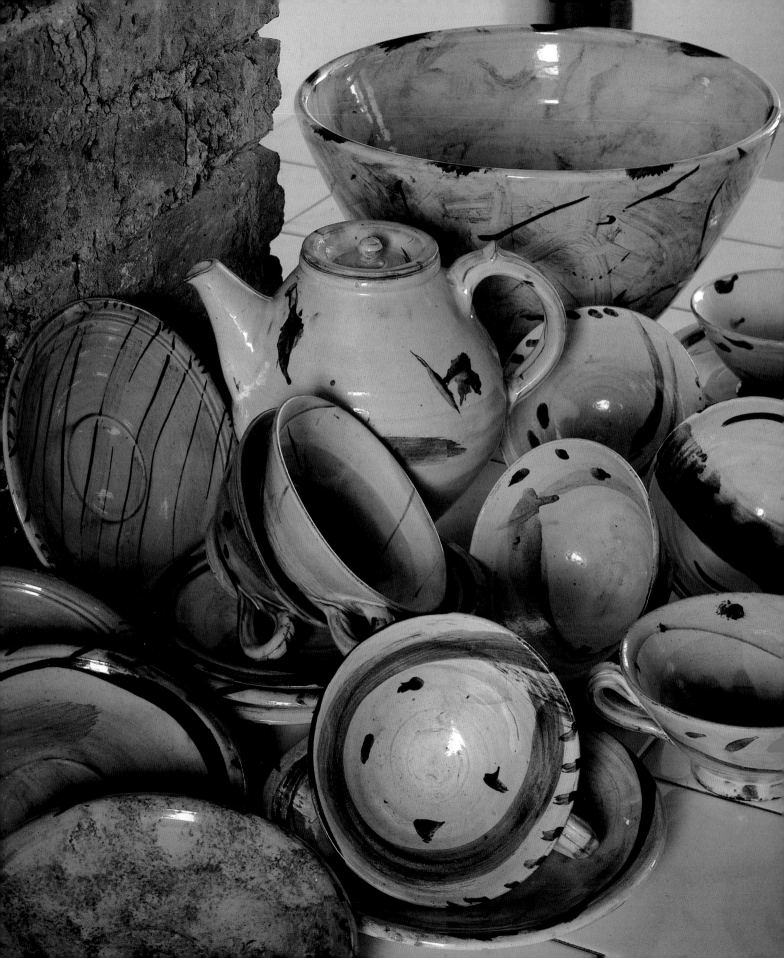

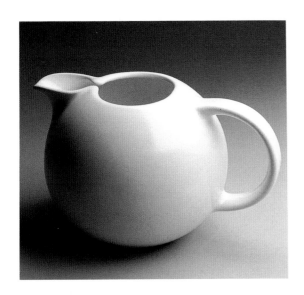

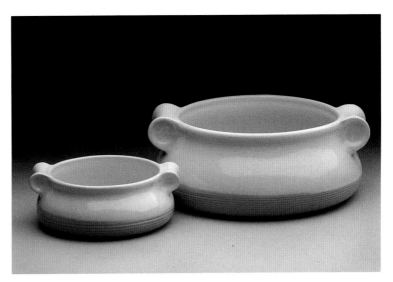

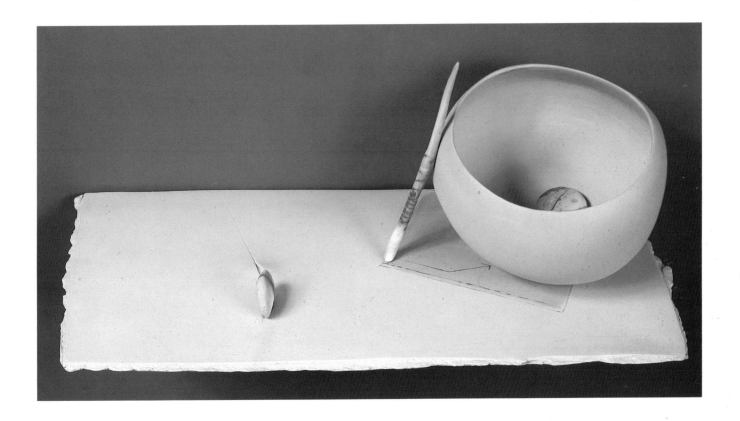

78 Domestic ware
David Garland
Thrown earthenware
h. 40 cm (bowl)
UK, 1984

79 Jug
Franco Bucci
Stoneware
h. 18 cm
Italy, 1969

80 Soup service
Franco Bucci
Stoneware
d. 14 cm, 26 cm
Italy, 1978

81 Soup Site II
Paula Winokur
Porcelain
l. 50 cm, h. of bowl 15 cm
USA, 1983

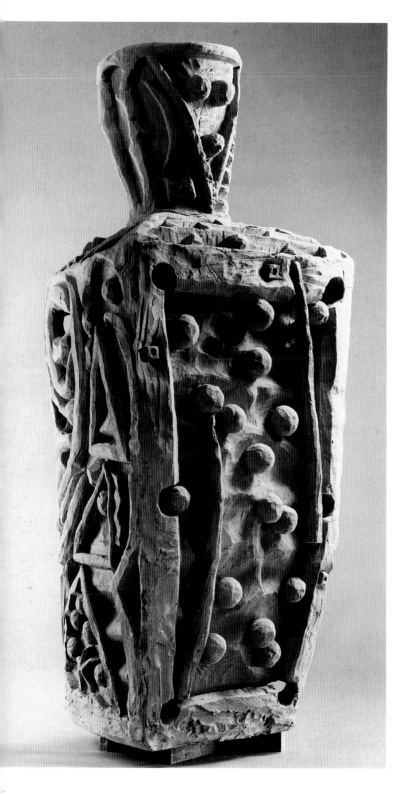

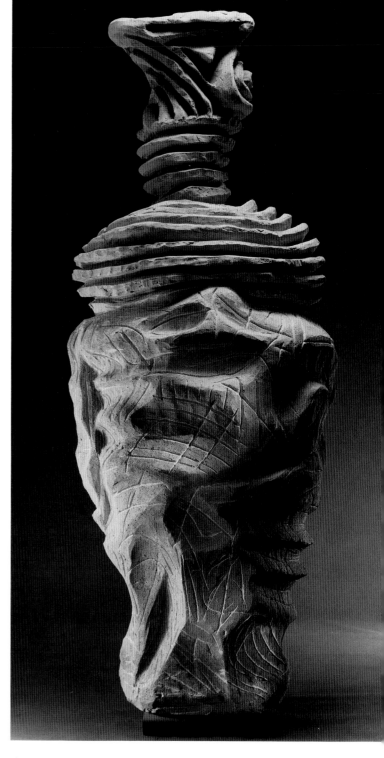

82 Untitled
Arnold Zimmerman
Earthenware
h. 2.5 m
USA, 1985

83 Untitled
Arnold Zimmerman
Earthenware
h. 2.5 m
USA, 1985

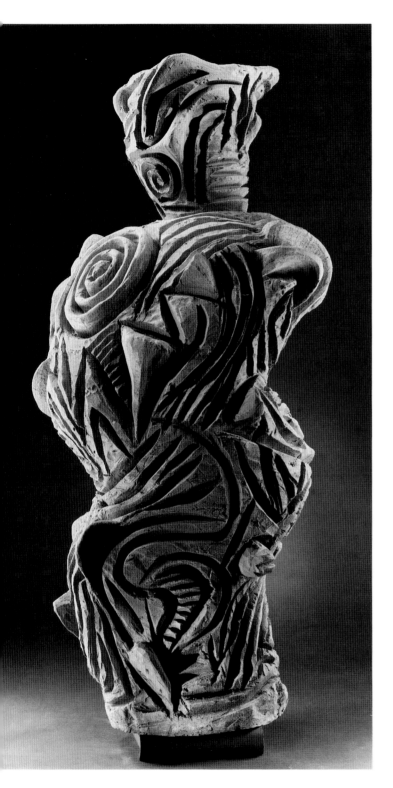
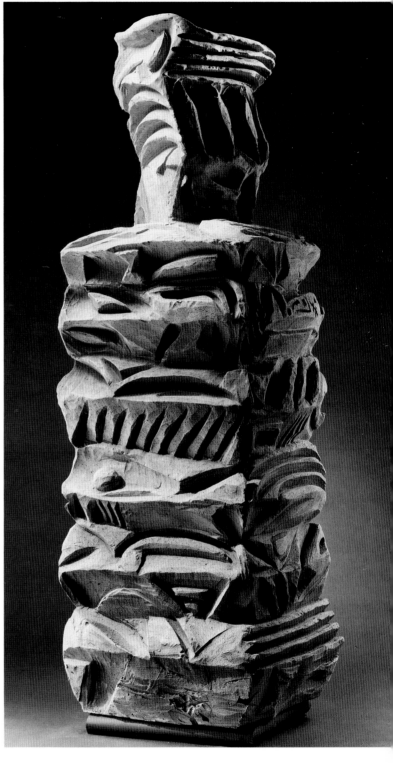

84 Untitled   85 Untitled
    Arnold Zimmerman   Arnold Zimmerman
    Earthenware   Earthenware
    h. 2.5 m   h. 2.5 cm
    USA, 1985   USA, 1985

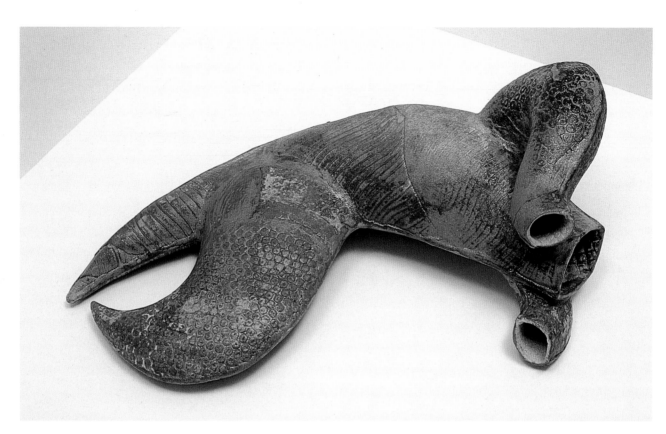

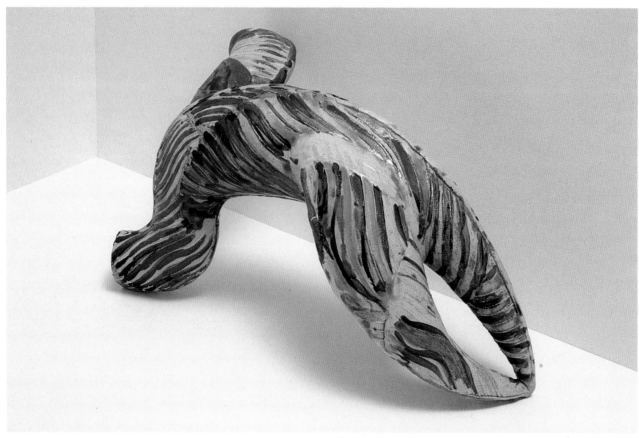

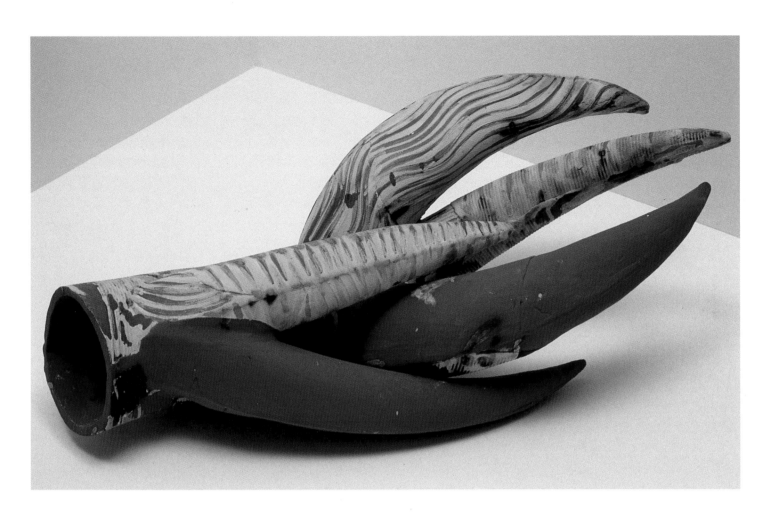

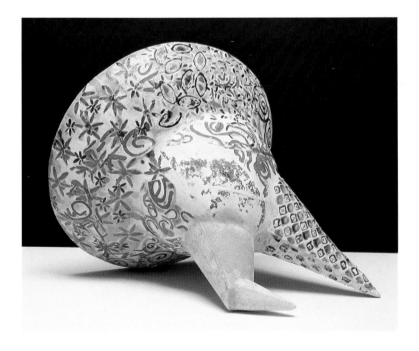

86 Form
Jacqui Poncelet
Stoneware
l. 60 cm
UK, 1985

87 Form
Jacqui Poncelet
Stoneware
l. 45 cm
UK, 1985

88 Form
Jacqui Poncelet
Stoneware
l. 70 cm
UK, 1985

89 Form
Jacqui Poncelet
Stoneware
l. 50 cm
UK, 1983

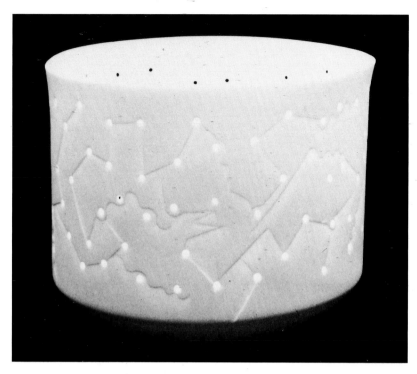

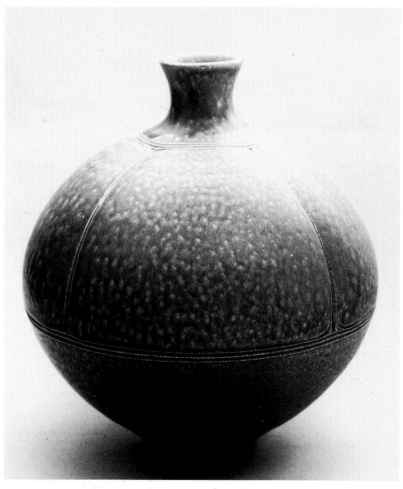

90 Bowl
Jacqui Poncelet
Bone china
h.8cm
UK, 1974

91 Bottle
John Dermer
Salt-glazed stoneware
h.50cm
Australia, 1985

92 Bowl
Lucie Rie
Pitted stoneware
h.11cm
UK, 1960

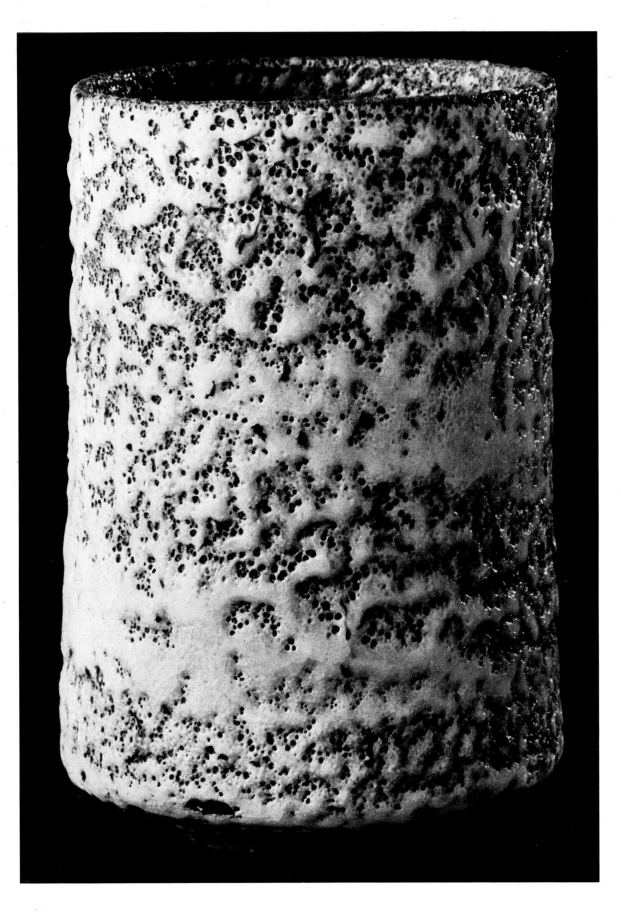

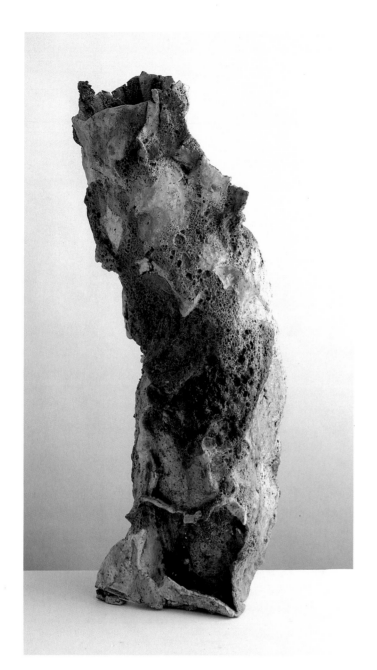

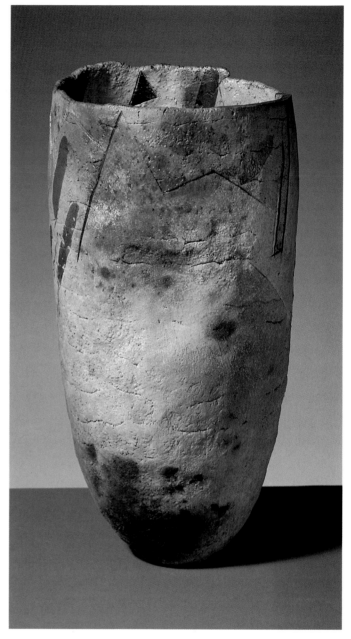

93 Vessel
   Ewen Henderson
   Laminated stoneware and
      bone-china mix
   h. 75 cm
   UK, 1986

94 Wild pot
   Peder Rasmussen
   Raku-fired earthenware
   h. 36 cm
   Denmark, 1985

95 Jar
   Janet Mansfield
   Wood-fired stoneware, salt-glazed
   h. 49 cm
   Australia, 1985

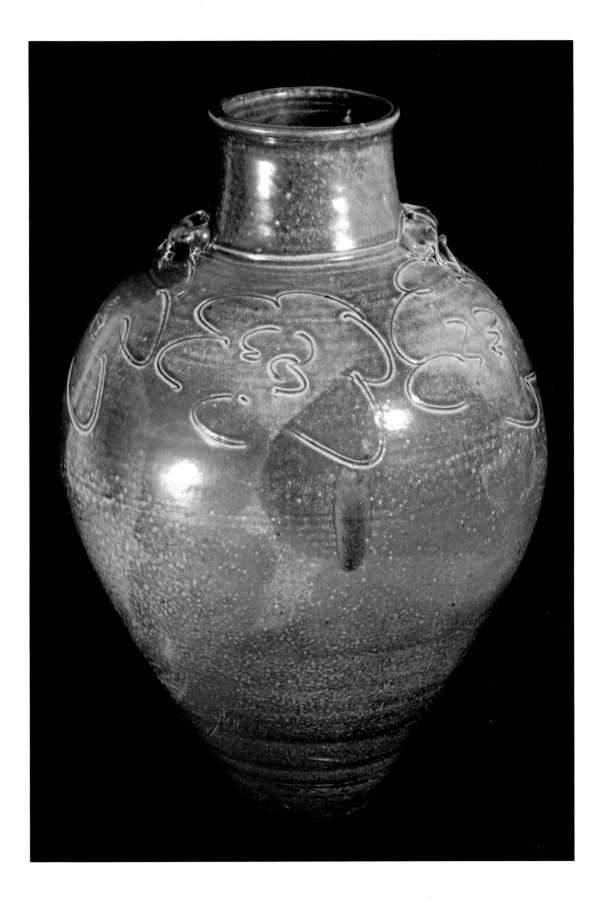

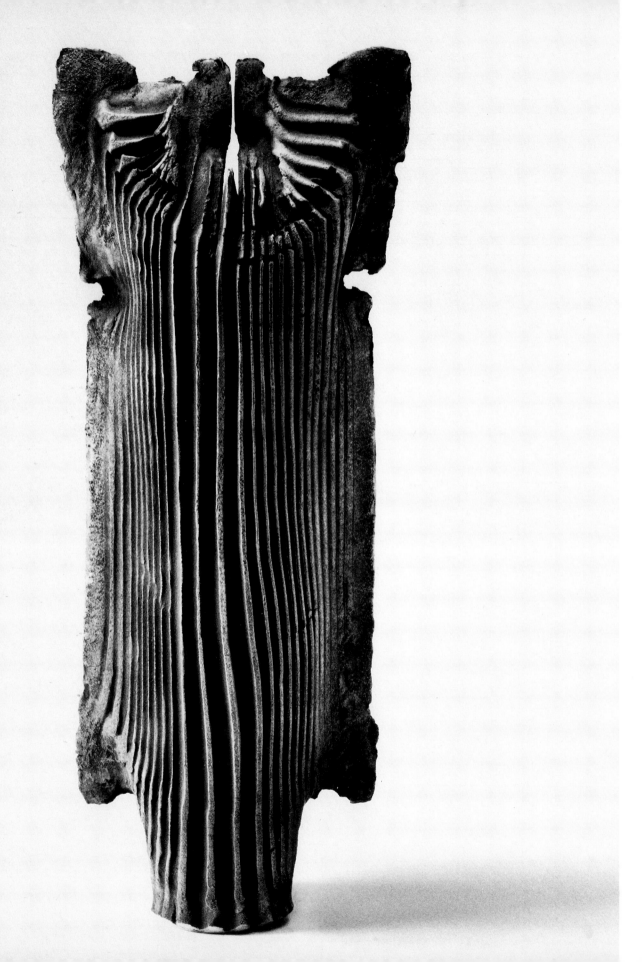

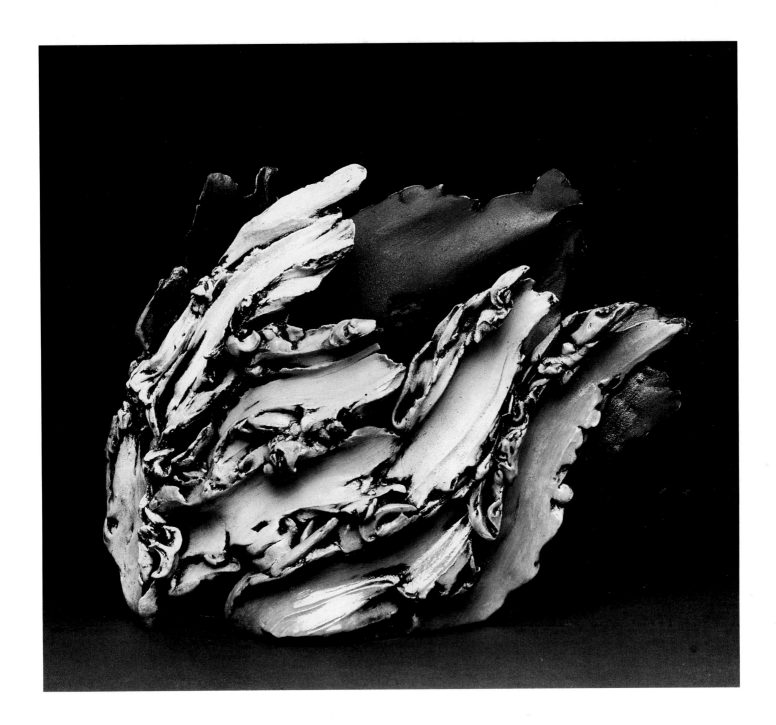

96 Figurine
   Christa Gebhardt
   Stoneware
   h. 35 cm
   West Germany, 1984

97 Vase
   Irene Vonck
   Stoneware
   h. 50 cm
   Holland, 1985

98 Handled vessel
Jeff Mincham
Raku earthenware
h.28cm
Australia, 1985

99 Cone Stand
Robert Hawkins
Stoneware
87 × 35cm
Australia, 1984

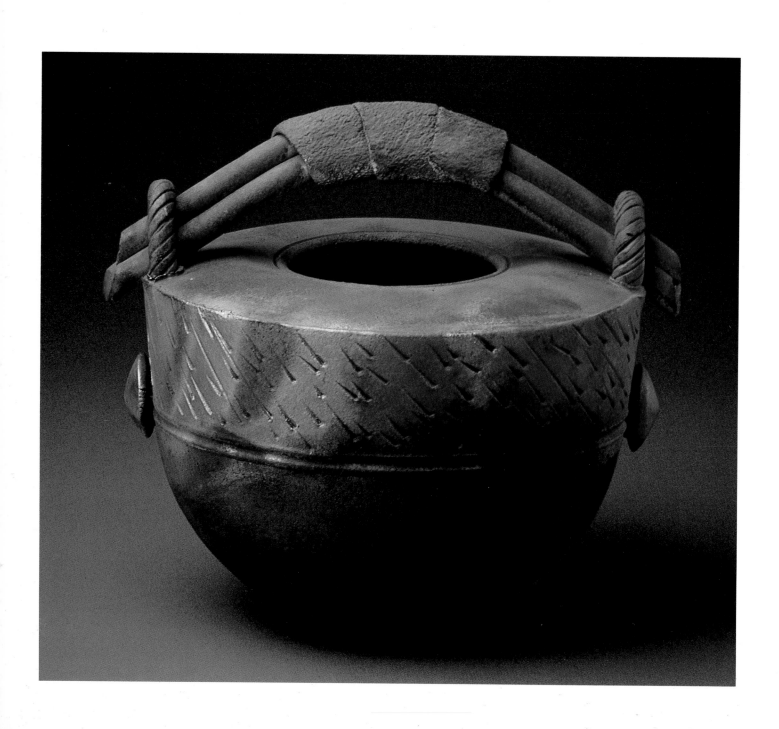

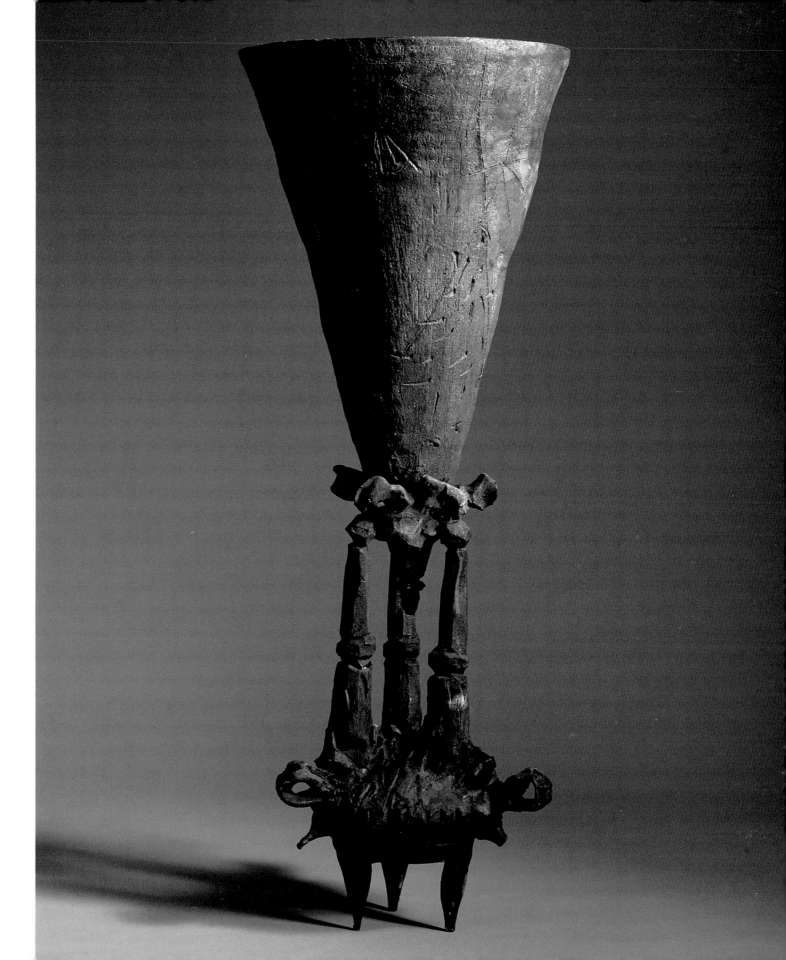

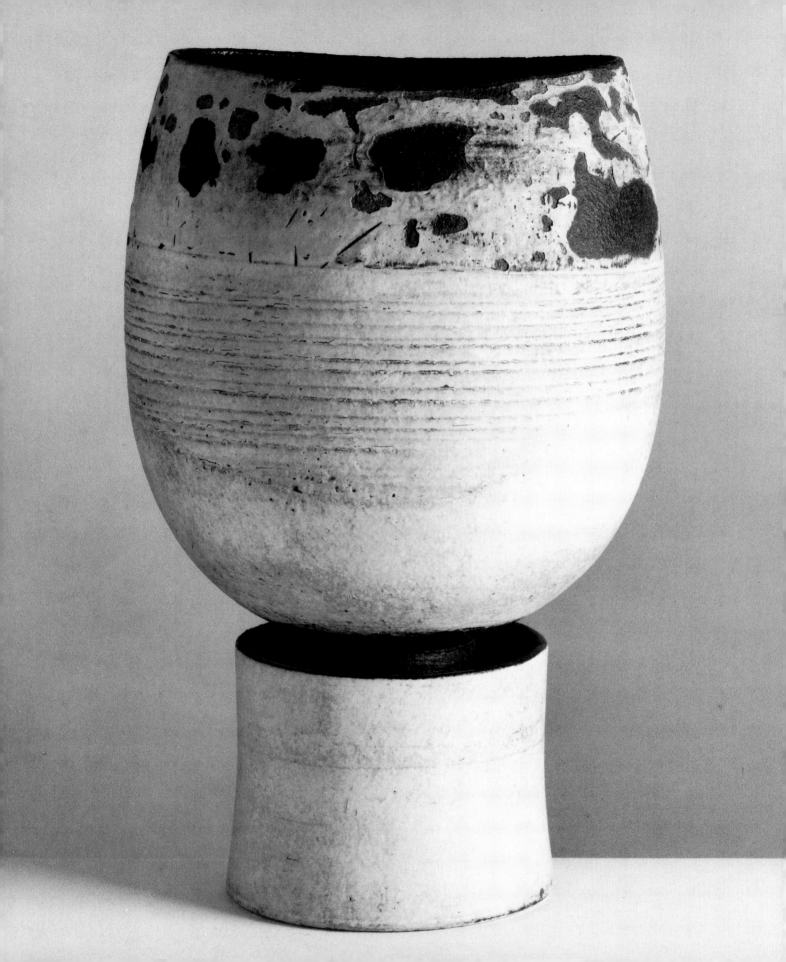

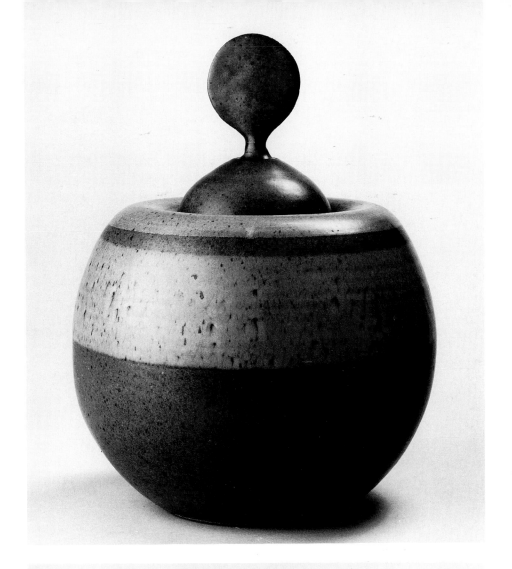

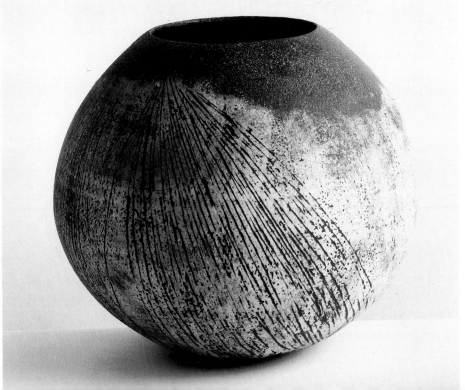

100 Vessel
Hans Coper
Stoneware
h. 15 cm
UK, 1975

101 Apple Roll Top jar
Val Cushing
Stoneware
h. 37.5 cm
USA, 1979

102 Spherical Pot
Hans Coper
Stoneware
h. 32 cm
UK, 1956

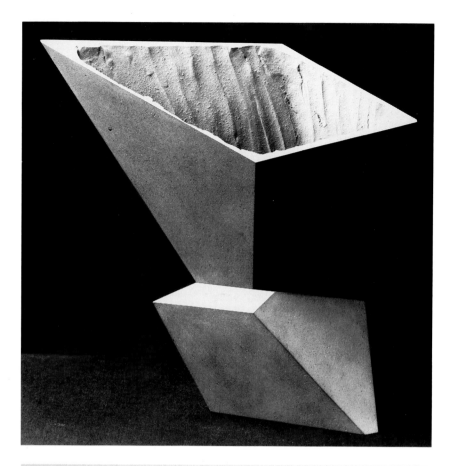

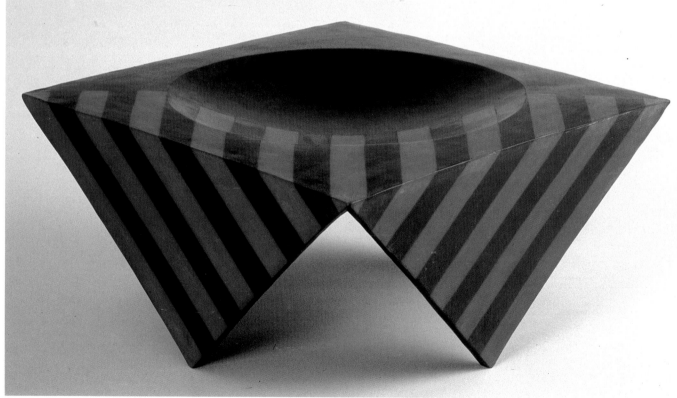

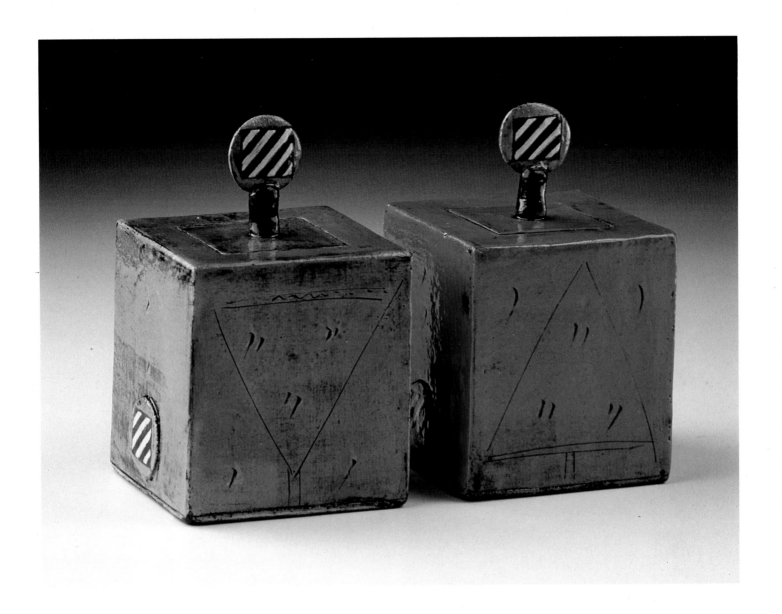

103 Vessel on plinth
Martin Smith
Redware
h. 29.5 cm
UK, 1979

104 Sacrificial bowl
Fritz Harstrup
Earthenware
h. 17 cm
Norway, 1985

105 Two boxes
Ingrid Mortensen
Earthenware
h. 13 cm
Norway, 1984

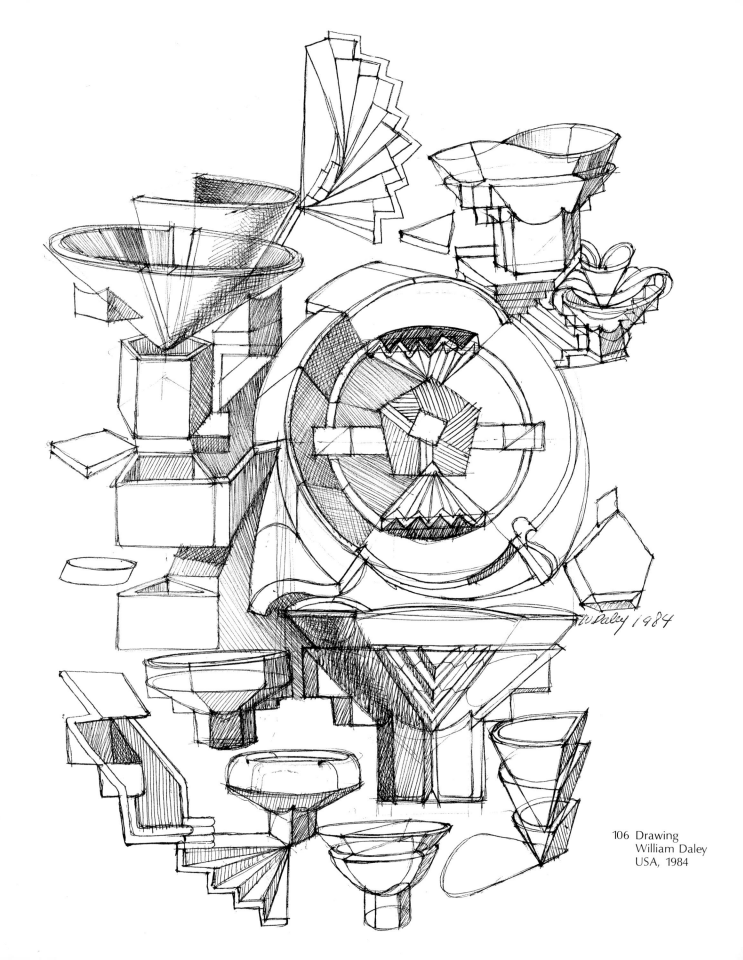

106 Drawing
William Daley
USA, 1984

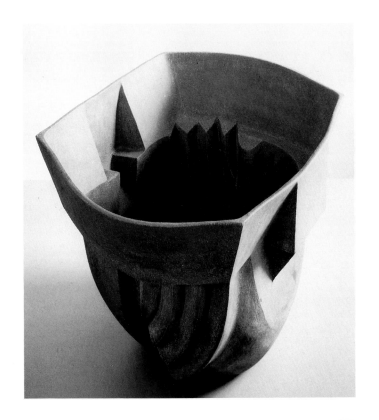

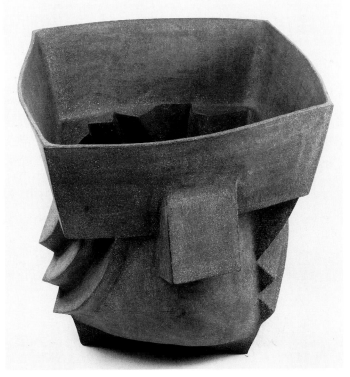

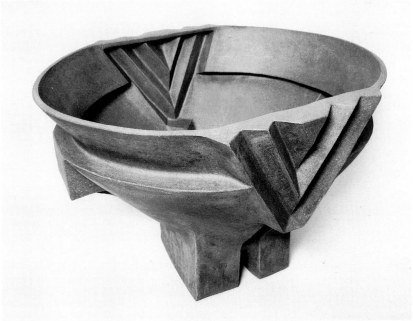

107 Friendly Location
    William Daley
    Stoneware
    h.43cm
    USA, 1983

108 To Josiah W
    William Daley
    Stoneware
    h.46cm
    USA, 1980

109 Vessel
    William Daley
    Stoneware
    h.43cm
    USA, 1983

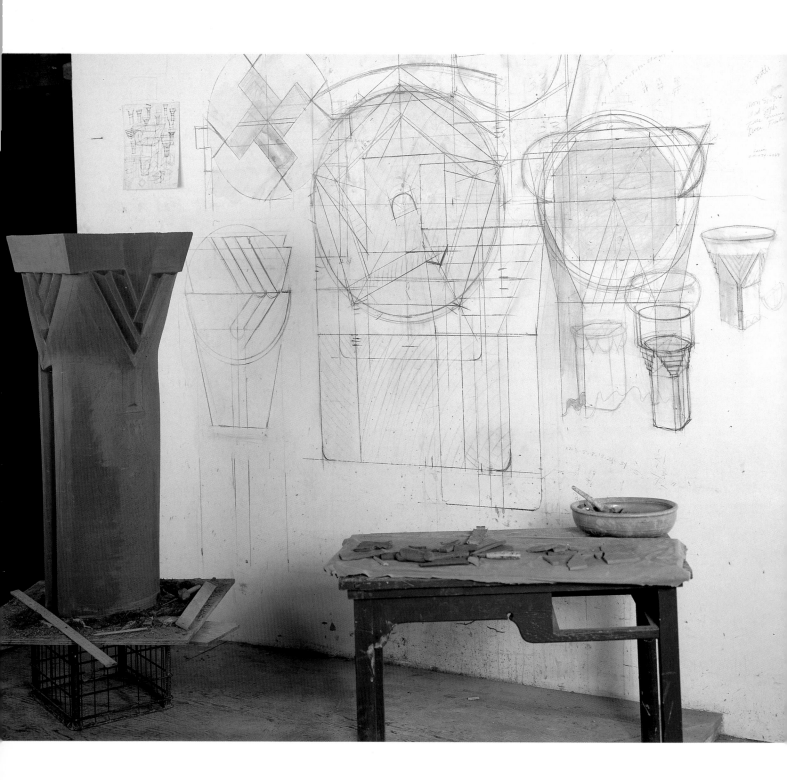

110 Drawing Wall
William Daley
Stoneware vessel
h. 80 cm
USA, 1981

THE PAINTED POT

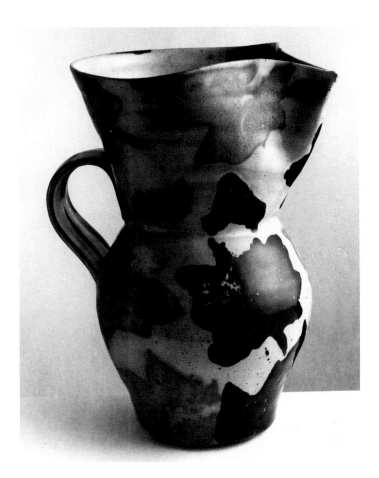

Jug. Janice Tchalenko. Stoneware. h. 30 cm. UK, 1984

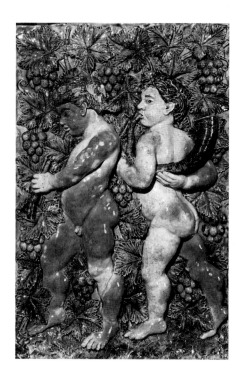

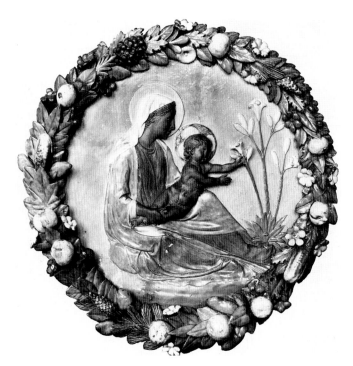

In recent years we have grown accustomed to seeing either no decoration or very simple decoration. Modern plastic surfaces, for example, tend to be patterned with straightforward abstract designs or texture effects. Decorative detailing on buildings has been minimal and kept to two basic effects, the smooth and the rough – either roughened concrete or marble veneer. Inside the building there has been little employment for the artisan skilled in decorative plasterwork, or the metalsmith, or even the wallpaper designer.

The absence of decoration amounts first of all to an absence of variety in texture. We are unaccustomed to feasting ourselves on a piece of intricate carving or flamboyant plasterwork, or relishing the quiet feel and tone of surfaces that are subtly grained and polished to modulate the light rather than to reflect it harshly. Equally, we have tended to forget that decoration can also contain figures, patterns and symbols that mean something; we need reminding that ornament can have themes.

After so much brush-and-dab work it is therefore refreshing to see ornament by Frank Fleming (USA). Fleming's *Where the Corn Grows Sweet* is straight out of the Della Robbia 120 tradition. This famous Florentine family of sculptors produced tin-glazed earthenware reliefs of a very decorative nature in the 15th and 16th centuries. A common Della Robbia composition is a plaque, with a frame of tightly packed leaves and fruit, and a religious subject as the

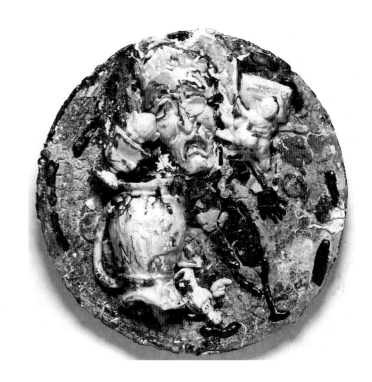

Opposite page
Left, Putti playing musical instruments.
William de Morgan. Earthenware. UK, 1885

Right, Virgin and child. Della Robbia.
Ceramic. d. 1.20 m. Italy, early 16th century

This page
Pitcher and mask of tragedy. Viola Frey.
Earthenware. d. 67 cm. USA, 1984

centrepiece. In a Della Robbia certainly, and to an extent with Frank Fleming, what we have is a liveliness of surface texture together with ornament which we can 'read'.

Fleming offers, then, a sense of ceramic tradition and continuity – his work is a 'quotation' from ceramic history. Moreover, we can easily understand that the content, made clear by the inscriptions – 'American by Birth – Southern by The Grace of God' – comes both from the heart, and from the head. Fleming is a Dixieland freak; he loves the South. He is also a modern ceramist and, although endorsing sentiments about the South, he is tongue-in-cheek about the simple-minded, and indeed chilling, jingoism. Fleming is acting both as participant and observer – a role increasingly played by decorative artists, ceramists among them, at this point in our self-consciously sceptical century.

The fact that much successful decoration is symbolic rather than abstract is plain enough from our museums, though the most obvious examples are to be found in religious or civic architecture. However, by and large contemporary Western society is sceptical of religious and 'civic' pride and it is difficult for the applied artist or architect to devise alternative symbolic decoration that is both wanted and understood by the public. American architect and writer Charles Jencks, in his book *Symbolic Architecture* (1985), asks: 'What, in this agnostic age, is there to symbolise beyond the perennial themes of comfort and fashion?' Many contemporary 'serious-wit' and irreverent craftsmanship with the British sculptor, Barry Flanagan. Flanagan's leaping and dancing or boxing bronze hares, perched on anvils or elephants or helmets, are comic in the same way that Saxe's antelopes are. (Flanagan's own pots are witty in an opposite manner, through being so literal an interpretation of the technique of coiling a pot.)

To an extent, all this is contrived but not arbitrary. There is no way round contrivance for the modern, sceptical or ironic ornamentalist – there has to be a degree of invention in the absence of a shared system of belief. In fact the use by ceramists of art-historical references may be the closest the modern artist can come to finding imagery that a number of people can understand, simply because art history and the museums industry are almost the new 'religion' of our time – especially since museums have become *de facto* churches and churches have become *de facto* museums.

The question is whether this phase of 'knowing ornamentalism' is a temporary one or not: temporary because we are still in a transitional period between hard modernism and new decoration, and there is still some uncertainty as to whether or not it is legitimate to go 'over the top' with decoration just for the fun of it. The Chippendale pediment on Philip Johnson's AT&T building in New York provides an analogy: at first nervous architectural critics and architects rubbed their hands and described it as an ironic reference to ornament. Yet later buildings in

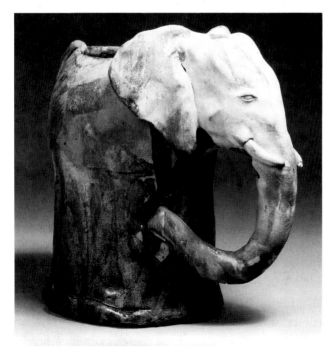

Elephant Vessel. Ann Adair. Raku-fired earthenware. h.24cm. USA, 1977. Collection of Joan Mannheimer

the so-called 'post-modernist' architectural style have been far more idiosyncratic, and neither critics nor architects refer to irony any longer. Now the AT&T building is accepted for what it is – rather odd, charming, a postwar Chrysler building. In time, will the commentary aspect of Slee's and Saxe's work drop away as the work itself is considered simply part of the late 20th-century decorative movement? Much art is bound to change its 'meaning'.

p. 117   Nevertheless, it will be interesting to see whether or not the ceramics community will ever make ornament such as that shown in the photograph of the 18th-century silver coffee pot just for its own sake and without feeling the need to hedge bets by introducing the element of commentary.

139, 160   Richard Slee's work also picks up ceramic history, especially late 18th-century and 19th-century industrial ceramics. But Slee is fond, too, of the ceramic ornament as it was used or as it developed for the ordinary English suburban home between the World Wars – nostalgia is a dominant thread in English culture and it is thus not surprising that it should consciously surface as one of the themes in a thoughtful potter's work. Slee is both intelligent and kind, and in his quotations from the past and his acknowledgment of the décor of the suburban home – a most mocked institution – there is more sympathy and pleasure than satire; the fun is good-humoured, not snobbish. Part of the pleasure in both men's work is, however, very straightforward – they are both good craftsmen.

140   The curious little work by Anne Kraus (USA) is in a similar category to that of Slee and Saxe except, of course, that Kraus has used illustration to give her decoration a content. Kraus's work is odd: it is gauche, it is 19th-century factory-ware in its appearance, but it is all based on Kraus's private musings – about loneliness, shyness, plainness and friendship.

136   Private and abstract decoration can also have a rich source material. Elizabeth Fritsch (UK) actually arrives at her work through a complicated set of allusions – literary, mathematical and musical – but her pots are not hard to understand or enjoy. They derive their coherence and interest from the variety of Fritsch's interests, yet you need not know or recognize her 'references'. It is equally true that those who want to follow Fritsch's ideas can do so (the clues to the source material are provided by her elaborate titles); thus the complexity of interest is an addition to the original and continuing pure enjoyment of the work.

Decorated versus Decorative

The work I have been considering falls into the category of decorative pottery, as opposed to decorated pottery. George Woodman, American painter and writer, made this distinction in the *American Ceramics* article already referred to by Alison Britton in the Introduction. He said that a decorative pot is there to embellish something else, a room perhaps or a table, whereas decorated pots are usually very simple affairs – and could be said to exist more or less complete even without their decoration – the decoration is an extra not a necessity. An Elizabeth Fritsch pot is simply not complete until the painting, or rather the firing of the painting, is accomplished. By contrast most pots made in the Bernard Leach tradition are not greatly altered by the addition of decoration. Indeed, someone like David Leach, a very skilled craftsman who has produced some beautiful, simple forms, is much more successful when he does not attempt decoration.

The simple pot has nothing to do except be itself, but modern potters have – as Wayne Higby, for one, amply demonstrates – more complicated ambitions. Consider Higby as an example. George Woodman says that his natural affinity is with painting. To begin with, he is using

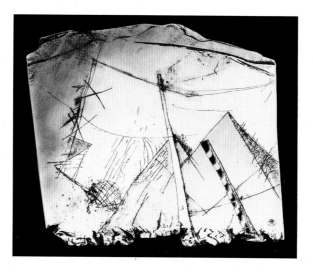

An Edge at Mt Isa. Vincent McGrath. Earthenware. h.60cm. Australia, 1983

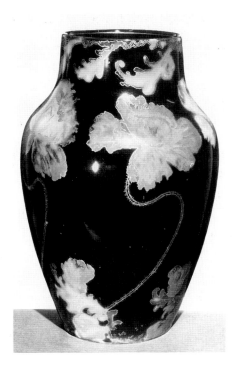 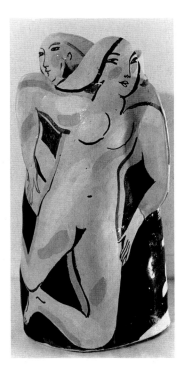

Right, Vase. Bernard Moore. Porcelain. h.24cm. UK, c. 1900

Far right, Daughters of the Finnish Witch. Rudy Autio. Stoneware. h.85cm. USA, 1983

landscape – the landscape outside his studio window in Alfred. Higby says that he started throwing bowls on the wheel in order to get a form that was appropriate to what he saw as a softness in the landscape. However, although the landscape gives him a theme, the result is not illustrative but metaphorical. It is not a pot decorated with a country scene like a tourist gift pot. You get no sense that you could pull off the 'picture' from the pot as though it were a transfer. For one thing Higby uses the whole pot to create crossovers and references from the inside to the outside – the photographs show how the parts of a Higby painting-pot connect with or echo one another. He contrives to give a sensation of space and distance, and his nearest equivalent in this is, perhaps, Elizabeth Fritsch. The work becomes a piece of interpretation, not mimicry. Andrea Gill, who works with Higby at Alfred University, says that to her mind Higby's pots look like the countryside as it appears when you drive through it. If so, she must be driving rather slowly.

148–50 Higby himself has said: 'I like to think that there's an equal tension or balance between the three-dimensional form and the drawn illusion of projecting and receding space. It's a balancing. . . As the bowl radiates outward, it becomes a metaphor for human consciousness and our strange existence in space. The bowl form has that potential resonance; it can deal with finite space and infinite, illusory space – things that also exist in our psyches.'

Landscape continues to provide the theme for several potters – in a secular age, nature is one of the few sources of imagery that people can be expected to recognize. Kari Christensen's (Norway) porcelain work is drawn strongly from her love of landscape and animals, but she, like Higby, is an interpreter and not an illustrator. Allowing imagery to become more ambiguous and less factual allows for the possibility of metaphor and also allows the viewer to bring into play his or her own associations. Decoration that is too specific wraps everything up – like a magazine picture. Such a literal approach can be seen in Lene Regius's work (Denmark), in which the pot has been pushed into two dimensions to accommodate the picture. The result may be described as 'attractive' – it has that cool, rational, well-mannered 'Scandinavian' quality much admired by the British, but it is a long way removed from the transformational process employed by Christensen or, for that matter, Ingrid Mortensen (Norway). Mortensen's boxes and plates are the epitome of Norwegian architectural scenery – not through any literal picturing but through the quality of the colour and the proportions of the pattern, which both coincide with what you can see for yourself in the buildings in Norway. There is a special quality of Scandinavian grey or crimson which is typical of the area and which is seldom successfully reproduced by artists, designers or architects elsewhere in Europe.

And even where one comes across a piece of pure illustrative pottery, such as that in Jo Buffalo's (USA) endearing Russian *Princess* pot, it is still noticeable that the maker felt it necessary to mess around with the pot – interfere with the literalness – and in this instance the pot has been deliberately broken and reconstructed.

12, 193–4

163–4

195

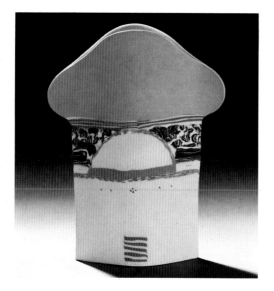

Vase. Lene Regius. Porcelain. h.25cm. Denmark, 1983

High Art, Low Art

There remains, however, a deep suspicion among many potters and critics about decoration – a suspicion which, in part, is as old as the debate about good and bad 'taste' in art itself. Decorative pottery of the kind pursued by Adrian Saxe is regarded in some quarters, notably among painters I am told, with puzzlement. They do not know whether it is high or low art.

The art historian, Ernst Gombrich, has written extensively about decoration and in his essay 'Visual Metaphors of Value in Art' he examines the split between low art, which historically is supposed to appeal only to the eye of 'simple-minded people', and high art, which appeals to the intellects of the cultured. Gombrich mentions a story from Vasari's *Lives* in which Pope Sixtus IV promised a prize to the artist who would acquit himself best out of four employed in the Sistine Chapel. While the true masters, Botticelli, Perugino and Ghirlandaio, gave of their best, the fourth, Cosimo Rosselli, knew that he was 'poor in invention and weak in design'. Much to the amusement of his colleagues he plastered his fresco with gaudy colours, ultramarine and gold, to cover up its shortcomings. But the Pope, knowing nothing of art, awarded the prize to Rosselli, and insisted that the others gave their work a sprinkling of gold as well.

This century there has been in the crafts movement a debate between the lobby for pots dependent upon form and the lobby for decorative work. This debate is rooted in arguments about good and bad taste, but is more importantly bound in with the early 20th-century ideology of the craft movement, with its central idea of humble, plain wholesomeness as the virtuous aesthetic. The plain pot syndrome. Classic plain pots are found all over the place and George Woodman is more right than he knows when he says in his article that there is plenty of life left in the plain pot – it was, for example, surprising for me in December 1985 to find in a beautifully eroded farmhouse, up a farm track in a Tuscan valley, a young Italian potter, Pietro Maddelena, turning out very good, classical Leach, brown pots. Maddelena had, in fact, trained with David Leach and is not at all interested in decorating his work. Nevertheless, he is a little uncomfortable to be working in a manner so at odds with both contemporary Italian design and the Italian tradition of maiolica (tin-glazed, brightly decorated earthenware).

However, 'plainness' is open to abuse. The appearance of honesty and wholesomeness and integrity has frequently been hijacked. Notoriously since the last World War it has been hijacked by food manufacturers. Entrepreneurs have learned fast that breadcrumbs are the equivalent in food covering to 'honest' brown glazes on pots – the texture and colour convey the value 'goodness'. As a consequence, the breadcrumb technologists have had a marvellous time teaching the food industry how to conceal all kinds of less than natural foods with a wholesome-looking covering. I mention this only to reflect, by comparison, upon the success of the brown-pot industry. Looked at commercially, the success of the latter, especially in Britain and America, is based largely on simple associations between brownness, wholesomeness and nostalgia. Just as brown breadcrumbs are attractive because they allude to wholesomeness and homemade rather than factory-made food, so too does the brown-glazed pot epitomize good, 'old-fashioned' values. (In fact, although domestic brown pots are handmade, they are made semi-industrially in a form of batch production.) The association of 'goodness' with plain brown pots still makes older potters and purchasers of craft pots resistant to the charm of painted pots.

At the same time, the plain pot is also emerging in other styles, as we saw in the previous chapter with the work of Italians such as the Memphis group designer Matteo Thun and Memphis designer-craftsman Alessio Sarri. And the Englishman, Martin Smith, for example, 16, 103 produces 'plain' pots, but they are like the Memphis wares in that they have a very obvious intellectual pedigree, even though we are unlikely to unravel the thinking that went into their creation. There is a category of plain pot that is very far from being simple – there is, for instance, no connection between Martin Smith and, say, Svend Bayer (UK), whereas there is a link between Smith and Thun, despite the fact that the one has emerged from a craft tradition and the other would insist on his design pedigree.

The Italian design influence, more so than the Dutch – whose ceramics are also design-orientated – may have implications for the development of contemporary studio ceramics. The point is that all applied art needs subject matter, and subject matter itself needs replenishing from time to time. The development of American ceramics shows how rapid changes in subject matter can be. There appears now to be a distinctive break or separate development in ceramics which is bound up with the new – and self-conscious – revival of decoration: the intellectual pot. The dominant – and entirely reasonable and pleasurable – trend in 20th-century craft and studio pottery has until recently been towards producing either simple plain pots, or pretty decorative pots, or obviously self-expressive pots of the put-your-whole-body-and-mind-into-the-clay kind bequeathed us by Peter Voulkos. By contrast, Matteo Thun and other Memphis colleagues provide us with examples of the intellectual pot, as do, in their own way, Higby, Saxe, Robert Hawkins and Jacqui Poncelet.

In a perceptive essay entitled 'The Potted Word', Martina Margetts, editor of *Crafts*, pointed out that much was now being 'said' in clay; potters were creating their work as containers of

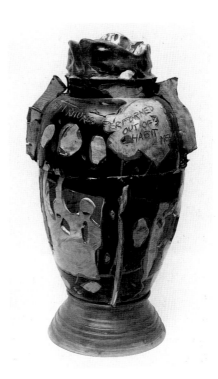

Vase. Penny Kokkinos. Earthenware.
h.56cm. Canada, 1985

thought and meaning. Given that the newer potters are aware that decoration and ornament demand a content, it is understandable that they should reach out to literature or music or history in order to make themselves some symbols. 'But', asks Martina Margetts, 'if conceptual thought precedes object-making, the pots themselves will begin to need special interpretation.'

How special? There is something ridiculous in the notion of a new school of criticism developing for the purpose of decoding the inner messages of pots, although we are getting accustomed to just that phenomenon in architecture. Pots are essentially for people to enjoy and comprehend – how far do they want their familiar forms to become ironic or polemical?

It is a matter of degree. Pottery, like any other applied art, has to quote from its past or from outside itself to gain a content. In England, for example, Janice Tchalenko looks to, among others, Bernard Palissy (16th-century French potter and naturalist), and Carol McNicoll is excited by Oribe ware (Japanese, but the antithesis of the work admired by Bernard Leach). None of these quotations need matter very much to the observer and user of the pottery; their main importance rests with the maker by providing a subject matter and a theme. What matters to the user is that the forms and decoration should make intuitive sense.

In fact I believe that, as pottery has become more decorative and figurative, it has become – whatever ironies or hidden meanings are intended by its makers – more and not less accessible

153–4, 159

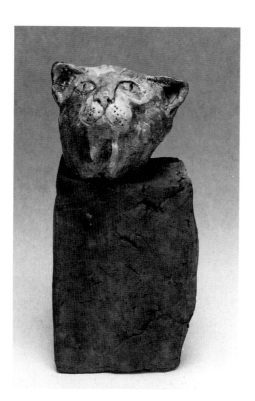

Cat. Jill Crowley. Stoneware.
h. 30 cm. UK, 1980

to the eyes and minds of people outside the pottery world. Lay people find it harder to come to terms with the 'truth to material' expressionist school of potters such as Peter Voulkos and Robert Turner. These potters (whom I much admire) appear to relate to nothing except very general ideas like volume, gesture and 'landscape'. Their pottery thus appears to many people as uncomfortably abstract and unlovely. Such popular evaluation is, I think, ill-informed, but none the less raises an issue if you believe that pottery is first and foremost a popular art form. People, I suggest, either want more symbolism and more figuration in their pottery, or they want the absolute reverse – an obvious pot-like pot: plain like a Lisbet Daehlin (Norway), or glazed like 15, 51 a Gaby Koch (West Germany, but she is working in the UK), or apparently useful like a David 167 Leach (UK) teapot which 'quotes' Japanese and Korean pottery. p. 33

One of the more interesting 'tests' of accessibility and popularity in pottery is to note what influence certain trends and styles in the craft movement have had on the mass manufacturers; for example, the Leach-style influenced factory potteries in the late 1960s and 1970s to the extent that they began producing dinnerware in the form of a kind of middle-class folkware. More recently, it has been interesting to note that in Italy the pottery produced by the Memphis group is being mimicked and marketed in popular gift shops.

Ornament is an evolutionary rather than a revolutionary activity: it evolves with society or with an institution. In the West we have had some problems with the revival of ornament and decoration simply because of the long break with decoration that has been fostered by a certain kind of modernist architect, designer and art-school teacher. Decoration and symbolism in ornament has to emerge from common ideas and practice; if they have long been unfashionable, then the initial steps at rediscovery will appear arbitrary. Indeed, they *are* arbitrary, because the ornamentalist, be he potter or architect, is starting afresh.

One of the interesting phenomena of the latter part of this century is the way that design, rather than fine art, is now generating new images and metaphors. In the last five years, design, especially in Europe and Japan, has been liberated from the black-box/white-box syndrome by the development of micro-circuitry. Objects can still be useful but are metamorphosed into the most surprising shapes. Micro-circuitry has forced the designer to think of the imagery his packaging presents, because there is no longer an excuse for making things according to the old 'function dictates form' principle.

For the applied artist, including the potter, this trend is exciting – on the one hand, it ought to suggest to the potter that he or she can offer skills in decoration and ornament to the design world (this has happened a little in England with Janice Tchalenko and Carol McNicoll). On the other hand, the new upsurge of ornamentalist design provides all decorative artists with a wider source of images, together with a greater chance of public acceptability as more and more people become used to the variety of ways in which a thing – any thing – can look. Pottery, as a decorative art form, has much to offer contemporary designers and private patrons alike.

Opposite
111 Bowl
John Glick
Stoneware
d.45cm
USA, 1977

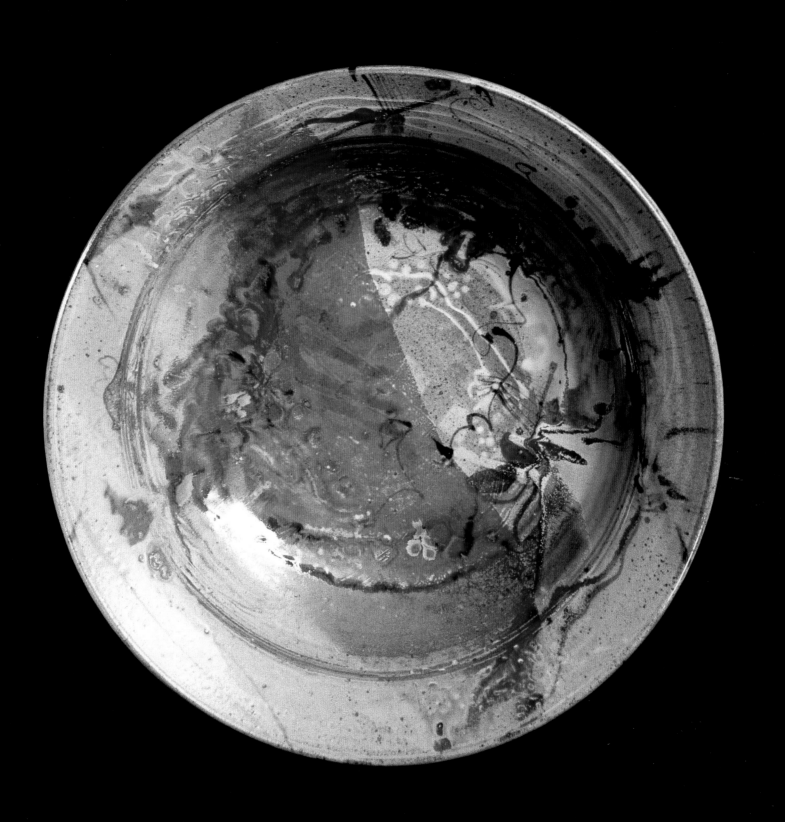

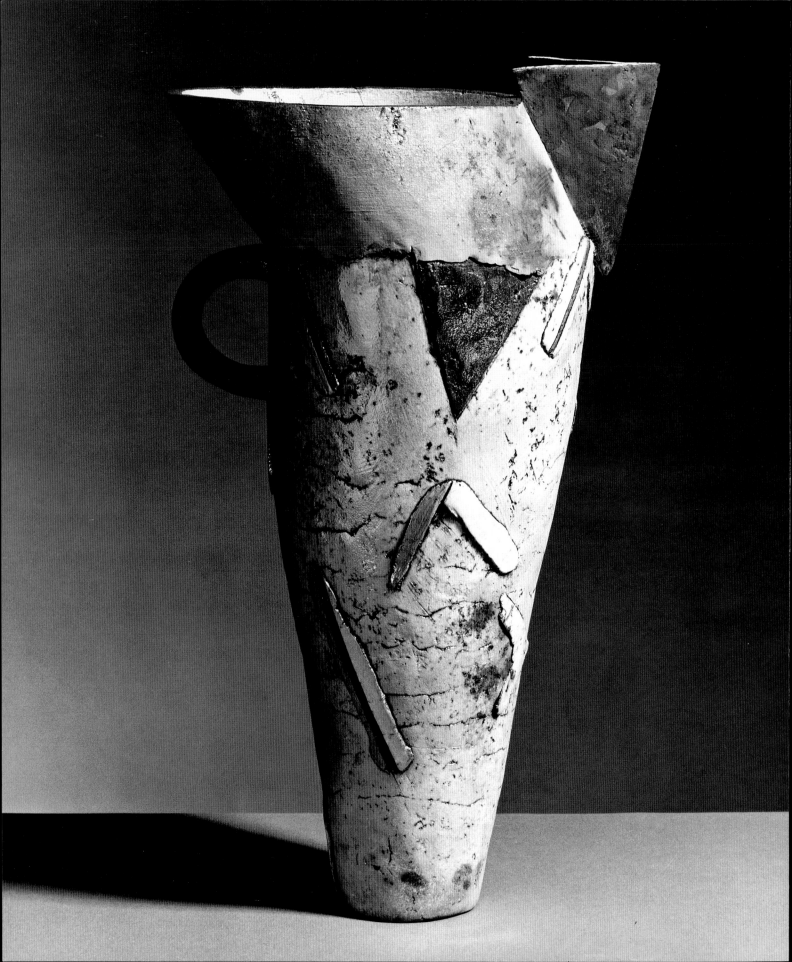

112 Big Jug
Peder Rasmussen
Raku-fired earthenware
h. 43 cm
Denmark, 1985

113 Box
Ingrid Mortensen
Earthenware
h. 15 cm
Norway, 1984

114 Jug
Alison Britton
Earthenware
h. 34 cm
UK, 1977

115 Bowls
Klaartje Kamermans
Earthenware
d. 40 cm
Holland, 1984

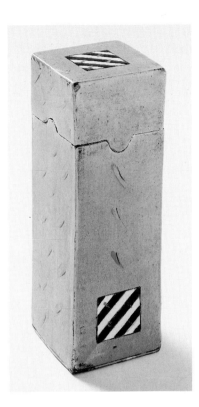
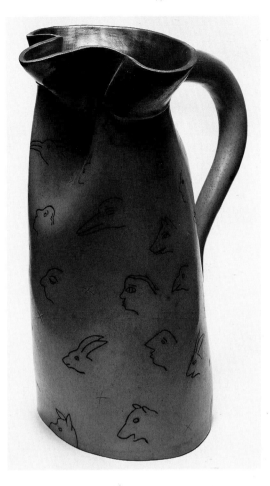
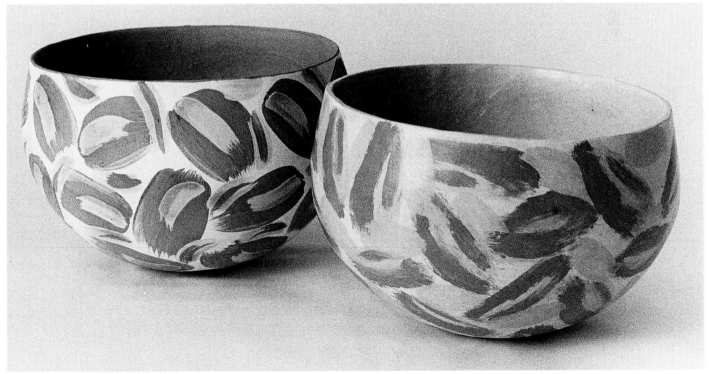

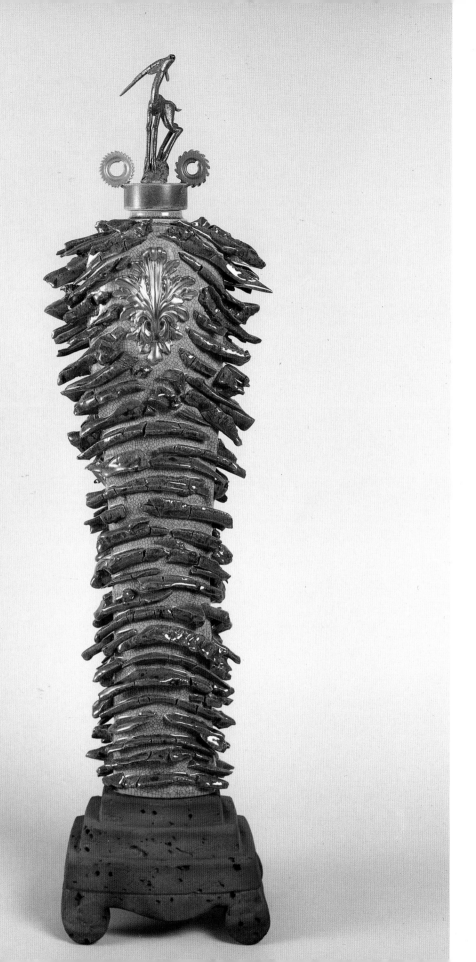

116 Untitled
     Adrian Saxe
     Raku and porcelain
     h. 26 cm
     USA, 1983

117 Untitled
     Anne Turner
     Stoneware
     h. 30 cm
     UK, 1985

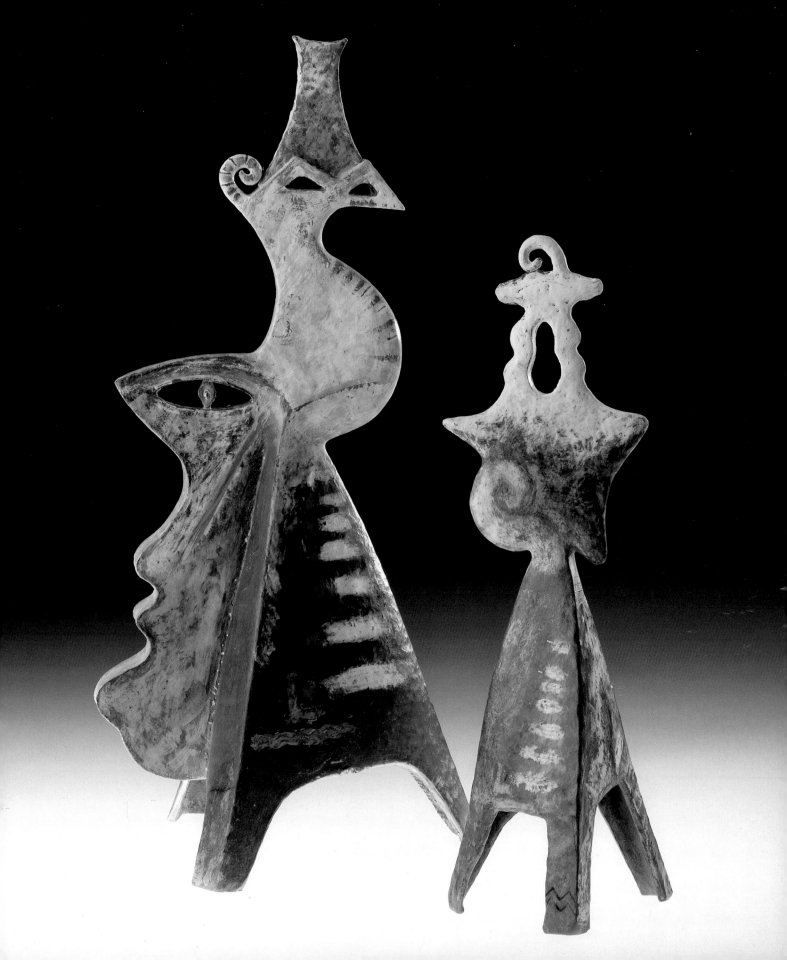

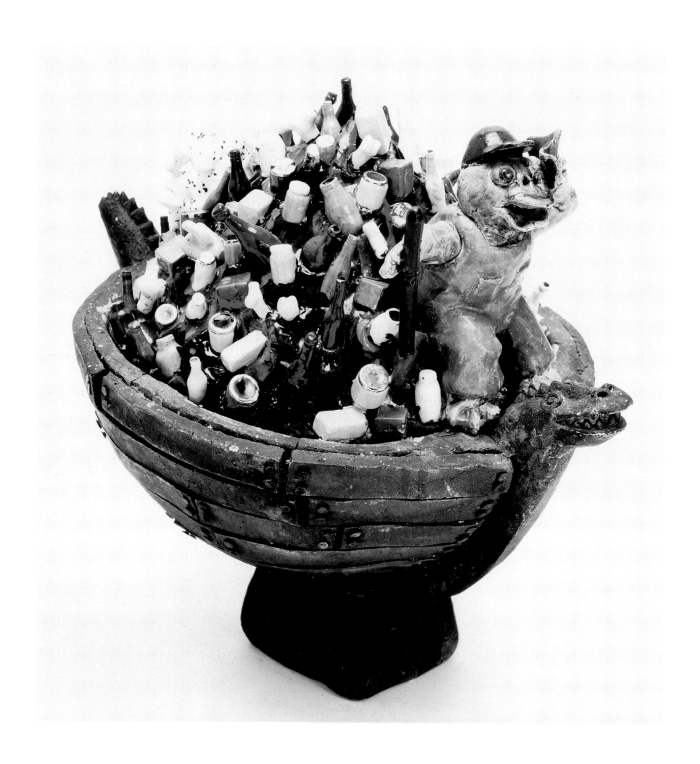

118 Garbage Ark
      David Gilhooly
      Earthenware
      h.55 cm
      USA, 1976

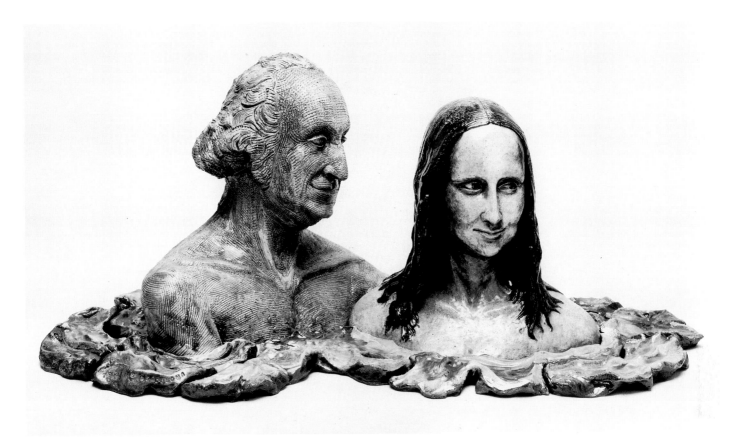

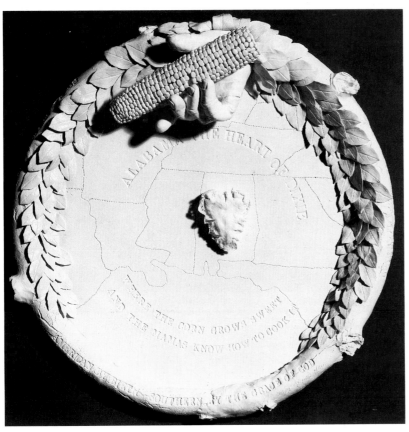

119 George and Mona in the
        baths of Coloma
     Robert Arneson
     Earthenware
     h. 60 cm
     USA, 1976

120 Where the Corn Grows Sweet
     Frank Fleming
     Porcelain
     d. 50 cm
     USA, 1983

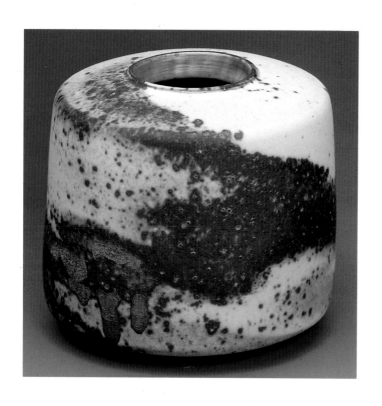

121 Vessel
Ursula Scheid
Stoneware, porcelain
h. 10 cm
West Germany, 1984

122 Casserole
Jane Hamlyn
Salt-glazed stoneware
d. 35 cm
UK, 1985

123 Vessel
Hans and Renate Heckmann
Stoneware
h. 41 cm
West Germany, 1980

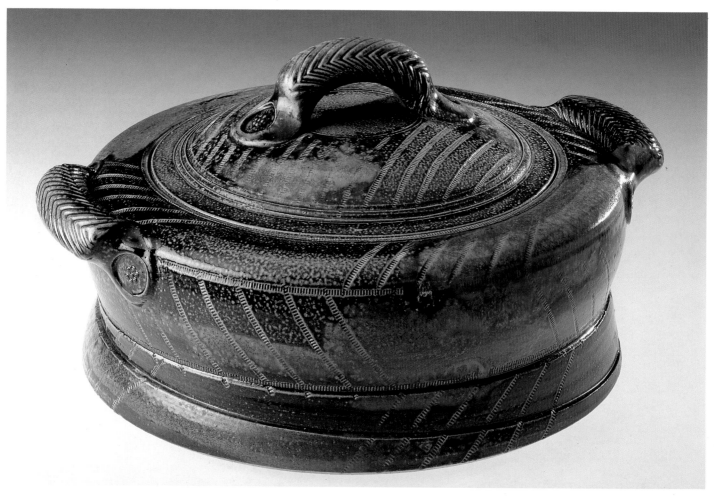

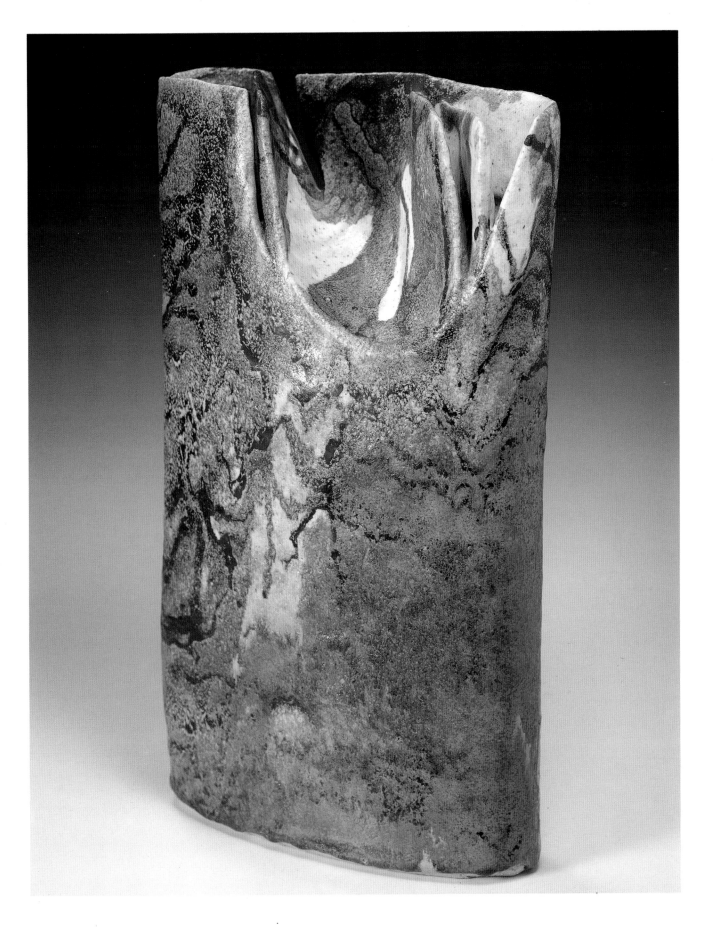

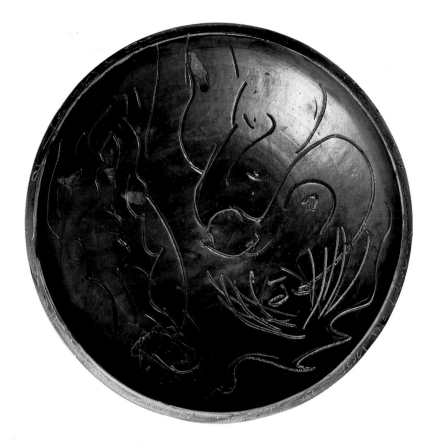

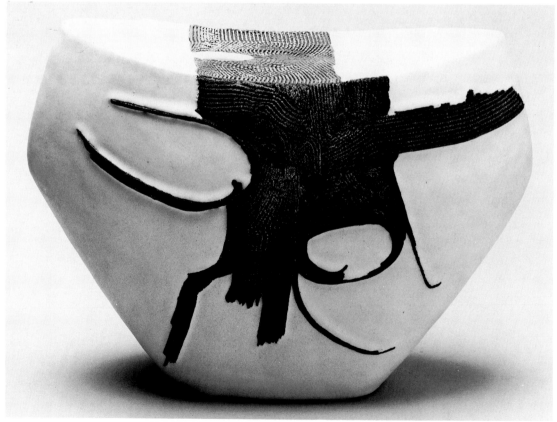

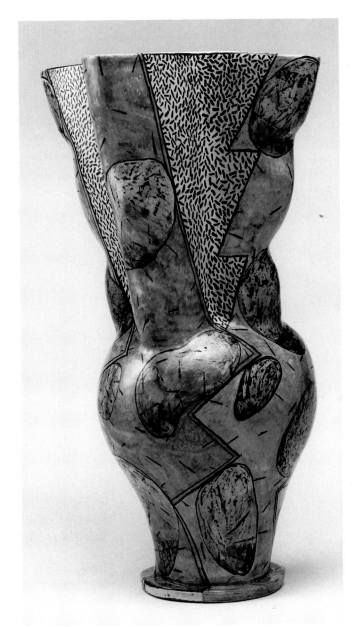

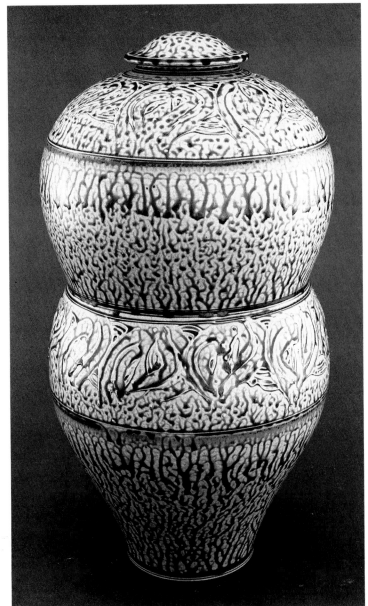

124 Adam and Eve
     Kenneth Ferguson
     Porcelain
     d. 43 cm
     USA, 1982

125 Barrier Reef Sanctuary
     Hiroe Swen
     Stoneware
     h. 28.5 cm
     Australia, 1981

126 Jelly Bean Vase
     Andrea Gill
     Earthenware
     h. 50 cm
     USA, 1983

127 Covered jar
     Tom Turner
     Thrown porcelain
     h. 50 cm
     USA, 1980

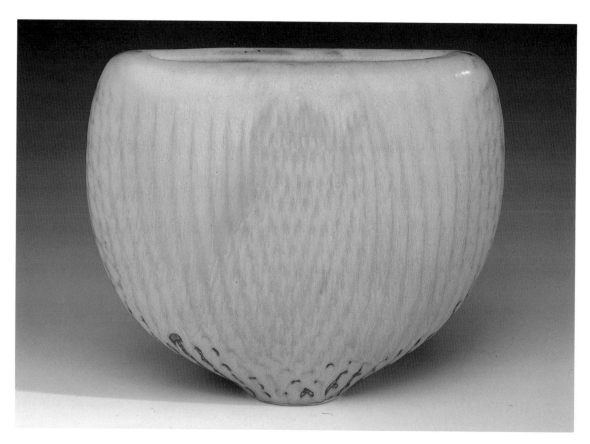

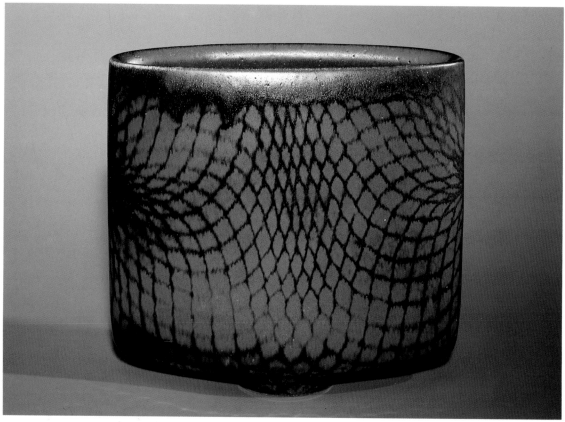

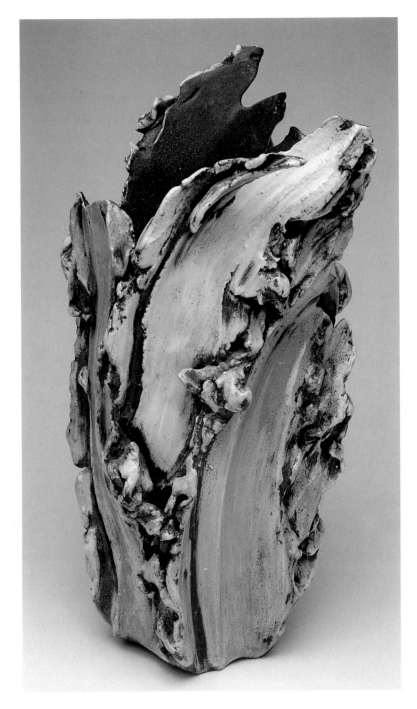

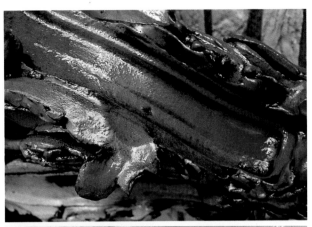

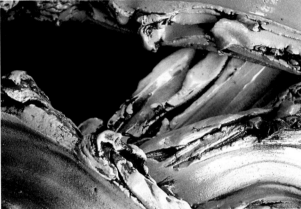

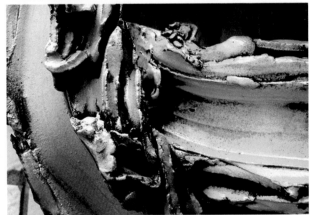

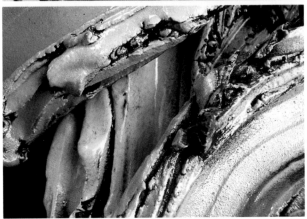

128 Bowl
   Gotlind Weigel
   Stoneware
   h. 17 cm
   West Germany, 1985

129 Bowl
   Gotlind Weigel
   Stoneware
   h. 18 cm
   West Germany, 1985

130 Vase
   Irene Vonck
   Stoneware
   h. 56 cm
   Holland, 1984

131 Details of large public
     wall-relief
     Irene Vonck
     Holland, 1985

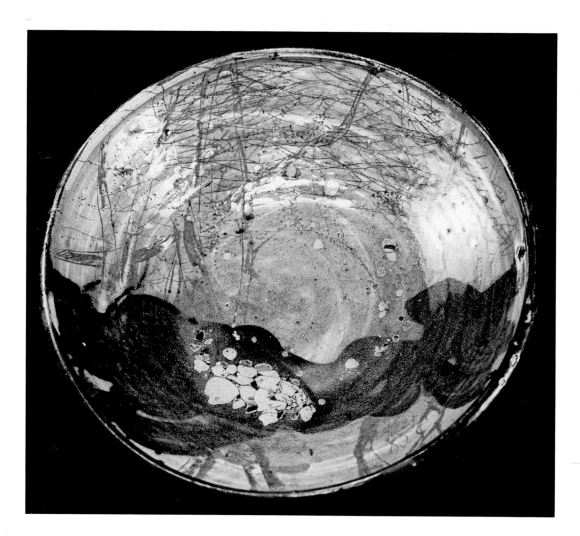

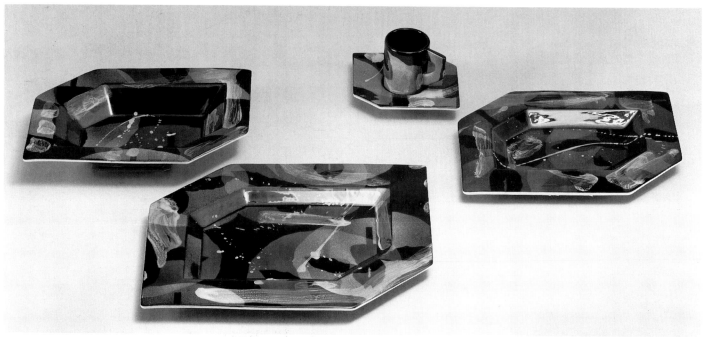

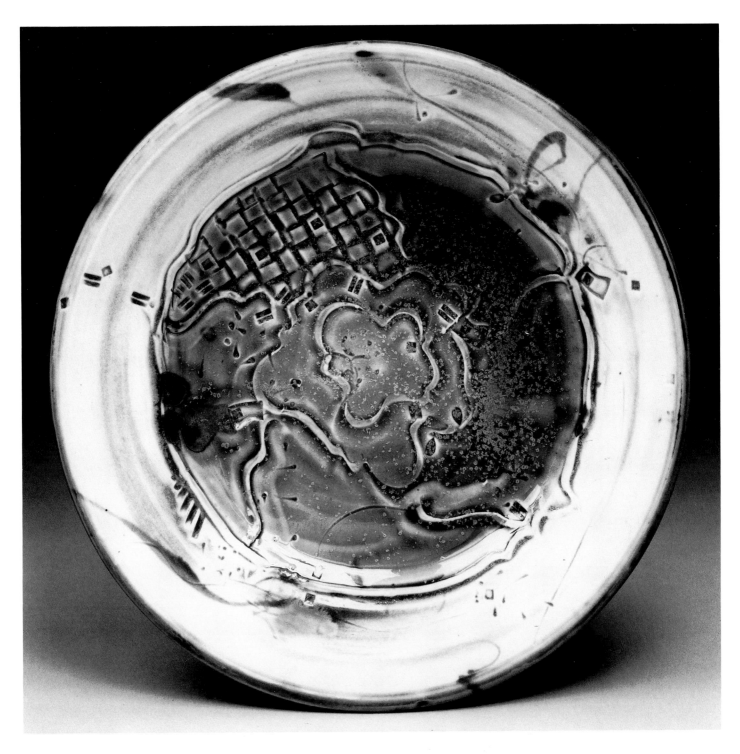

132 Bowl
Brigette Penicaud
Stoneware
d. 60 cm
France, 1985

133 Hexagonal dinner-ware
Billy Al Bengston
Earthenware
l. 30 cm
USA, 1976

134 Plate
John Glick
Porcelain
d. 29 cm
USA, 1979

Overleaf
135 Vase
Ann-Marie Wasshede
Stoneware
h. 40 cm
Sweden, 1985

136 Jar from Tlön (right)
Elizabeth Fritsch
Stoneware
h. 30 cm
Spiral jar (left)
Stoneware
h. 24 cm
UK, 1984

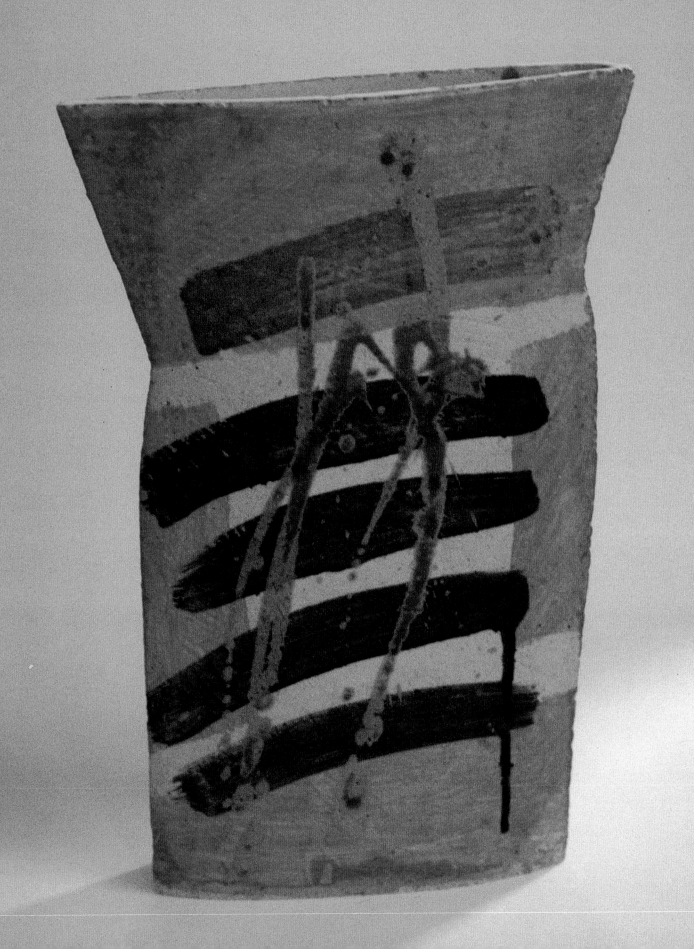

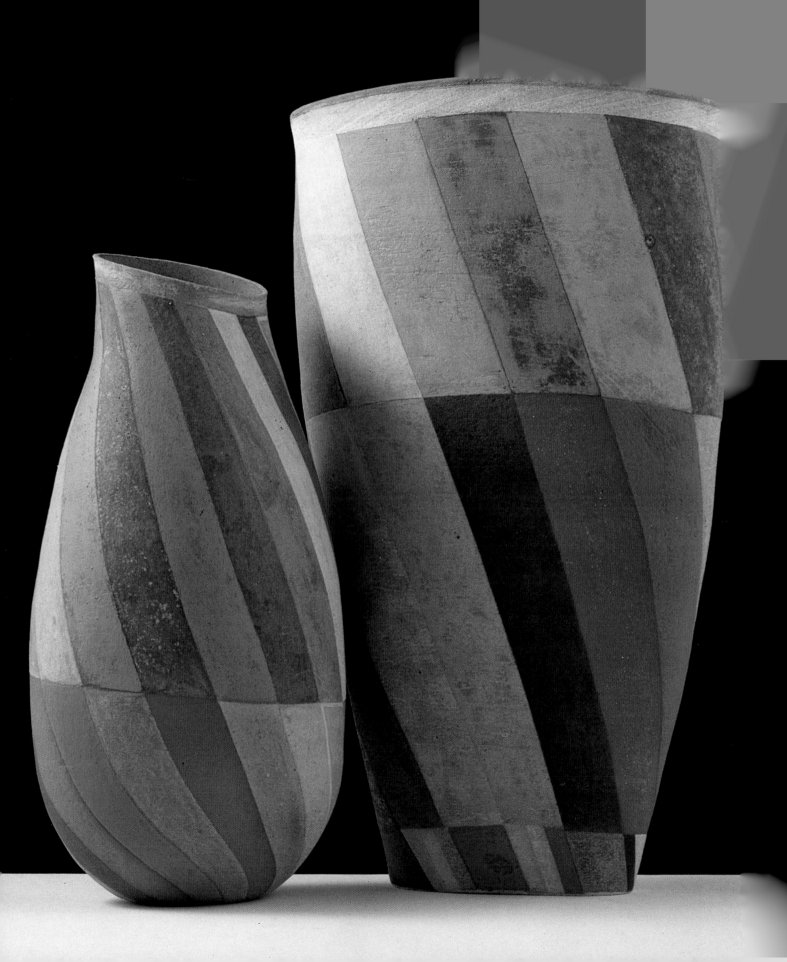

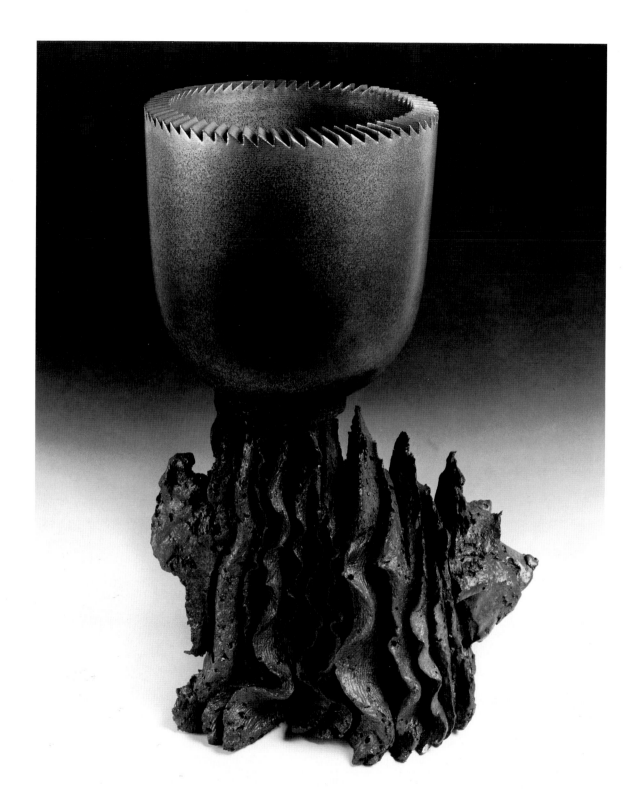

137 Untitled
   Adrian Saxe
   Porcelain, raku
   h. 14 cm
   USA, 1982

138 Blossom-shaped vessel
   Johannes Gebhardt
   Porcelain
   h. 31 cm
   West Germany, 1984

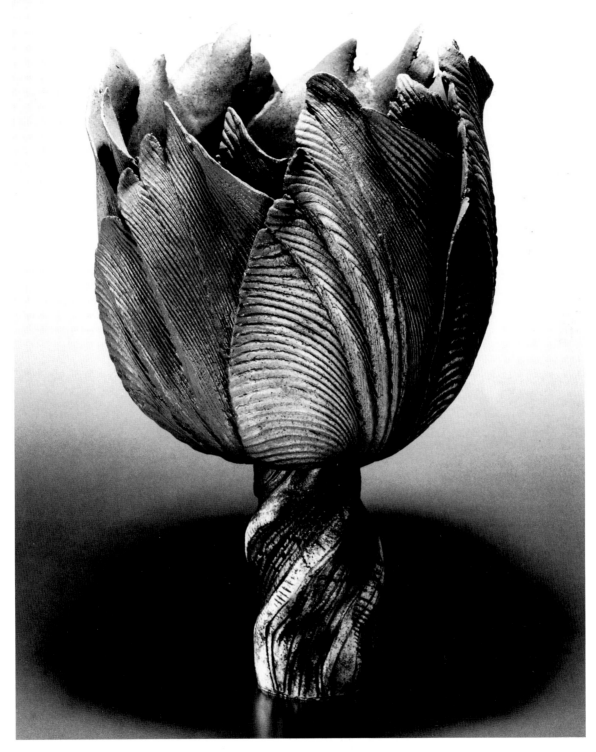

Overleaf
139 Untitled
    Richard Slee
    Stoneware
    h.40cm
    UK, 1984

140 Vase
    Anne Kraus
    Stoneware
    h.20cm
    USA, 1985

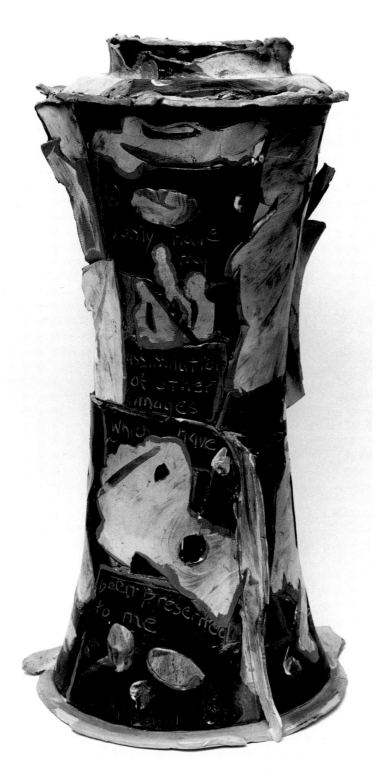

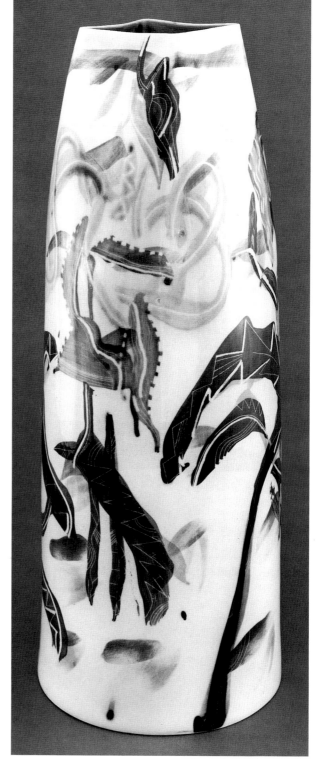

141 Jar
Penny Kokkinos
Earthenware
h.60cm
Canada, 1985

142 Vessel
Tom Spleth
Slip-cast porcelain
h.54cm
USA, 1979

143 Gemini Vessel
Rudy Autio
Stoneware
h.68cm
USA, 1984

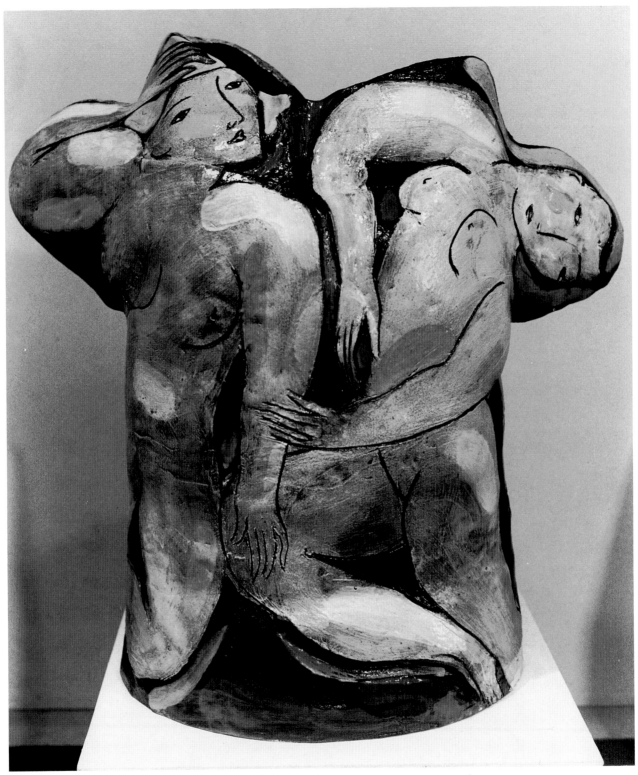

146 Hands
   Jill Crowley
   Earthenware
   h. 27 cm
   UK, 1983

147 Bowl, double portrait
   Andrea Gill
   Earthenware
   h. 30 cm
   USA, 1983

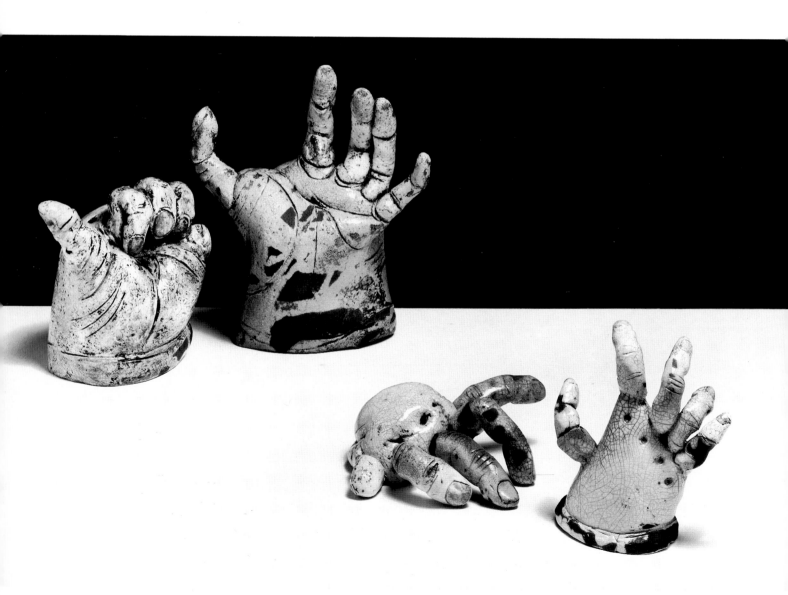

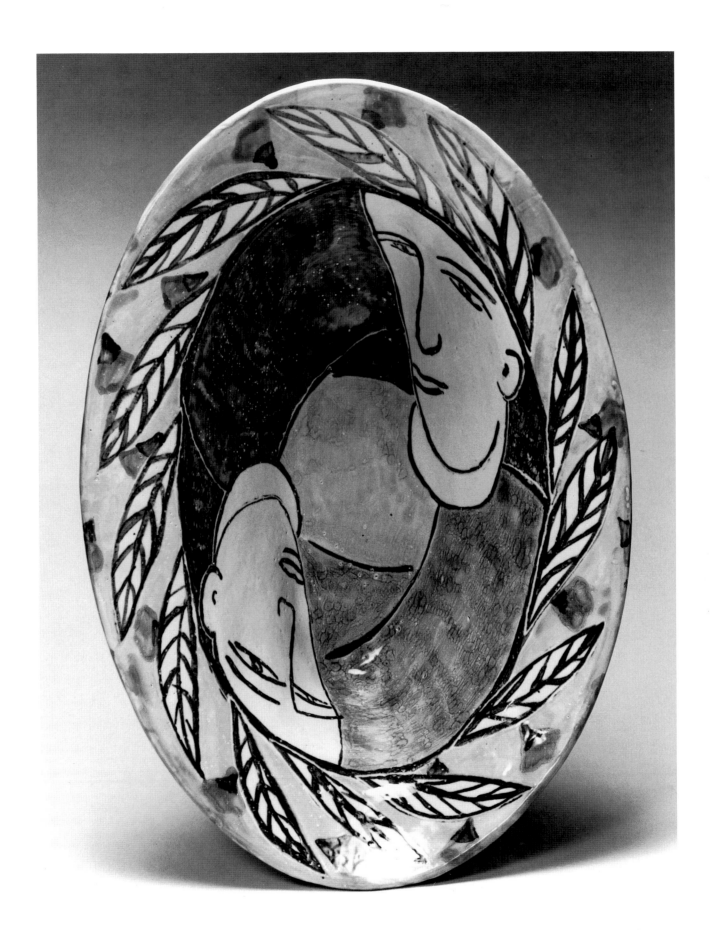

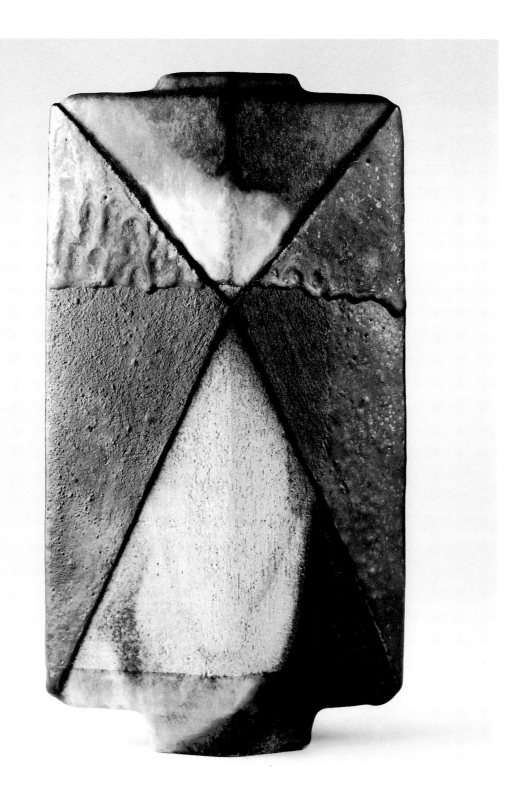

151 Vessel
Antje Brüggemann-Breckwoldt
Stoneware
h. 35 cm
West Germany, 1981

152 Goblet
Beatrice Wood
Earthenware
h. 24 cm
USA, 1976

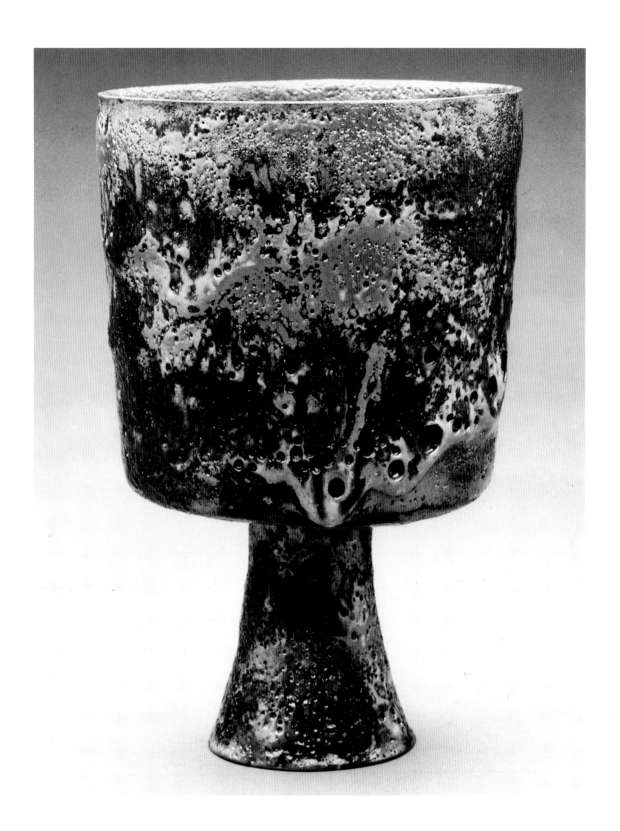

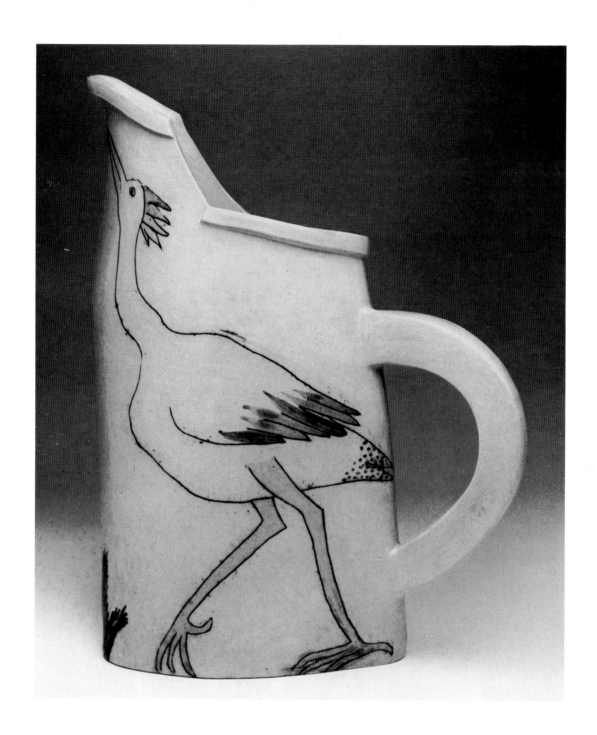

156 Stork Jug   157 Vase
    Alison Britton   Bernard Leach
    Earthenware   Stoneware
    h. 30 cm   h. 40 cm
    UK, 1977   UK, 1965

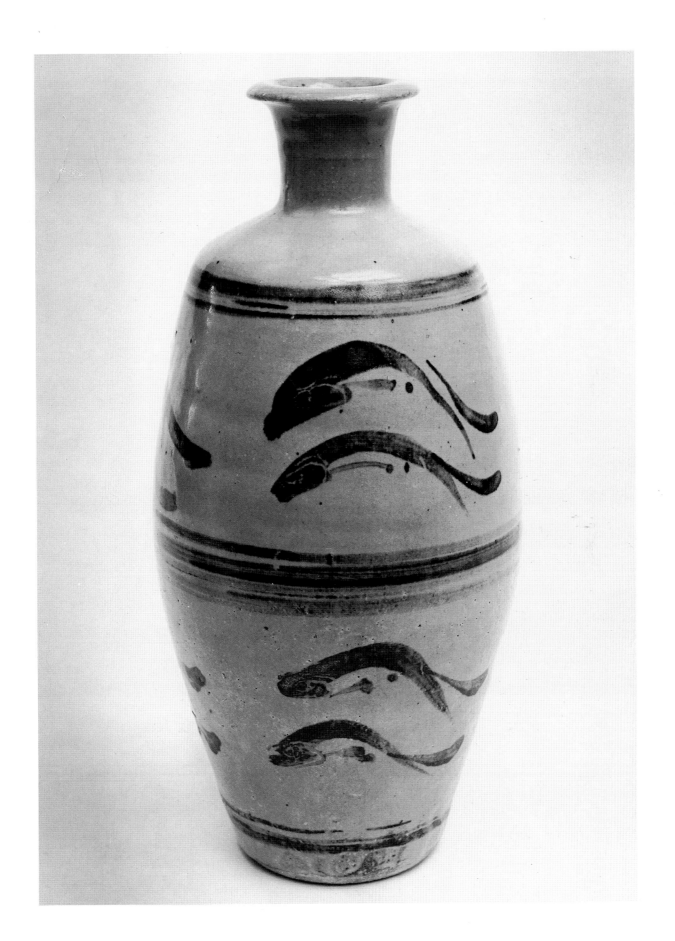

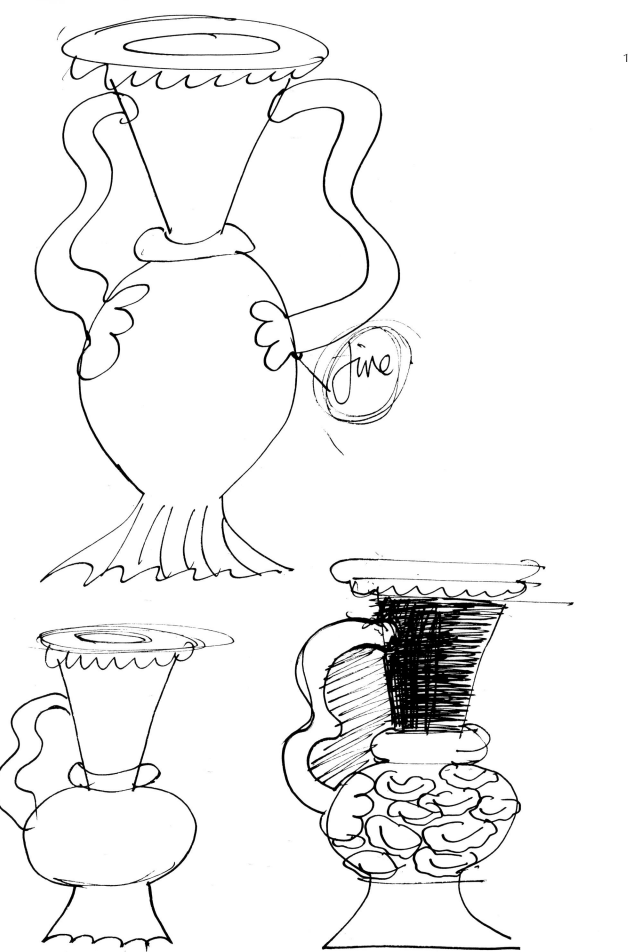

160 Drawing from
Richard Slee's
Sketchbook
UK, 1984

161 Land Form Teapot
(variation no. 6)
Richard Notkin
Stoneware
h.8cm
USA, 1983

162 Ritual No. 1
Jerry Rothman
Porcelain
h.37cm
USA, 1978

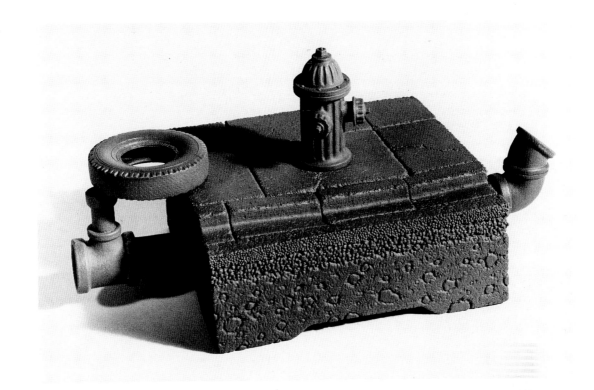

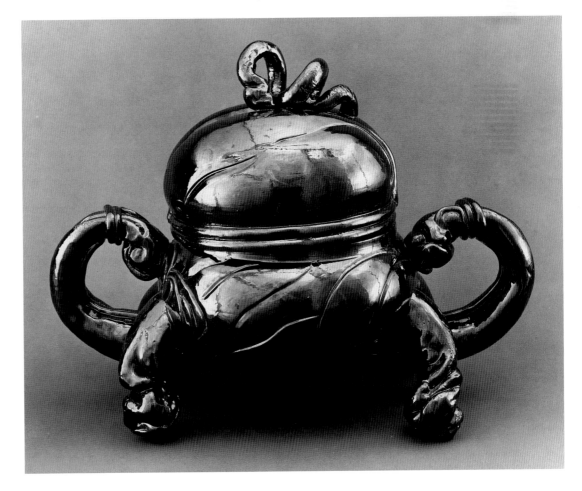

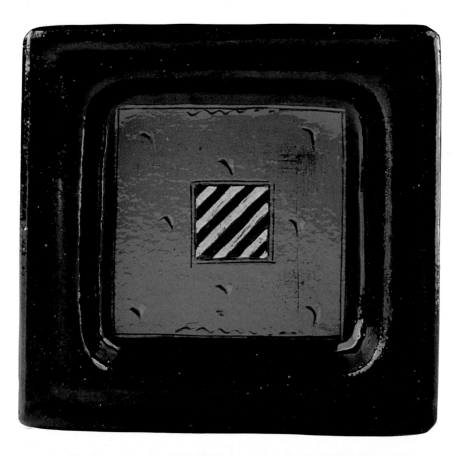

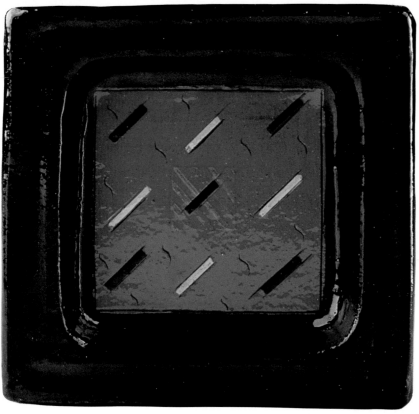

163 Plate
   Ingrid Mortensen
   Earthenware
   h. 14.5 cm
   Norway, 1984

164 Plate
   Ingrid Mortensen
   Earthenware
   h. 14 cm
   Norway, 1984

165 Vessels
   Ruth Koppenhöfer
   Earthenware
   h. 24 cm, 17 cm
   West Germany, 1980

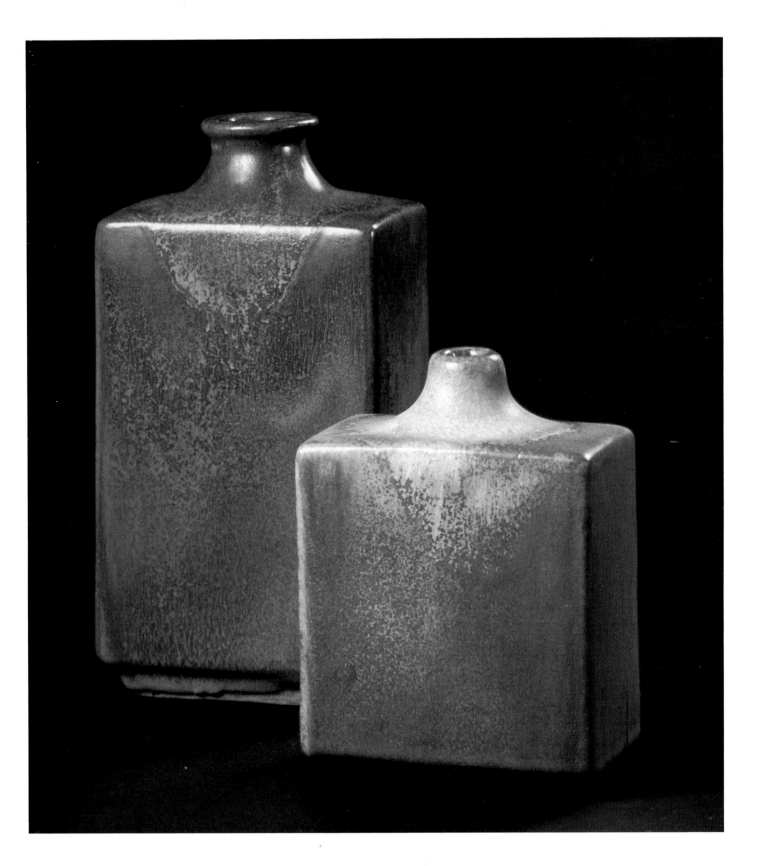

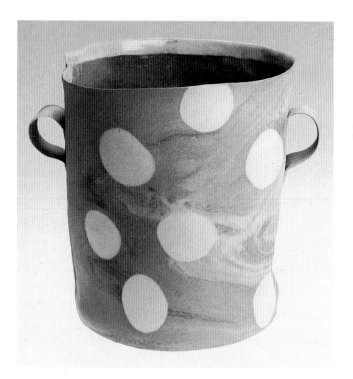

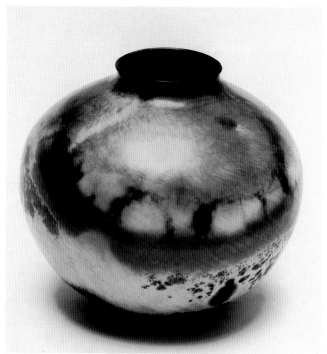

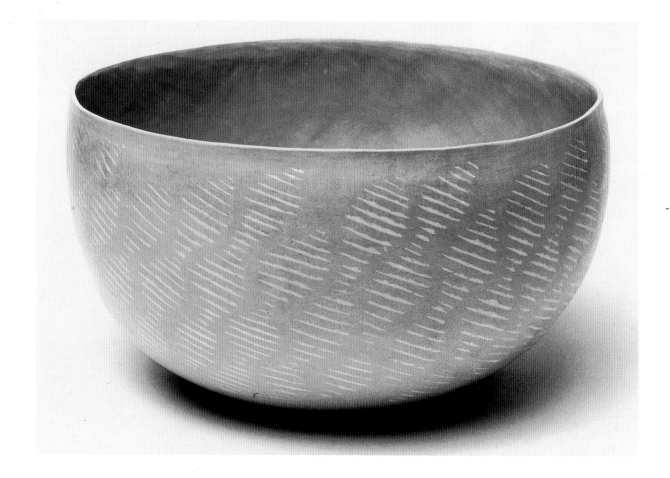

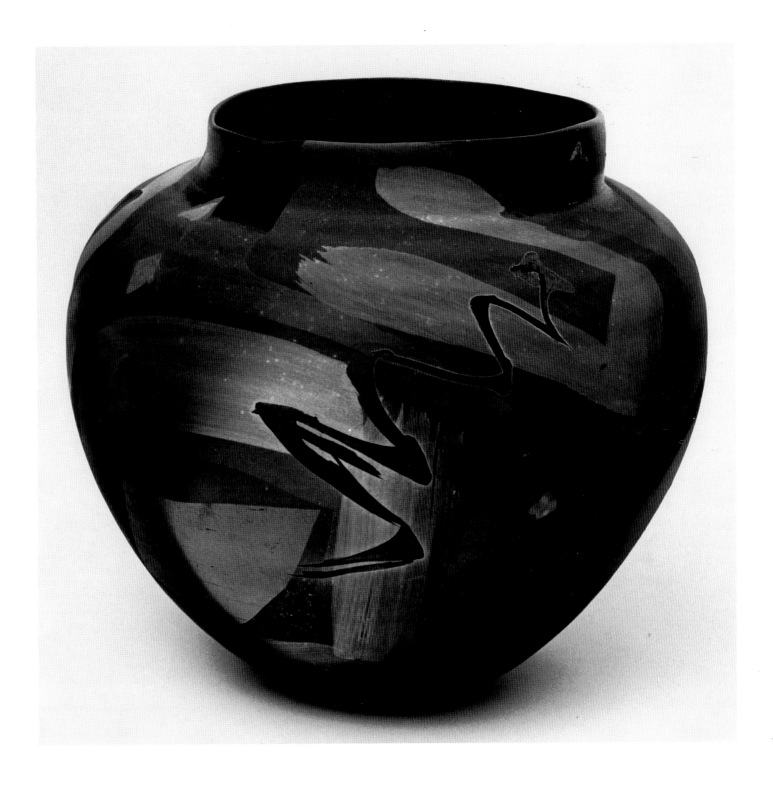

166 Polka-dot pot
   Johan van Loon
   Porcelain
   h. 24 cm
   Holland

167 Vessel
   Gaby Koch
   Stoneware
   h. 50 cm
   West Germany/UK, 1985

168 Bowl
   Klaartje Kamermans
   Earthenware
   h. 16 cm
   Holland, 1984

169 Bowl
   Nancy Solway
   Raku
   h. 37 cm
   Canada, 1985

170 Oracle
   Toni Warburton
   Earthenware
   h. 26 cm
   Australia, 1983

171 Two faces
   Babs Haenen
   Porcelain
   h. 19 cm
   Holland, 1985

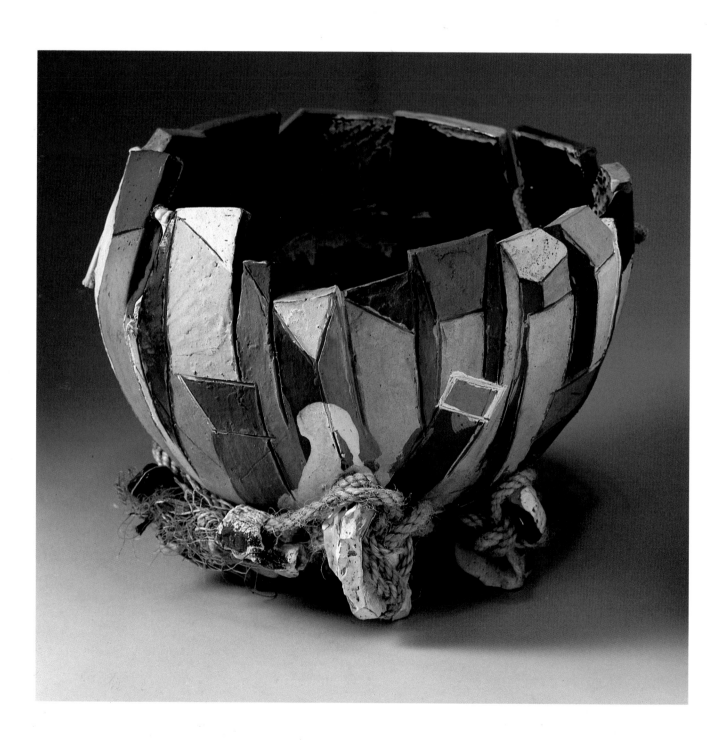

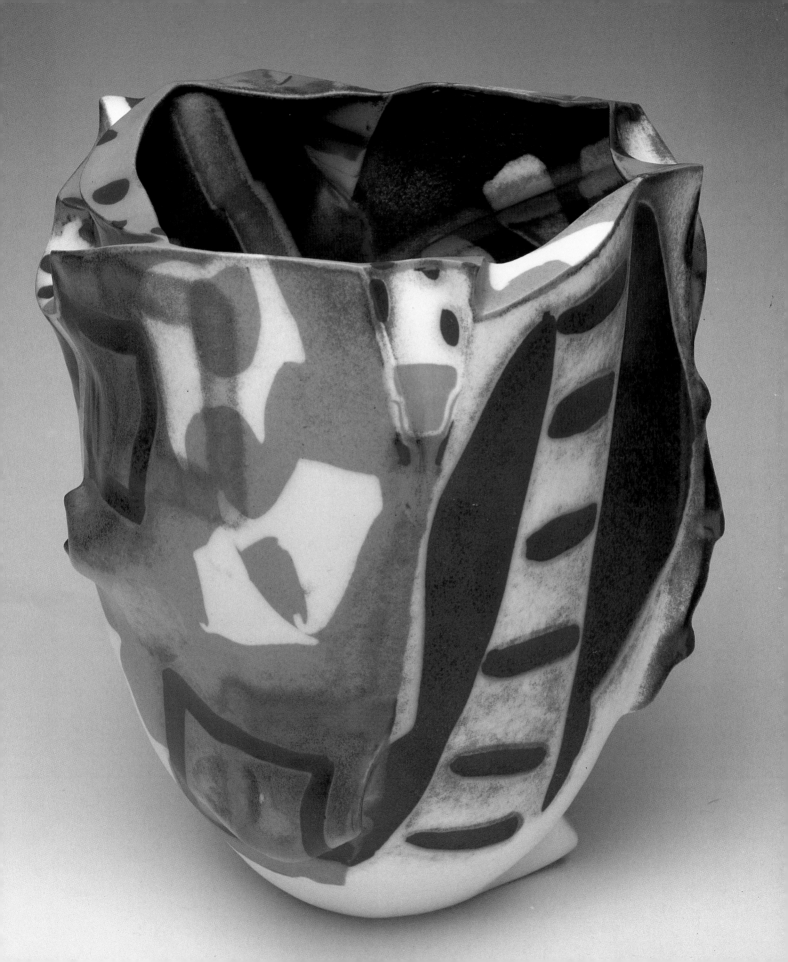

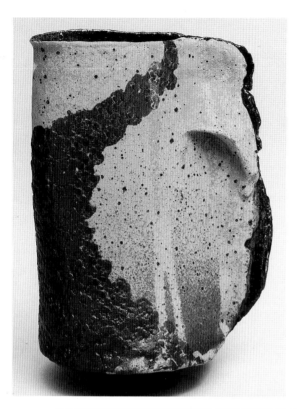

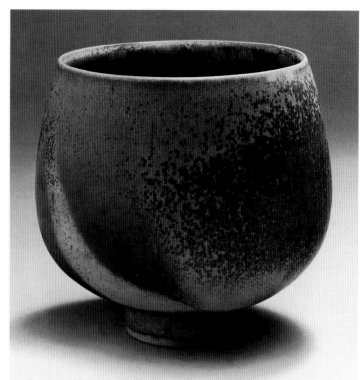

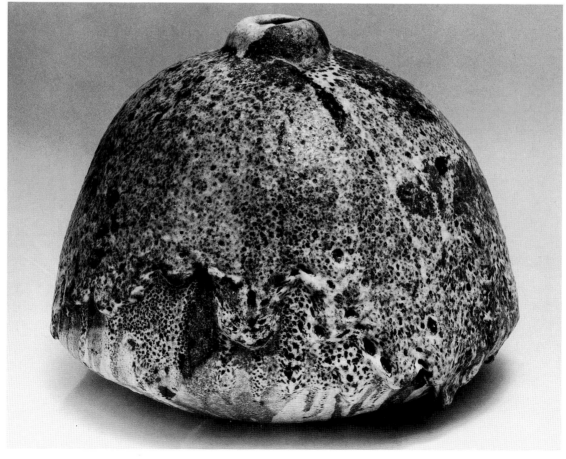

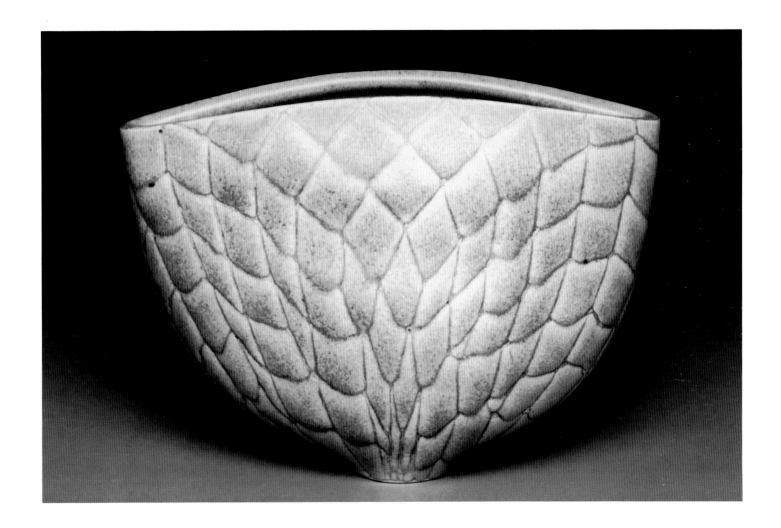

172 Vessel
    Signe Lehmann Pistorius
    Earthenware
    h. 25 cm
    West Germany, 1980

173 Bowl
    Hans and Renate Heckmann
    Earthenware
    h. 17 cm
    West Germany, 1979

174 Vessel
    Hans and Renate Heckmann
    Earthenware
    h. 29 cm
    West Germany, 1985

175 Vessel
    Gotlind Weigel
    Stoneware
    h. 23 cm
    West Germany, 1984

Overleaf
176 Decanter
    Gaby Sperer Scope
    Stoneware
    h. 15.5 cm
    Canada, 1992

177 Form
    Angus Suttie
    Stoneware
    h. 45 cm
    UK, 1985

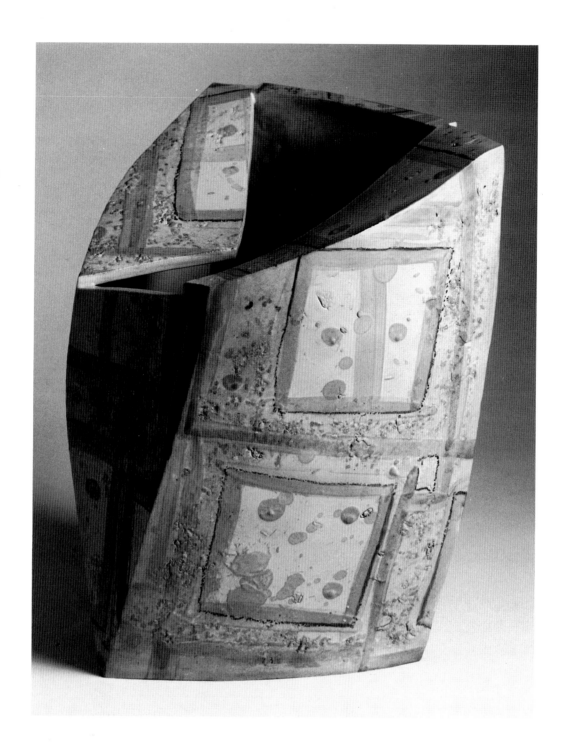

178 Big Yellow Pot
Alison Britton
Earthenware
h. 33 cm
UK, 1981

179 Equinox
Richard Deutsch
Porcelain
h. 27 cm
USA, 1979

180 Bowl
Klaartje Kamermans
Earthenware
d. 15 cm
Holland, 1985

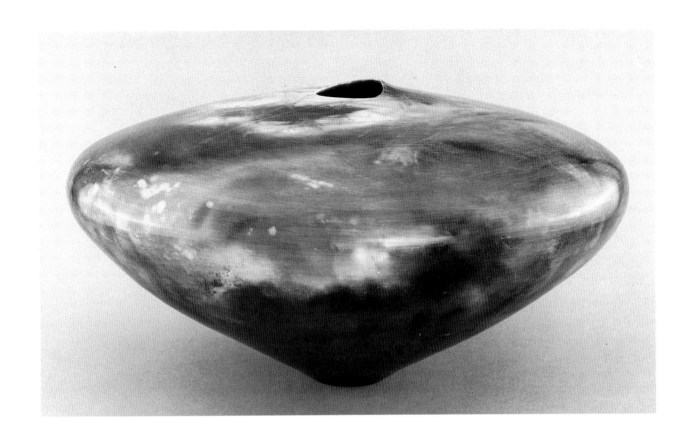

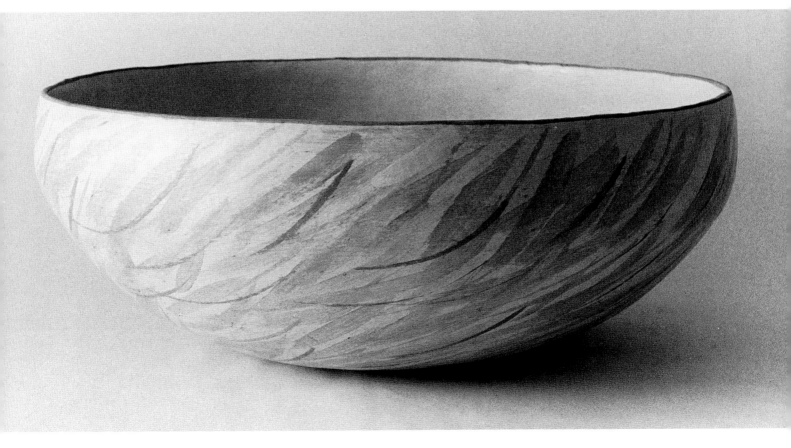

181 T'ang Pillow Pitcher
Betty Woodman
Earthenware
h.45cm
USA, 1982

182 Vessel on tray
Betty Woodman
Earthenware
h.27cm
USA, 1980

183 Beige-striped pot
Alison Britton
Earthenware
h.39cm
UK, 1984

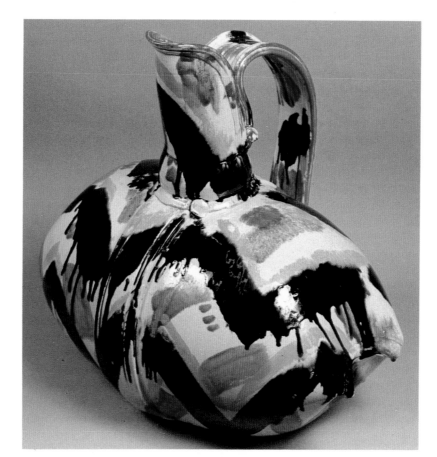

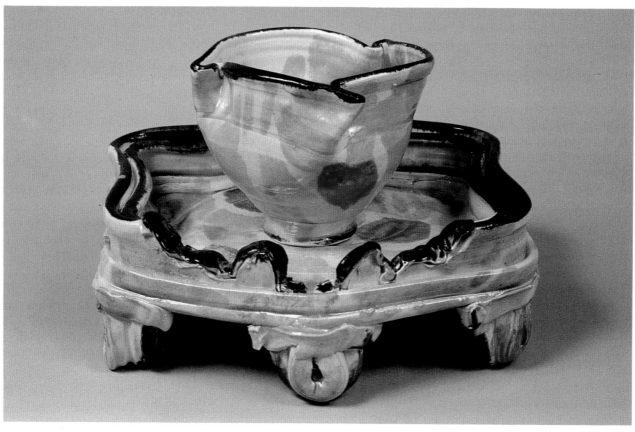

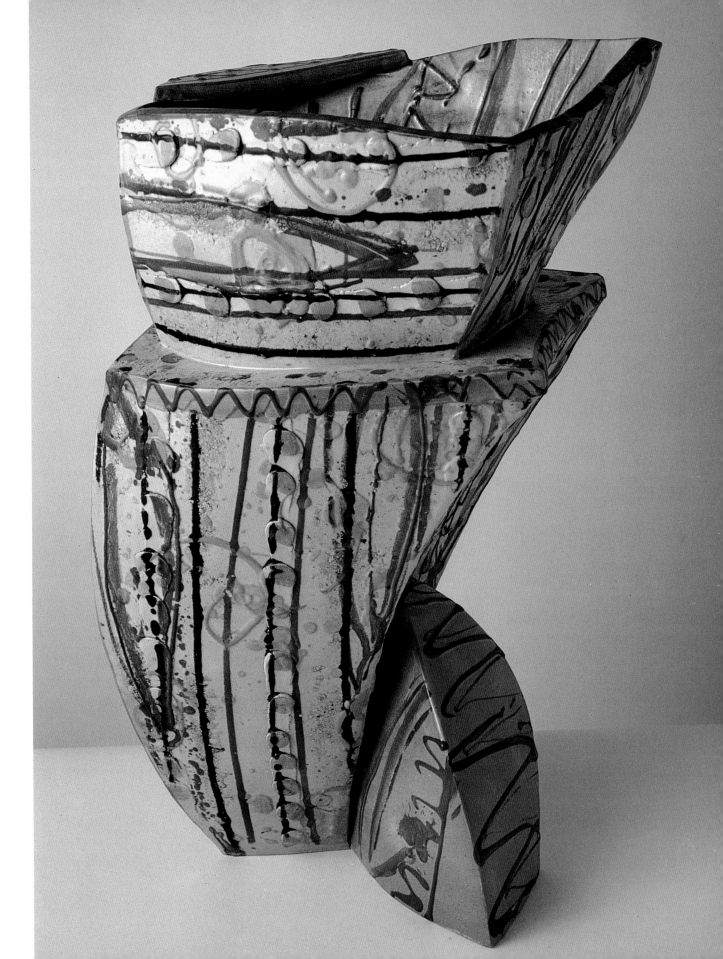

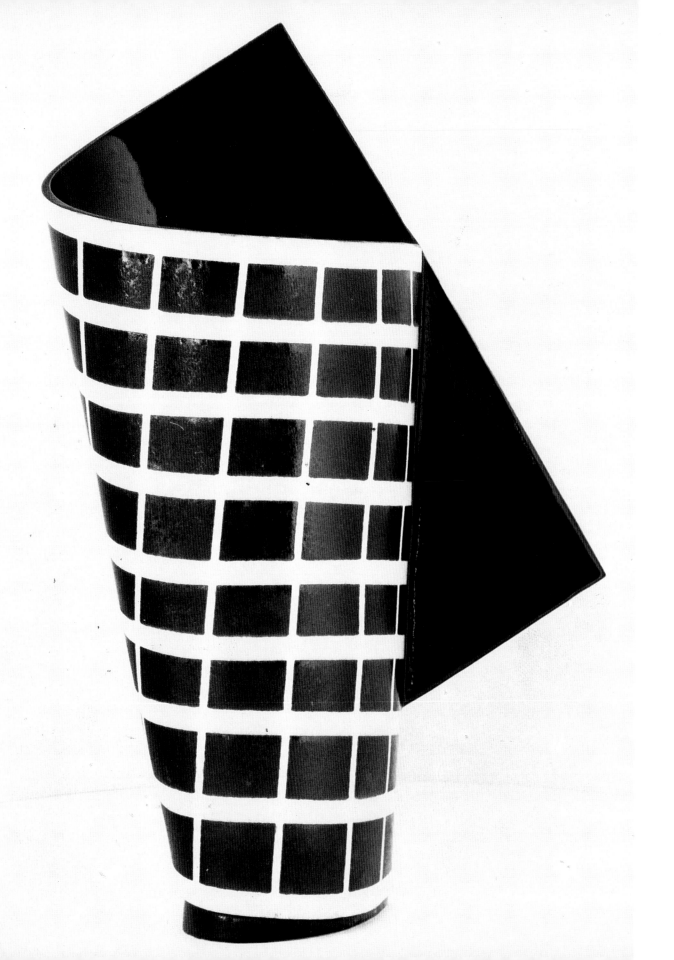

184 Folding vase
   Mieke Blits
   Stoneware
   h. 50 cm
   Holland, 1985

185 Optical pot
   Karen Bennicke
   Stoneware
   h. 19 cm
   Denmark, 1984

186 Platter
   Malcolm Stewart
   Stoneware
   d. 49 cm
   Australia, 1981

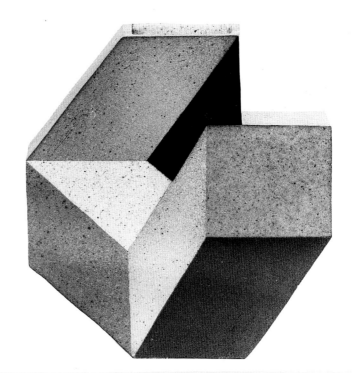

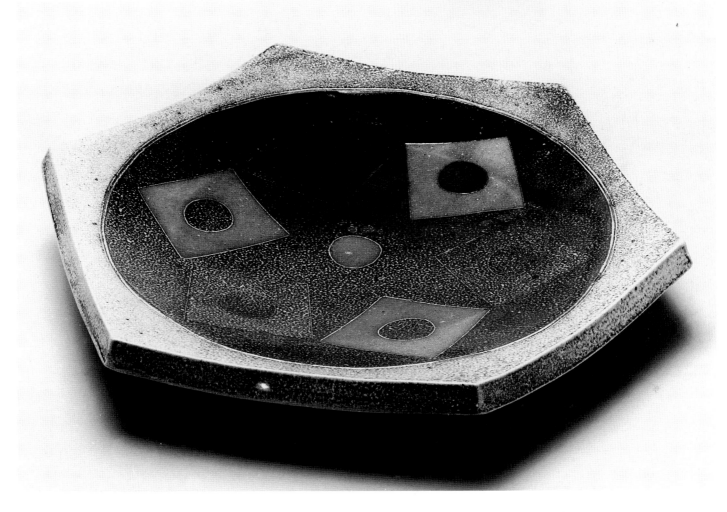

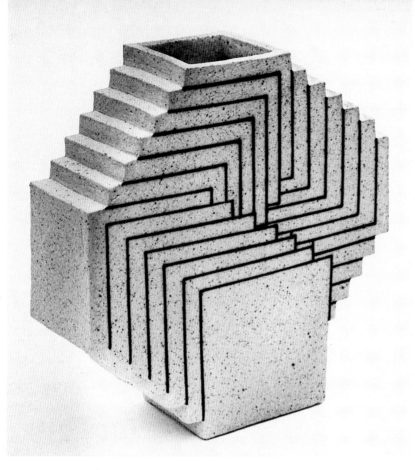

187 Optical pot
   Karen Bennicke
   Stoneware
   h. 47 cm
   Denmark, 1984

188 Line
   Philip Cornelius
   Porcelain
   h. 17 cm
   USA, 1985

189 Vases
   Karen Bennicke
   Stoneware
   h. 26 cm
   Denmark, 1984

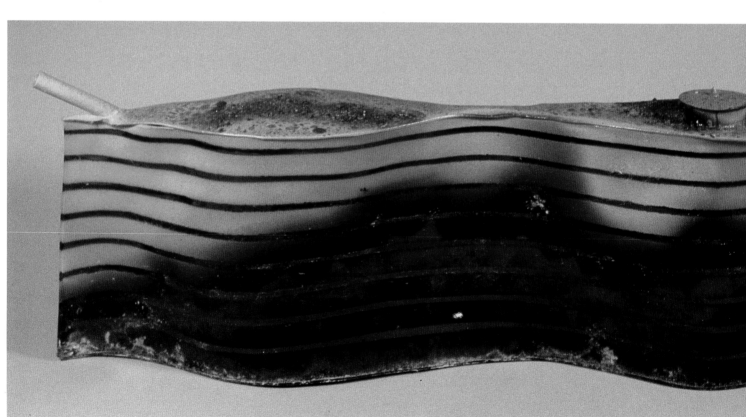

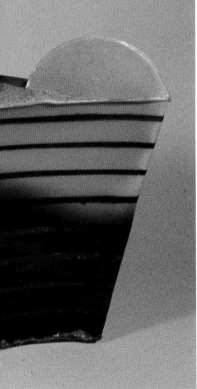

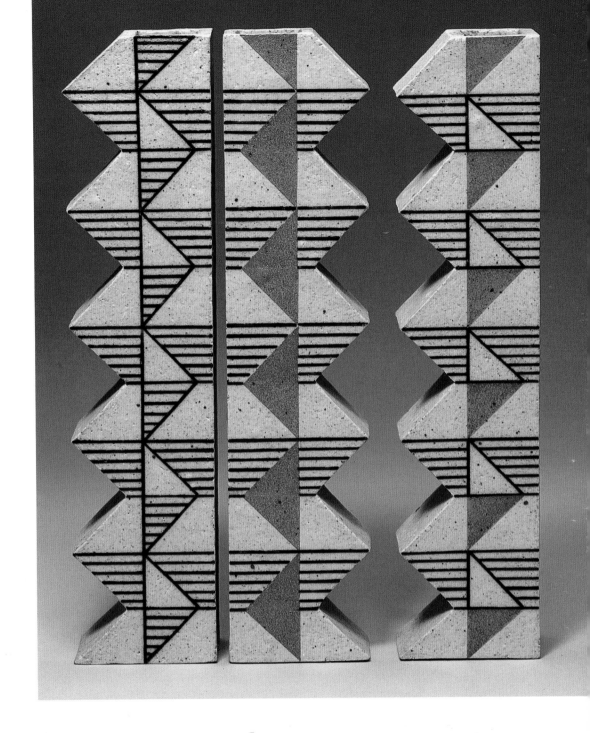

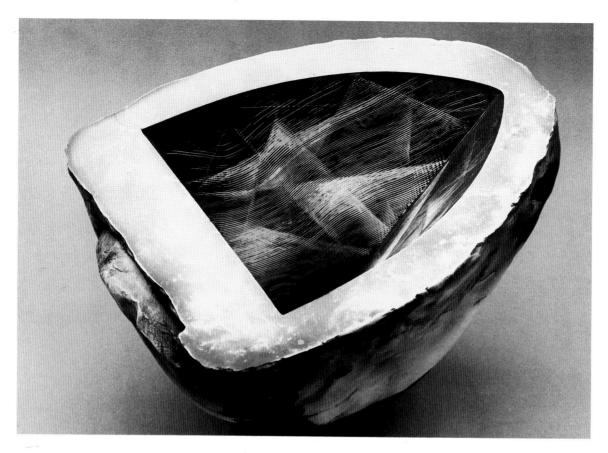

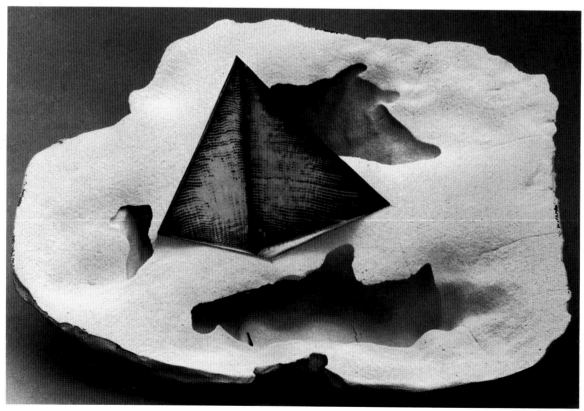

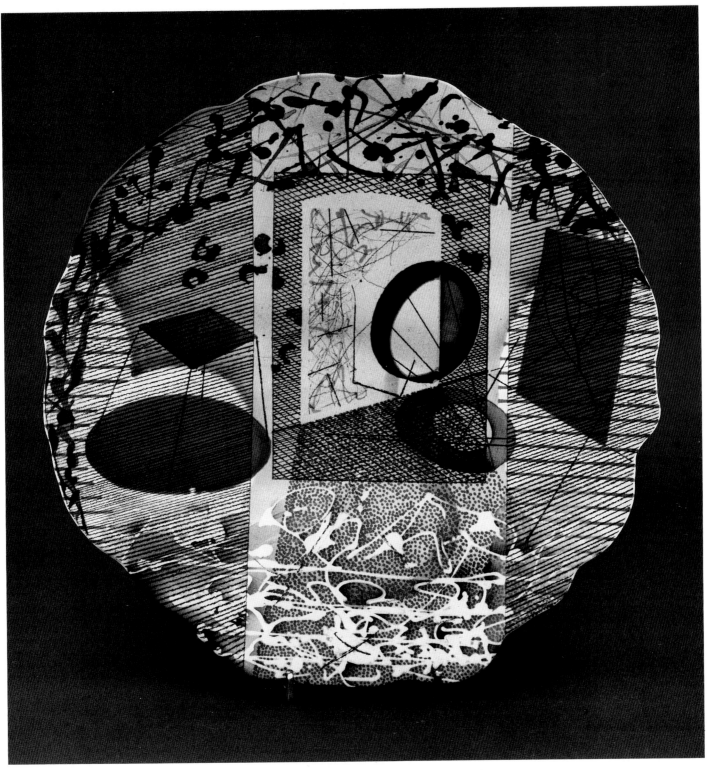

190 Vessel
Steve Heinemann
Earthenware
h. 40 cm
Canada, 1983

191 Form
Steve Heinemann
Earthenware
d. 50 cm
Canada, 1982

192 Tintype no. 1
Walter Hall
Porcelain
d. 49.5 cm
USA, 1977

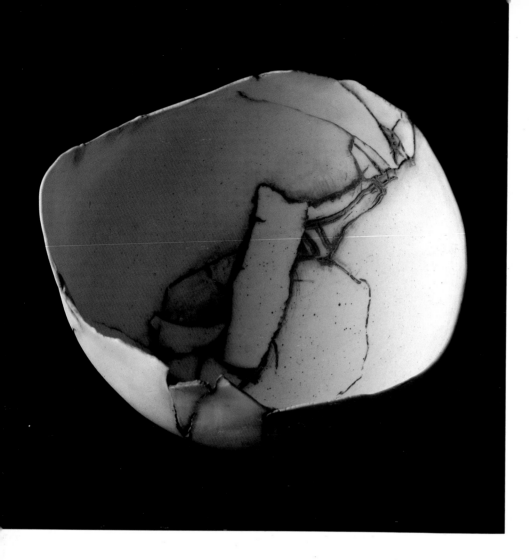

193 Bowl
Kari Christensen
Porcelain
d. 15 cm
Norway, 1976

194 Drawing by
Kari Christensen
Norway, c. 1976

195 The Princess and the Wolf
Jo Buffalo and
    Christopher Darling
Earthenware
h. 24 cm
USA, 1985

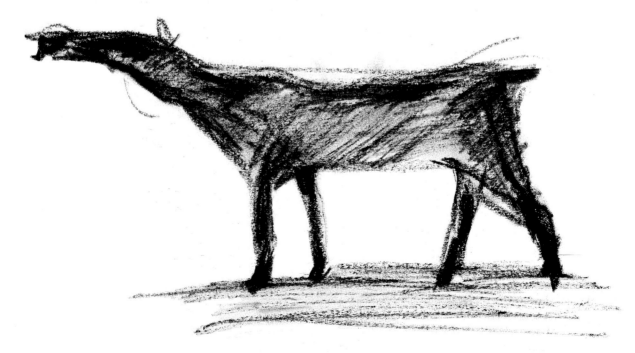

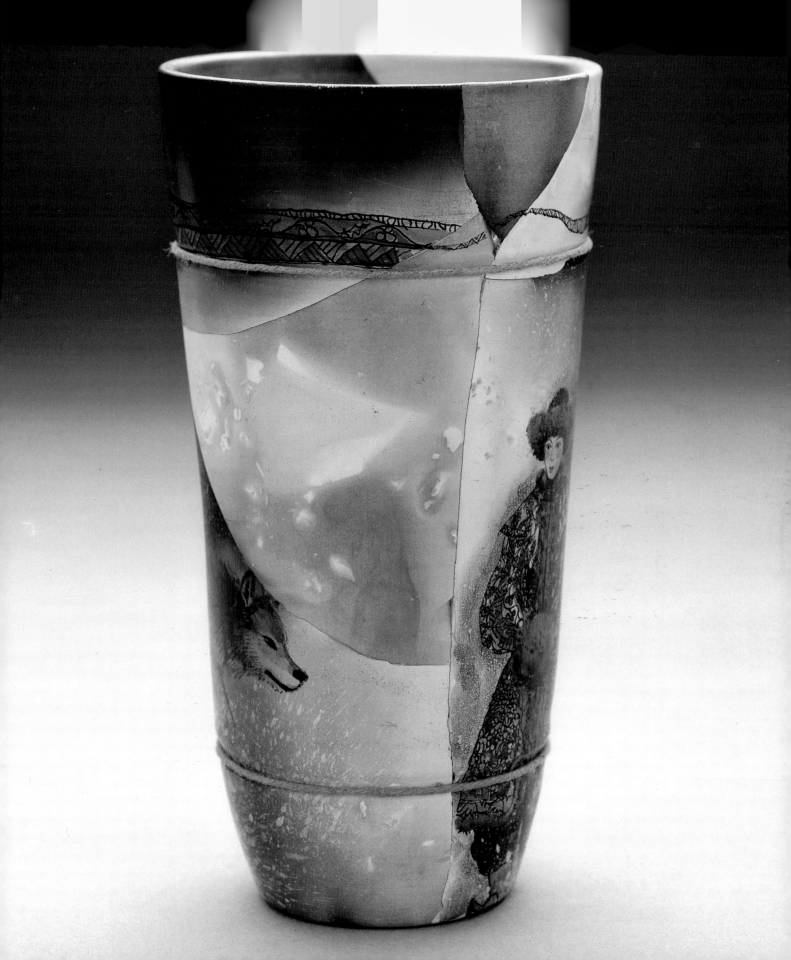

196 Fan-shaped tray
Ann Cummings
Earthenware
d.38cm
Canada, 1983

197 Vase
Claude Varlan
Earthenware
h.45cm
France, 1985

Overleaf
198 Vase
Claude Varlan
Earthenware
h.50cm
France, 1985

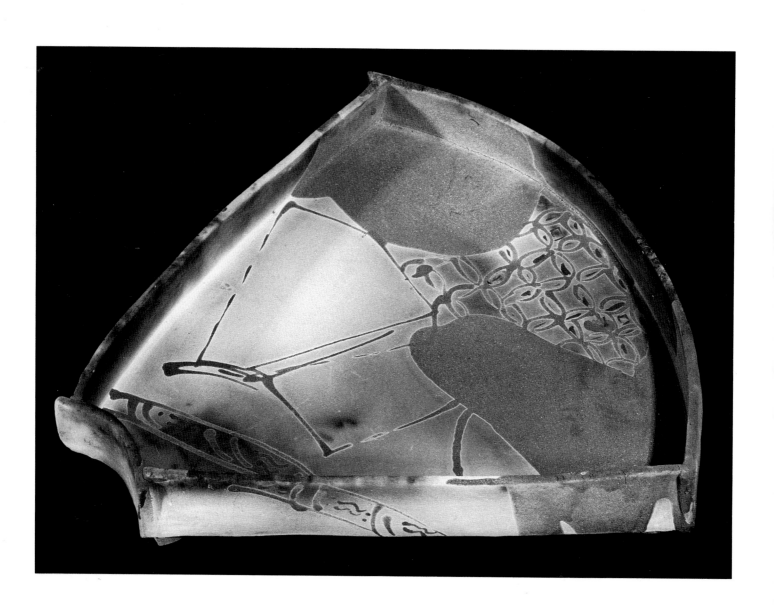

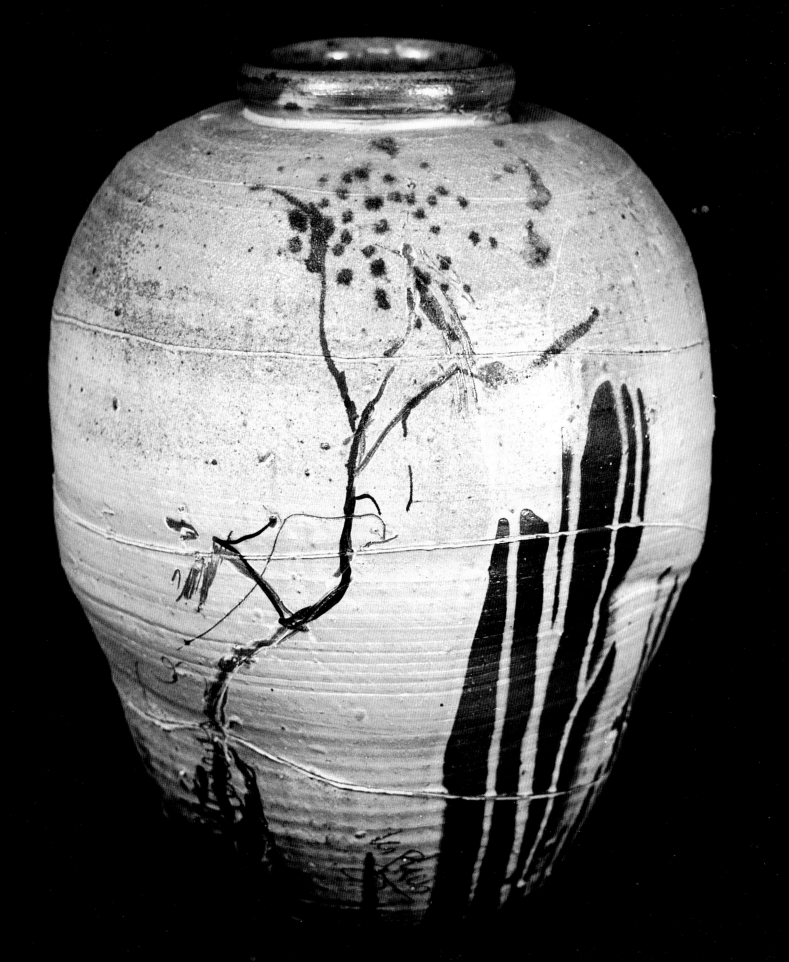

The Sculptural Ambitions of Potters

Since the mid-1980s the craft of ceramics has continued to change into a form of 'fine art'. There remain many potters producing functional hand-built or wheel-thrown ceramics, just as there remain industrial potters producing prototype designs for industry. And yet the functional potter is overshadowed by the steady emergence of the ceramic sculptor. The aspirations towards making sculpture *per se* are changing the nature of the hand-craft discipline of ceramics.

Of course, several of the functionalist or vessel-orientated potters featured earlier in this book have continued to refine and deepen their craft: Jane Hamlyn is a notable example. Nevertheless, both the concept and the practice of ceramics as a craft has ebbed in the art schools and among a new generation of ceramics graduates. Even the notion of ceramics as an applied art is harder to sustain in the 1990s than it was in the 1980s.

After all, the term 'applied' suggests not only utility but also a form of service: an applied art is one that serves architecture or provides the home with tableware or domestic ornament. These categories are no longer prominent in the ceramics of the 1990s. Where a ceramicist makes reference to architecture, then he or she is more likely to do so in terms of using the building as an ancillary part of his or her own art – as happens in installation art.

Consider, for example, the installations featured in this chapter by Yasutoshi Jinnai (Japan), Ellen Driscoll (USA) and Setsuko Nagasawa (Japan). These works stand in their own right: they are not an embellishment to the building; the building merely provides the space or the prop for the art. Even the exciting architectural embellishment provided by Alexander Brodsky and Ilya Utkin (Russia) for the Europees Keramisch Werkcentrum in the Netherlands (see p. 196) is in truth a free-standing art work rather than an architecturally integrated piece of decoration.

With regard to domestic craft, there is an interesting development from the USA that centres upon the home: it concerns the rise of a folk art in which ceramic containers or figures illustrate or narrate contemporary political or social themes. An example of this work is provided here by Matt Nolen (USA). More generally, it is also true that many sculptural ceramics are scaled – domestically – for the table, but the ideology that has brought these works into existence is rooted in the art gallery.

The ideology of the art gallery, together with the ambition to be seen as an individualistic sculptor, dominate endeavour in ceramics in the 1990s.

219
214, 206
212
209

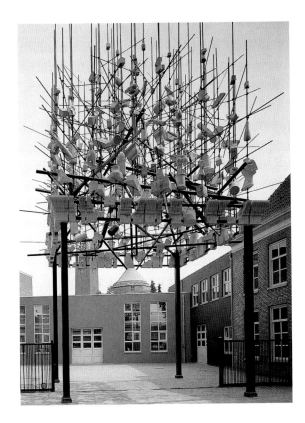

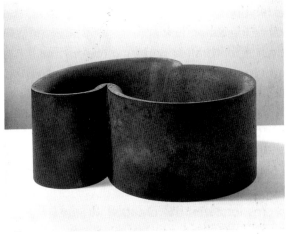

Left, Portal. Alexander Brodsky and Ilya Utkin. Stoneware. Russia/Holland (EKWC), 1992

Below, Substance and Shadow No. IV. Martin Smith. Raku. d. 40 cm. UK, 1993

Individualism and the sheer variety of output has affected notions of quality and connoisseurship. Indeed, just as the role of the art critic as a connoisseur of art has become less tenable, so too has that of the design or applied art critic. As the twentieth century closes, the situation that holds in the plastic arts makes it difficult and perhaps impossible to write coherently about quality. There is so much diversity. What, for example, are the coherent criteria for judging the relative quality of sculptures by the ceramicists Martin Smith or Kimpei Nakamura (Japan) and teapots by Gail Busch (USA)? Descriptions of form and texture are possible in each case, together with a discussion about the intention and the achievement of the individual ceramicist. Much can be said about the work of each potter – we can consider the minimalist form of Martin Smith's work as being part of a continuum of modern British sculpture, just as a provenance for Nakamura's extraordinary ceramic assemblage can be based on reference to Japanese pots in the tea ceremony. But these generalizations are more theoretical than real, they do not refer to a physical vocabulary of shared ornamental or sculptural devices, symbolism or metaphor that exists in the works themselves. The objects do not relate to one another. To say that each is well done is less meaningful than to say 'I like it'.

215, 205

Bechtold himself explains: 'All over the world you can find ruins, the remains of human wealth and power. At these ruins I can sit and contemplate for hours the mighty walls that now seem to have no other purpose than to fall apart . . . it's just as easy to look at today's big concrete and glass walls behind which captains of industry plan their games. I can't help but think about how they may look when our civilization is in decline. I sublimize these thoughts into porcelain. Porcelain because it is clean, pure, translucent – almost not of this earth.'

Ceramics has been a prolific generator of such sentiments. Moreover, and partly because clay objects are among the oldest and most common in our museums, contemporary ceramic artists have increasingly used 'history' and 'transcience' as a subject matter for their art. As the museum culture has develped, so clay artefacts have become identified as symbolizing the fragmented, half-understood past. Fired, glazed clay does not rot; that is why the material is such an abundant messenger from the past. The world's pots form a collective *memento mori*.

There is another aspect. It was noted above that contemporary ceramic sculpture is often quite small. It suggests an intimacy and a preciousness that most fine-art sculpture no longer has. Therefore it is possible to argue that work like Bechtold's is an art of private negotiation between one artist and an individual purchaser or collector – rather than one aimed at a public audience. The individual purchaser, attracted to the ceramic work, hears the story that accompanies it and takes both text and object away as a minor art work for his or her private contemplation and pleasure.

Presumably the romanticism that such work displays is a temporary, natural reaction against industrial design. However, when, as in Bechtold's work and other contemporary ceramics, each person becomes picturesque in his or her individual way, then the word is called upon to mediate between object and viewer.

The habit of the artist having to explain his or her work in some detail is now ingrained at art school, where the disciplines of the tutorial and the *viva voce* encourage the student to make up for obliqueness by offering an extended description of aims and intentions.

Not all ceramic artists want to make art that is dependent upon ancillary explanation. Consequently, alongside the more allusive and elusive ceramic art and installation work, there has been a revival of figurative and modern 'folk' art. Matt Nolen, mentioned earlier, produced a 'functional' tea set called *Foreign Interest Tea Set* which is decorated with dollar bills and other currencies. The cup handles are made in the form of dollar signs and the teapot handle has the shape of the yen. One of his other works, *Credit Card Reliquary*, is obvious enough in its meaning. The raw certainty of its design is rather startling because it is clearly deftly done and yet it also snubs all notions of good taste and finesse.

Another approach to figuration is taken by a young British ceramicist called Susan Halls. 213 Unlike so many ceramicists she does not have to search for or invent her subject matter. An

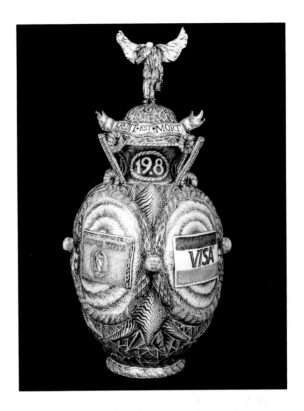

Credit Card Reliquary. Matt Nolen.
Porcelain. h. 66.5 cm. USA, 1991

extraordinarily fluent draughtswoman, she has passion for animals. She has written: 'I cannot remember ever lacking a sense of emotional connection with the natural world. To me, it seems right, and presents the most interesting, honest creative front. Nothing can excite me like an animal can. Dead or alive, the response may be different, but still as powerful. My work is not political, unless it can be said that my sense of seeing is a political act. I disapprove of any animal suffering, but my work is not driven by this. What my work says by this, if anything at all, is for the viewer to judge.'

Her fluency with clay and her analytical knowledge of animals gained through drawing gives her a freedom to invent and translate literal form. Her monkeys and apes need no explanation because they bridge that narrow – and often troubling – divide between apes and ourselves. For anyone who shares Hall's interest in animals and in the complexity of our relationship with them, then this work probably speaks quite clearly. Such non-equivocation is surprisingly rare. Mostly it occurs in the super-literal or propagandist work; Halls' work is neither.

But such judgments remain, for the time being, matters of opinion. No active genre of animal sculpture currently exists beyond the work of a few isolated individuals or outside the mass-produced ornament industry. There is little with which to compare Halls' work and for the

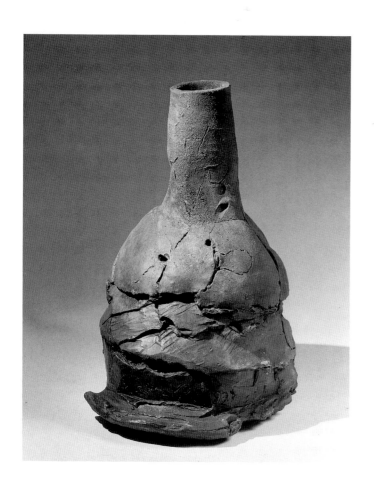

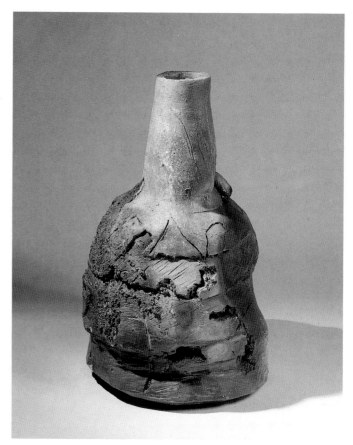

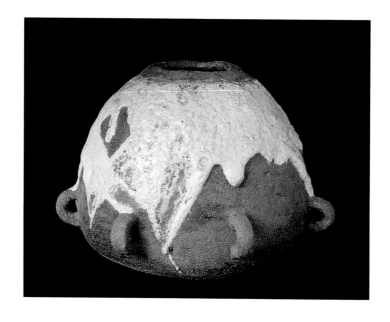

200 Sibley
   Peter Voulkos
   Stoneware
   h. 97.5 cm
   USA, 1992

201 Leyenda
   Peter Voulkos
   Stoneware
   h. 80 cm
   USA, 1991

202 Untitled
   Gaby Sperer Scope
   Stoneware
   h. 25 cm
   Canada, 1992

203 Le mont printanier
   Babs Haenen
   Porcelain
   h. 31.5 cm
   Holland, 1993

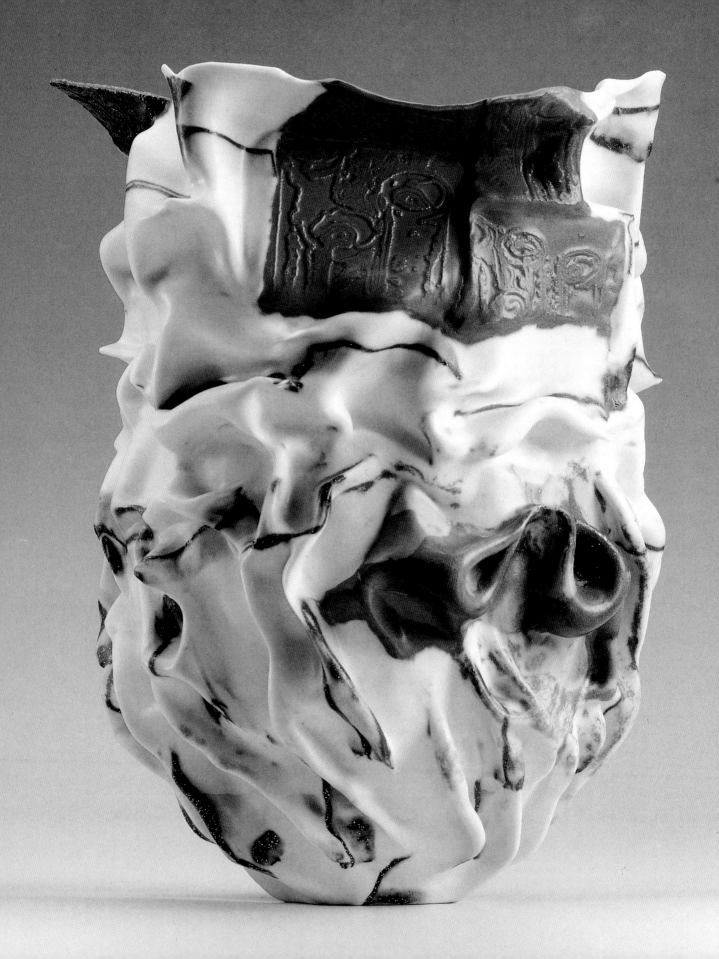

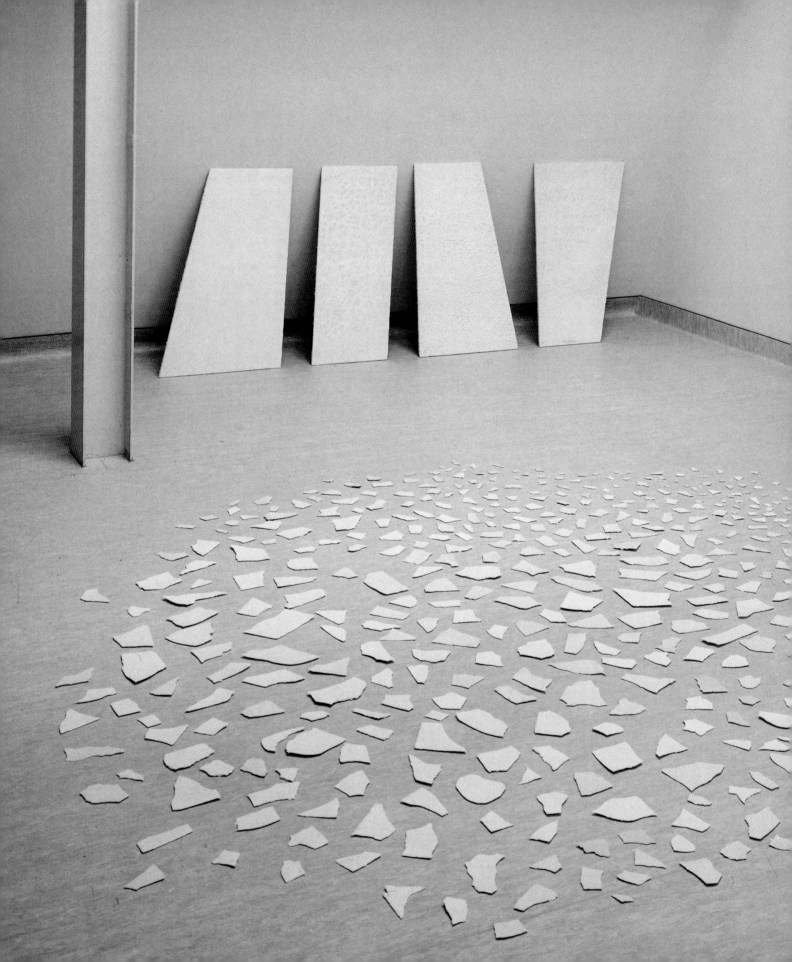

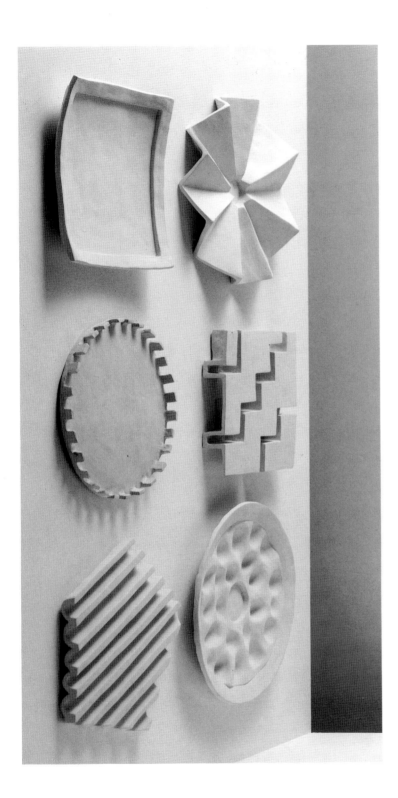

206 Installation
Setsuko Nagasawa
Stoneware
Japan, 1991

207 Forty Plates
(six illustrated)
Stephenie Bergman
30 × 30 cm each
UK, 1993

208 Lichtraum II
Johannes Gebhardt
h. 45 cm
Germany, 1991

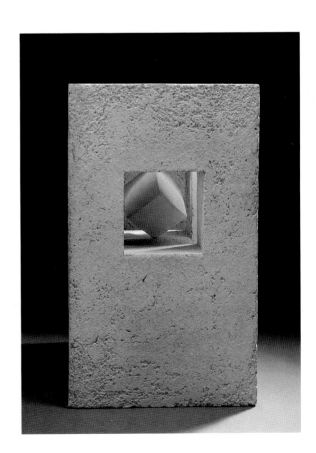

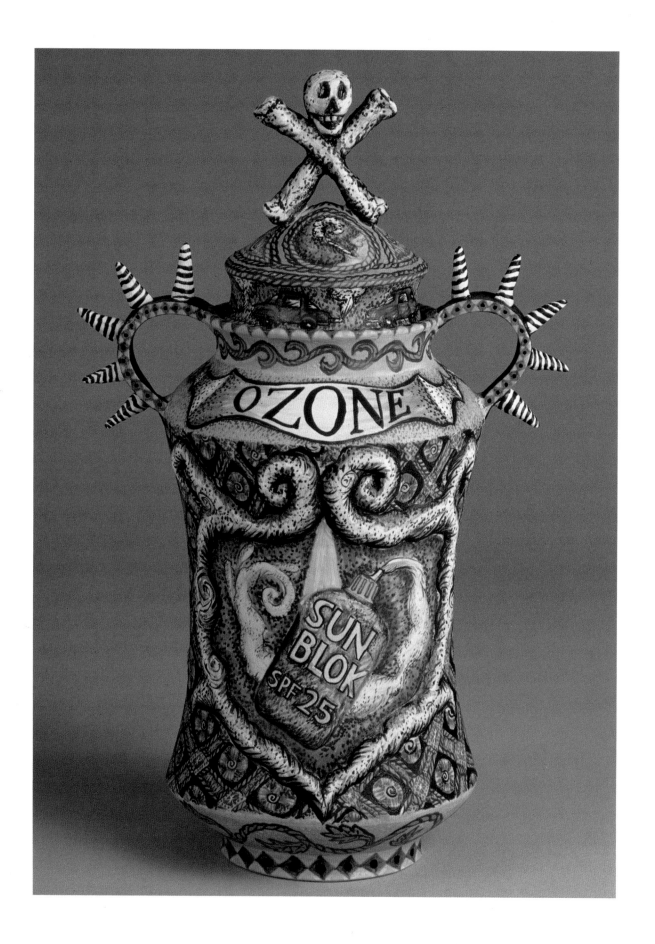

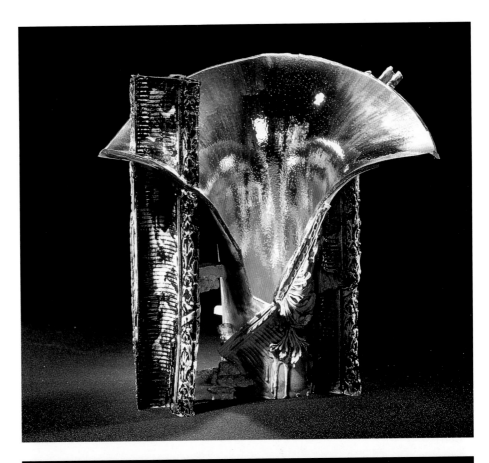

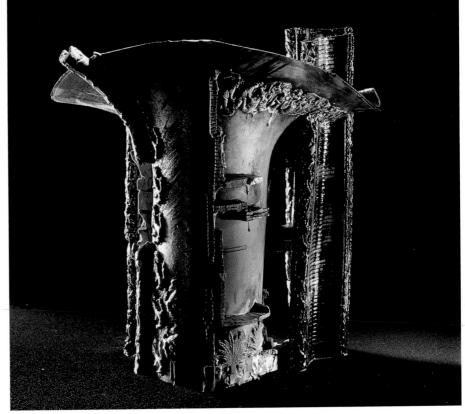

209 Apothecary Jar No.2: Ozone
   Matt Nolen
   Porcelain
   h. 48.5 cm
   USA, 1992

210 82nd reconstruction of the
   remains of the holy grail
   (Front view)
   Jeroen Bechtold
   Porcelain and gold lustre
   h. 48.5 cm
   Holland, 1992

211 82nd reconstruction of the
   remains of the holy grail
   (Back view)
   Jeroen Bechtold
   Porcelain and gold lustre
   h. 48.5 cm
   Holland, 1992

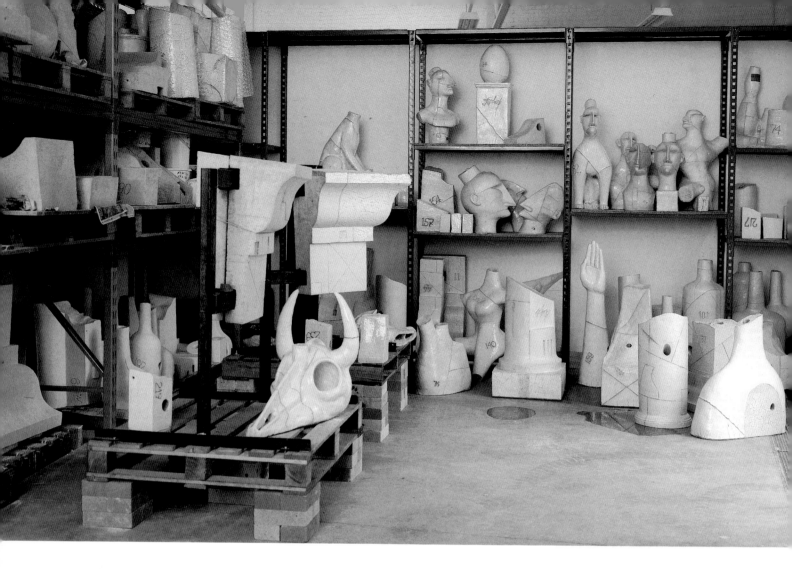

212 Portal
     Alexander Brodsky and
     Ilya Utkin
     Stoneware
     Russia/Holland (EKWC), 1992

213 Monkeys and Apes
     (11 illustrated from 20)
     Susan Halls
     Paper-clay, mixed media, raku
     10 cm each
     UK, 1992

214 The Art of Losing
     Ellen Driscoll
     h. 280 cm
     USA (EKWC), 1992

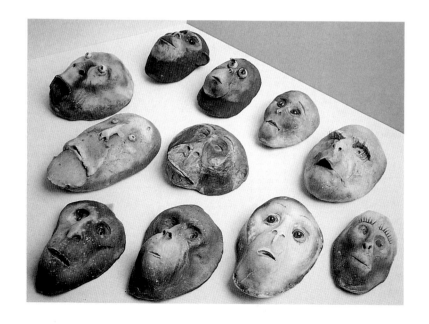

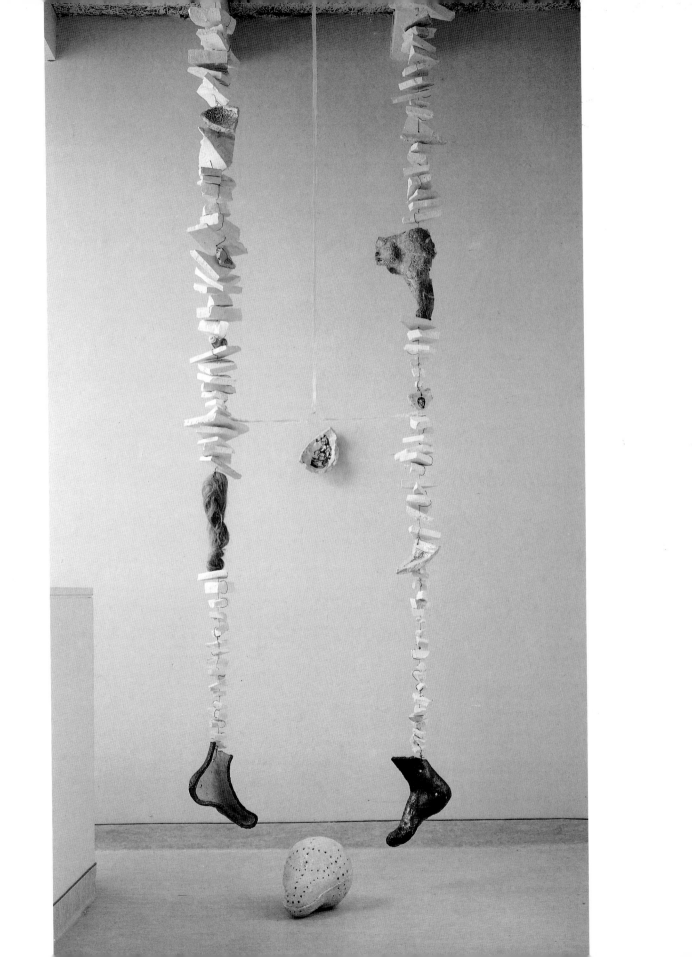

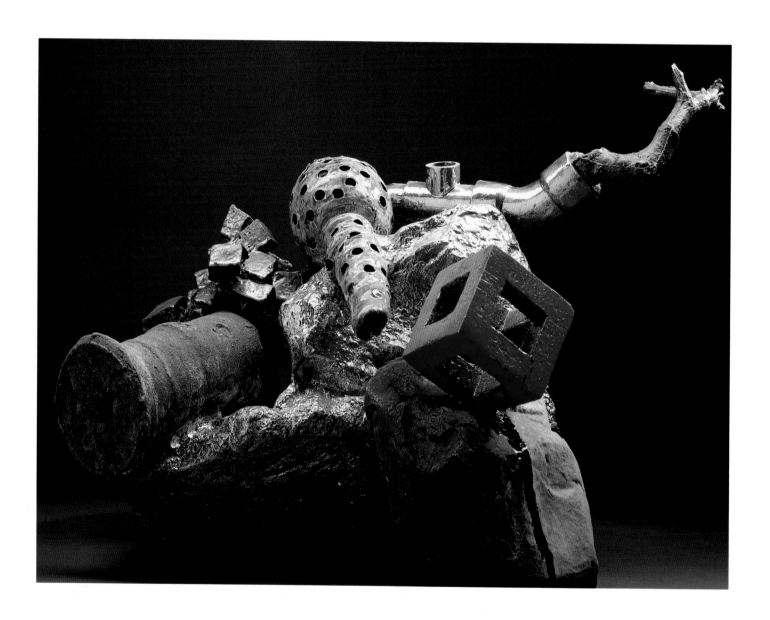

215 Where is Zen Spirit Now?
Kimpei Nakamura
Earthenware
h. 77 cm
Japan (EKWC), 1992

216 Installation
Pjotr Müller
Earthenware
l. 2.5 m
Holland (EKWC), 1991

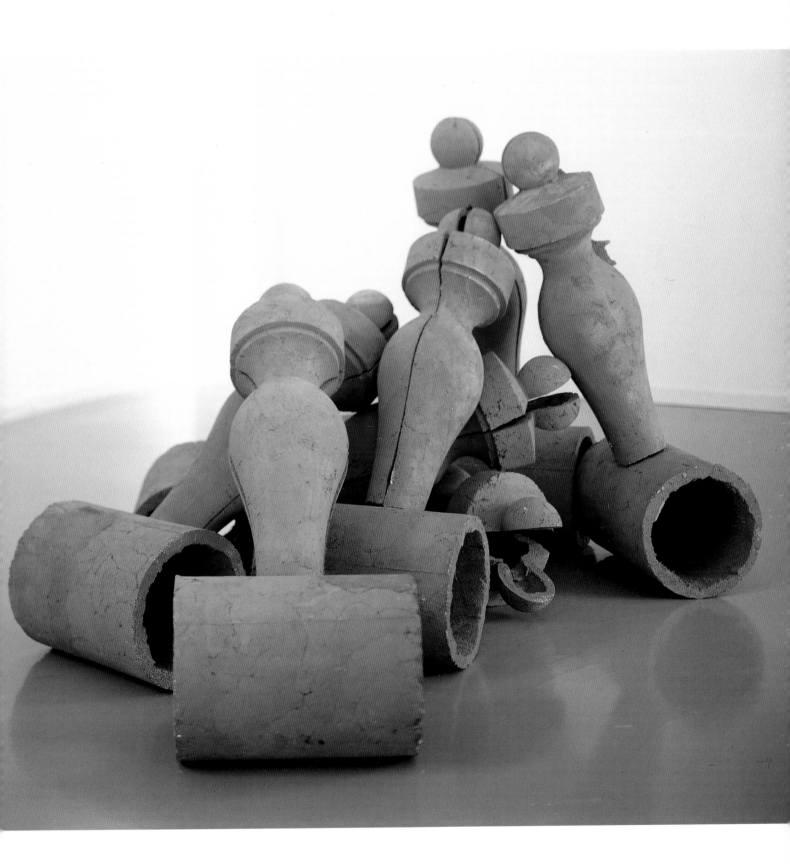

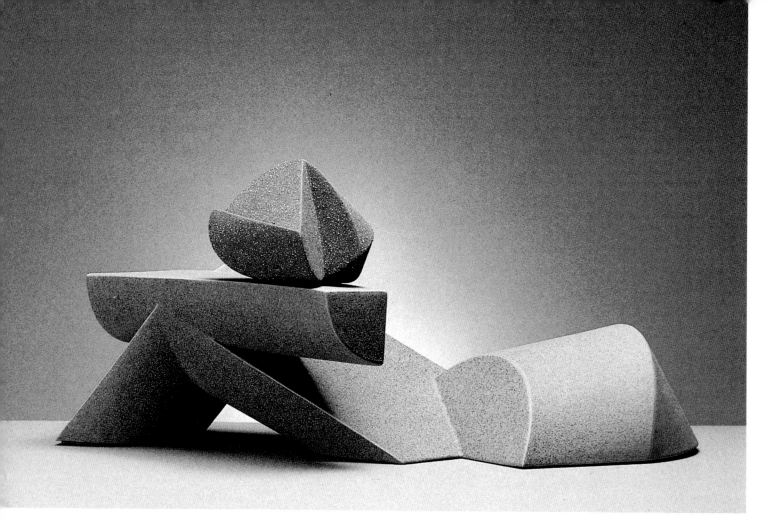

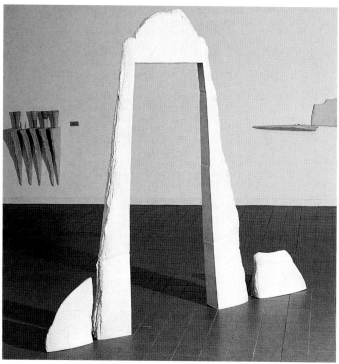

217 Angulated Still Life
     Anne Currier
     Glazed clay, sanded terracotta
     h.25.4 cm
     USA, 1992

218 Architectural Passage
     Paula Winokur
     Porcelain
     h. 2.4 m
     USA, 1992

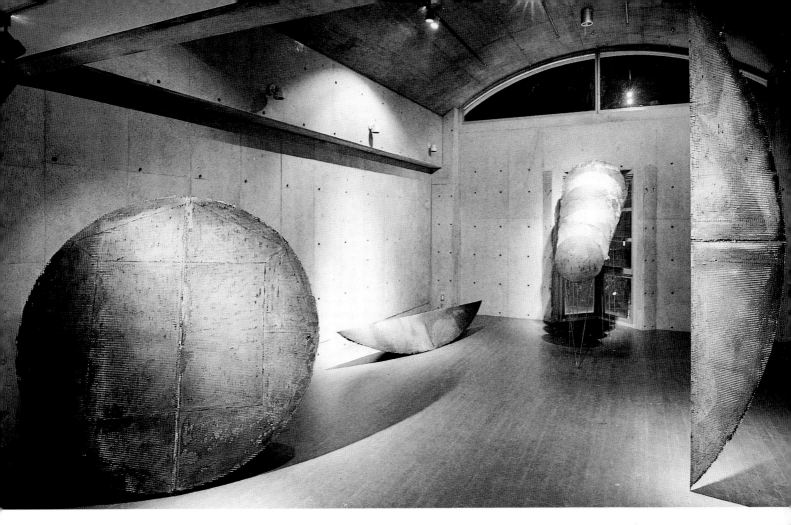

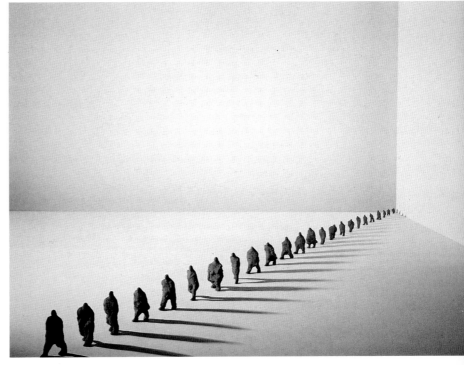

219 Installation
     Yasutoshi Jinnai
     Stoneware
     Japan, 1992

220 Twenty-Four Hours
     Antony Gormley
     Terracotta
     h. 2–30 cm
     UK, 1988

Overleaf
221 In Camera
     Tony Cragg
     Earthenware
     h. 77 cm
     UK, 1991

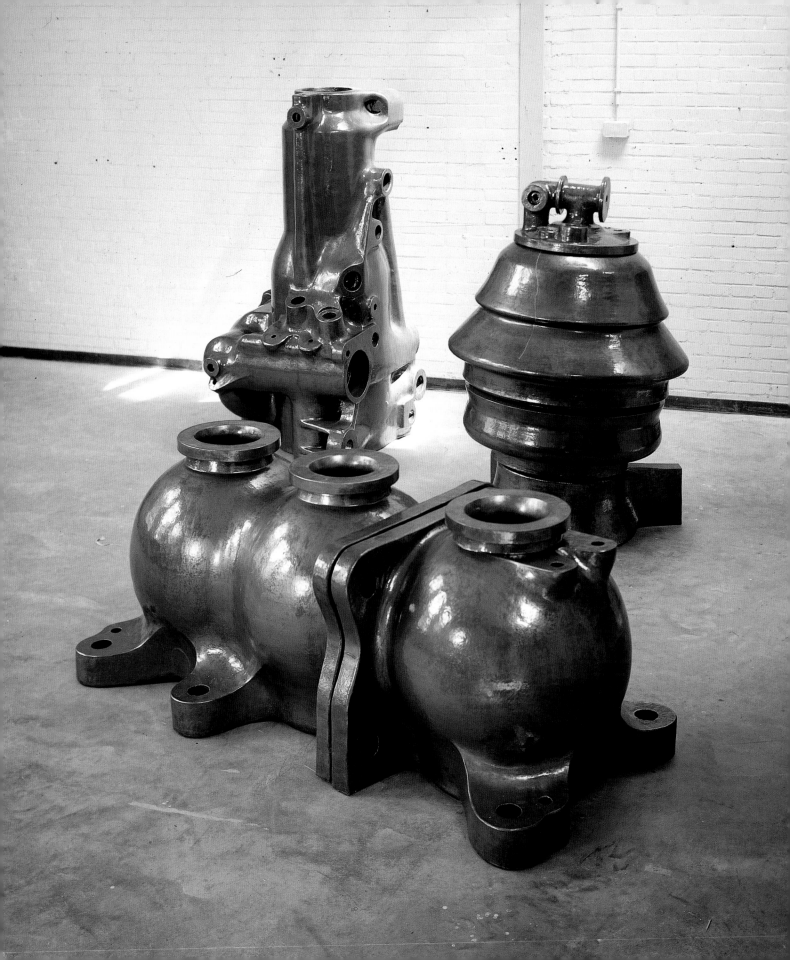

BIOGRAPHIES
Notes on selected ceramicists

Arneson, Robert 1930–92. Studied at the College of Marin, Kentfield, California; California College of Arts and Crafts, Oakland; Mills College, Oakland. In his later career, Arneson became an increasingly important figure as an artist and his connection with pottery became tenuous. But technically his virtuoso ceramic sculpture always interested potters and he has acted as a catalyst for new ideas. He kept alive the practice of figuration when there was a dearth of it in the visual arts. Nevertheless, his activity came to have more to do with painting, which is a better vehicle for comment. Later work by Arneson deals with the military establishment and the threat of nuclear war; he also did a series of works around the portrait of Jackson Pollock. He featured in the *Ceramic Sculpture* exhibition, alongside Peter Voulkos and others, Whitney Museum of American Art, New York 1981–82. Arneson continued his series of ironic figure studies until his death in 1992. He was a most interesting contributor to postwar figurative sculpture and much of his work commented upon that by other artists, especially Jackson Pollock. Arneson constructed *Guardians of the Secret*, a parody of Jackson Pollock's 1943 painting of the same title, as a sculpture in clay and other media (2m high by 3m long, 1989–90).

Åse, Arne b.Norway 1941. Studied at the National College of Art and Craft and Industrial Design, Oslo. Åse is one of Norway's leading potters. He is knowledgeable about the technology of pottery, but dislikes potters making a fetish of technique. Åse believes there is no virtue in doing things in an old-fashioned manner for the sake of it. A lot of his pots are wheel-thrown, with the emphasis on decoration. He has concentrated on brushwork and says: 'Two or more brushes are always used, very often combining the stroke of a big, flat, stiff brush with that of a small, soft one. Find what a brush can do, then take advantage of the possibilities.' His work is exquisite, but full-blooded. He has exhibited widely in Norway and in Germany, with work in the National Museum of Art and Craft and Industrial Design, Oslo. See also: Arne Åse, *Ceramics Monthly*, May 1985. Åse was co-organizer of the 1990 International Ceramics Conference in Oslo whose theme was 'research in ceramics'.

Autio, Rudy b.USA 1926. Studied at Montana State University; Washington State University. He became the resident artist at the Archie Bray Foundation in Helena, Montana, and worked with Peter Voulkos. Garth Clark argues that Autio is one of the most important talents in American ceramics and likens the raggedness and energy of the work to Jean Dubuffet's *art brut*. Among the public collections where Autio's work may be seen is the Everson Museum of Art, Syracuse.

Bayer, Svend b.1946, UK resident. Studied with Michael Cardew as an assistant. Bayer makes large glazed stoneware garden pots - handsome, and well thrown. Also produces smaller items, such as jugs and plates. He had a large solo exhibition at the British Crafts Centre, London 1985, and is represented in the Crafts Council collection, London.

Bayle, Pierre b.France 1945. Studied at the studios of various ceramists in Paris and the provinces. He has had several group and solo exhibitions – recent exhibitions include Galerie Sarver, Paris 1982 and 1984. In 1981 he won the 1st prize in the Châteauroux Biennale. Work can be seen in the following public collections – Musée des Arts Décoratifs, Paris; Musée de Sèvres; Musée d'Art Moderne du Nord, Villeneuve; Musée de Stuttgart; Fitzwilliam Museum, Cambridge, UK. Ceramics specialist, Henry Rothschild, has said: 'Bayle has perfected the control of glazing and subtle colouring on his upright forms, which often end in a fine point. The variety and harmony of his work, within his closely controlled shapes, is the great attraction.'

Bechtold, Jeroen b.Holland 1953. Studied at the Gerrit Rietveld Academie, Amsterdam, in 1981, and designs glass and porcelain for Rosenthal of Germany. He has his own gallery in Amsterdam. All his porcelain is hand-thrown and then modified. He has had a number of solo exhibitions in European galleries, including Arte Fiorentini, Pavia, 1988; D. Grutzmacher, Enschede, 1992; Galeri Norby, Copenhagen, 1992; Galeri Studio Maastricht, 1994. Among the recent articles discussing his work is 'A Flow of Frozen Thoughts' by Nel Kooy for *Ceramics: Art & Perception*, No. 8, 1992.

Bengston, Billy Al b.USA 1934. Studied at the Manual Arts High School, Los Angeles; Los Angeles City College; Otis Art Institute, Los Angeles. Bengston switched from ceramics to painting, but he produced some dinner-ware of great quality for the *New Works in Clay by Contemporary Painters and Sculptors* exhibition at the Everson Museum, Syracuse 1976 – these plates are now part of the Everson Museum permanent collection. Bengston is one of the early innovators who worked with Peter Voulkos.

Bennicke, Karen b.Denmark 1943. Apprentice in different potters' studios in Denmark, 1957–60. She established her first studio in 1960. Initially she was influenced by Mexican ceramics, and ornament has been a consistent interest of hers. In 1980 she was a co-founder of the Danish group of ceramists called Multi-Mud. Her work has been exhibited in Germany and Holland, as well as Denmark and Sweden, and is in public collections, including the Museum of Arts and Crafts, Copenhagen; Keramikmuseum Westerwald, Höhr-Grenzhausen, Germany; and Röhsska Konstslöjdmuseet, Gothenburg, Sweden.

Bergman, Stephenie b.UK 1946. Graduated from St Martin's School of Art, London, in 1967, moved to the USA and won a Gulbenkian Foundation Award, 1975–77. For several years she has been known mainly for her textile hangings, but has also been working extensively in clay. Her recent work, using non-functional, wall-mounted plates, shown in the travelling exhibition *The Raw and The Cooked*, 1993–95, was a way of stopping making vases and getting back to the wall territory familiar to her from her textile work. She lives and works in France.

Bonovitz, Jill b.USA 1940. Studied at the Moore College of Art, Philadelphia; Columbia Teachers' College, New York; Columbia University, New York. She has produced public commissions and participated in many group exhibitions. Her work can be seen in the Helen Drutt Gallery, Philadelphia; Montreal Museum of Decorative Arts, Montreal.

Britton, Alison b.UK 1948. Studied at Central School of Art, London; Royal College of Art, London. Was one of a small number of British women studio potters to emerge in the early 1970s whose work owed little either to the Anglo-Oriental tendency of Bernard Leach or to the quasi-Scandinavian look prevalent in the UK in the 1960s.

Britton quickly established herself and was given a solo exhibition at the Crafts Council Gallery, London1979. She has exhibited widely in Europe and has become a respected writer about the applied arts. Some of her peers now have an equivocal relationship with ceramic sculpture, but Britton has kept to the vessel – she remains, determinedly, a potter. She says: 'My work belongs on the "outer limits" of function – where function, or a reference to a possible function, is crucial but is just one ingredient in the final presence of the object, and not its only motivation.' Her work is slab-built, earthenware and decorated with underglazes and coloured slips; it can be seen in many public collections including the Crafts Council, London; Victoria and Albert Museum, London; Leeds City Art Galleries; Boymans-van Beuningen Museum, Rotterdam; Kruithuis Museum, 's-Hertogenbosch, Holland; Kunst und Gewerbe Museum, Hamburg, Germany.

Brodsky, Alexander b.Russia 1955 *and* **Utkin, Ilya** b.Russia 1955. Both are architects: they are among the leading 'paper practitioners' of radical architecture in Russia – 'paper' because there was great difficulty getting radical architecture built in the former USSR and economic problems since 1990 have also been a hindrance. Apart from solo exhibitions in the USA, they have contributed to many group shows, including *Between Spring and Summer: Soviet Conceptual Art in the Era of Late Communism*, 1990 and 1991. They did an artist's placement August 1991–January 1992 at the Europees Keramisch Werkcentrum, Holland, where they gave an exemplary demonstration of ceramics as a medium for contemporary architectural decoration.

Brüggemann-Breckwoldt, Antje b.Germany 1941. Studied with Jan Bontjes van Beek, a pioneer of 20th-century German ceramics and an influential teacher. Exhibited widely in Germany and other parts of Europe, and has also shown in Japan and Canada. Her work displays the excellent handling of glazes which is characteristic of German potters. However, Brüggemann has developed in recent years a more architectural range of forms which distinguishes her work from the preoccupation with organic forms favoured by her peers. A good catalogue of her work documents her retrospective exhibition held at the Kunstammlungen der Veste, Coburg 1983.

Buffalo, Jo b.USA 1948. Studied at Syracuse University. She has worked as a scientific illustrator and archaeological technician. Participated in the *New Works in Clay III* exhibition, Everson Museum, Syracuse 1981. Her vessels are the result of collaborations with potter Christopher Darling (USA). The imagery in her work, which includes wall pieces, paintings and illustrations, is gleaned from interests spanning art, biology, archaeology and physics. With Darling, she breaks the pots into shards which are then reassembled. This approach brings in an association with archaeology and also breaks up the illustration, so that it is not too literal and pristine – it introduces further possibilities for metaphor.

Casson, Mick b.UK 1925. Studied at Hornsey School of Art, London. As well as a respected potter of functional stoneware and porcelain, he is also an important educator. With Victor Margrie (former Director of the Crafts Council, London), he ran the influential Harrow School of Art ceramics course which produced potters such as Janice Tchalenko and Wally Keeler. He has exhibited extensively and been a good publicist for craft pottery, presenting such television programmes as the BBC series, 'The Craft of The Potter'.

Champy, Claude b.France 1944. Studied at the Ecole des Métiers-d'Art, Paris. Champy is a member of l'Academie internationale de la Céramique. He has exhibited frequently throughout France and is gradually achieving an international reputation. He combines restrained forms with highly variegated or textured surfaces.

Christensen, Kari b.Norway 1938. Studied at the National College of Art and Craft and Industrial Design, Oslo; Royal Danish Academy,

Copenhagen. For five years she designed for the Royal Copenhagen Factory. All her work is handbuilt, much of it porcelain, and deals with private stories or her particular interests in animals and landscapes. She does not, however, put her observations directly on to her pottery – her decoration is more allusive, more metaphorical than that. She has exhibited widely in Norway and has shown work in Germany, Italy and the USA. Christensen was a gold medal winner at an international ceramics exhibition held in Florence in 1971, and her work can be seen in various public collections, including the Kunstindustrimuseum, Oslo; Hetjens Museum, Düsseldorf.

Coper, Hans b.Germany 1920, d.Britain 1981. He studied textile design in Dresden, but emigrated to Britain in 1939 and joined Lucie Rie in her studio in London in 1946. Coper is, with Bernard Leach, the twin pillar of British 20th-century pottery. Posthumously, his pots have become immensely valuable, each one fetching thousands of pounds at auctions. His work is sculptural and eclectic, and more obviously intellectual than Leach's. He had a considerable impact on those whom he worked with or taught; former students frequently state their indebtedness to him. It is a tribute to his pedagogic modesty that he has spawned no clones. Coper's pots may be seen in the Victoria and Albert Museum, London; Sainsbury Centre, Norwich; Crafts Council collection, London.

Cornelius, Philip b.USA 1934. Studied at San Jose State University, California; Claremont Graduate School, California. Cornelius's pots are interesting because they sometimes depict some object such as a warship or a tank whose real-life construction and function is inimical to clay. But at the same time these pots manage to look like seascapes or landscapes. Cornelius plays ping-pong between a variety of objects and ideas within the same, often overtly, decorative piece. See the catalogue to the *American Porcelain* exhibition, Renwick Gallery, Washington D.C. 1981.

Cragg, Tony b.UK 1949. Graduated from Wimbledon School of Art, 1972; Royal College of Art,1977; then moved to Germany. He is emphatically not a ceramicist or a craftsperson but an 'artist'. None the less, his recent sculptures using clay (made with the help of a ceramicist) have exited a lot of interest in the European 'clay' community. A former Turner prize winner (1988), he explains his philosophy in a long artist's statement called *In Camera* (1993), accompanying his artist's placement at the Europees Keramisch Werkcentrum.

Crowley, Jill b.Ireland 1946. Studied at Bristol Polytechnic; Royal College of Art, London. She is particularly known for her acerbic, decorative, figurative sculptures of middle-aged men. More recent pieces have included ornament on the theme of a child's hand. She has made her ornaments take on a life of their own – in the late 1970s she put together collections of her teapots which almost crawl or scurry across the table. Her work has been widely exhibited and may be seen in the Victoria and Albert Museum, London; Crafts Council collection, London.

Cummings, Ann b.Canada. Studied at Wayne State University, Michigan, USA. She explains that she likes to keep her work simple, using one glaze and firing raku. All of it is handbuilt in stoneware, with decoration being done by slip-trailer and brush. She has exhibited regularly throughout Canada and is represented by Prime Gallery, Toronto.

Cushing, Val b.USA 1931. Studied at the New York State College of Ceramics, Alfred (where he is now a Professor). A review of a solo exhibition at the Helen Drutt Gallery, Philadelphia 1984, captures his aspirations: 'Featured in the exhibition are handsome, practical casseroles, dinner plates, ample platters with handles, big lidded jars, large scale cylinder vases and a few non-utilitarian pieces. To encourage people to touch these pieces, Cushing has gone out of his way to give them sensuous qualities. The inspiration for his work comes from nature . . . he favors a clear cut contour, he may make a jar by joining a smooth upper section to a textured lower section, thereby enhancing the contrast.' Widely exhibited, his work can be seen at the Everson Museum of Art, Syracuse; the Renwick Gallery, National Museum of American Art, Smithsonian Institution, Washington D.C.; other public collections; also in independent galleries, such as the Helen Drutt Gallery, Philadelphia.

Daehlin, Lisbet b.Denmark 1922, resident in Norway. Studied at the College of Art and Design, Copenhagen, followed by workshop practice in Paris and Copenhagen. She admires Bernard Leach, but has found her own, distinctive style. Her work is always very simple, a demonstration of why the plain pot will always survive. It has been shown extensively in Norway and has also been exhibited in W. Germany, Belgium, the UK and the USA. Among the public collections holding her work are the Cooper Hewitt, New York; Museums of Applied Arts, Oslo and Trondheim.

Daley, William b.USA 1925. After wartime experiences in a bomber crew and as a P.O.W., studied at Massachusetts College of Art, 1950; MA Columbia University, 1951. He teaches at the Philadelphia College of Art. Daley's pots explore the ritualistic quality of geometry. Sometimes the geometry is determined by Daley's fancy, sometimes by the practical demands of structure. He explains that he is strongly helped by his wife, Catherine, and William Parry says in his essay (see below), 'Daley is pleased to describe his debt to a father, who was a house painter who could quote A. E. Housman endlessly.' Daley's vessels are made in unglazed stoneware. Drawing is very important in his work. He makes initial sketches, which are then drawn up full-scale before he makes styrofoam templates and forms from which to make the pots. The pot is constructed with preshaped clay slabs, upside down, on the styrofoam forms. After the outside seams are completed, the pot is turned upright, the styrofoam removed, further clay slabs added and all inside seams sealed. Daley has exhibited extensively for thirty years. He exhibits with the Helen Drutt Gallery, Philadelphia; Exhibit A, Chicago; and Garth Clark, New York and Los Angeles. A retrospective of his work was held in 1982 at the Massachusetts College of Art. Publications about his work include essays by William Parry for the 1982 retrospective; by Garth Clark in *American Potters*, 1981; by Michael McTwigan, 'Duality in Clay', *American Craft*, December 1980.

Dermer, John b.Australia 1949. Studied at the Royal Melbourne Institute of Technology. Dermer is a production potter mostly making tableware. During a stay in the UK he spent two months with Michael Leach (second oldest child of Bernard). Dermer says: 'This time throwing entirely on a kick wheel made me feel I had learned more about throwing than in four years at College.' He uses porcellaneous stoneware, and his main glaze is a high calcium matt, with oxides sprayed on to enrich the surface. Dermer has exhibited extensively and his work is in the majority of the Australian public collections, including the Australian National Gallery, Canberra; Brisbane Art Gallery; National Gallery of Victoria; Museum of Applied Arts and Science, Sydney.

DeVore, Richard b.USA 1933. Studied at the University of Toledo, Ohio; Cranbrook Academy of Art, Bloomfield Hills, Michigan. From 1966 to 1978 DeVore was Head of Ceramics at Cranbrook, since then at the University of Colorado. For a while he explored the sculptural – including figurative – possibilities of ceramics, but for many years now has concentrated on the aesthetics of the vessel – his work being in clear and obvious contrast to the constructivist-expressionist trend in American ceramics. It is reassuring that DeVore is content with the title, 'potter'. It is his simple, refined stoneware vessels that most aptly fill the role of the pot as a

domestic art form. In a sense much of the eclecticism of our age has been sifted by DeVore – his work shows traces of the Oriental influence, but the geometry is contemporary and Western. He shows work with such galleries as the Garth Clark Gallery, New York and Los Angeles; Helen Drutt Gallery, Philadelphia.

Driscoll, Ellen b. USA. Awarded a Guggenheim Fellowship, 1987; Bunting Fellowship, Radcliffe College, Harvard, 1990. She is an installation artist using clay as a medium and her solo exhibitions include Damon Brandt Gallery, New York, 1990; *The Loophole of Retreat* installation, Whitney Museum of American Art, New York, 1991; Contemporary Art Center, Cincinatti, Ohio, 1992. She did an artist's placement at the Europees Keramisch Werkcentrum, Holland, August 1991–January 1992.

Ferguson, Kenneth b.USA 1928. Studied painting at the Carnegie Institute of Technology, Pittsburgh; New York State College of Ceramics, Alfred. A constant theme in his pottery, one way or another, is sex. The curiously flesh-like quality of some of his pots is, in part, derived from a combination of swelling form and irregular shape. One of the influences on his work, according to critic Michael Rubin, is the Japanese Oribe ware: 'The bold designs and fluid decorations manifested in Oribe pots – such features as sagging spouts, flap strap handles, and runny green glazes – often find their way into Ferguson's teapots, enlarged to a bolder scale.' He draws well, has had many exhibitions and is an influential teacher.

Fleming, Frank b.USA 1940. Studied at Florence State University, Alabama. He is a sculptor as much as a potter, and his themes are similar to those of Robert Arneson – nuclear war, and the world of the post-nuclear war. He is also strongly rooted in Alabama, coming from one of a family of seven children born to a cotton and corn farmer there. His affection for the American South and for the land is another important theme in his work. Janet Koplos has written an excellent article in *American Ceramics* (Vol.4, no.2, 1985) about Fleming.

Frey, Viola b.USA 1933. Studied at the California College of Arts and Crafts, Oakland; Tulane University, New Orleans. She should properly be included in a book of sculpture, although her plates and plaques overlap with pottery. In many ways her work fits well into the new figuration movement, that oddly appropriate style of the 20th century which is half-cartoon, half-expressionist and always visceral. See Garth Clark, *A Century of Ceramics in the United States*, 1979; Jeff Kelley, *American Ceramics* (Vol.3, no.1, 1984).

Fritsch, Elizabeth b.UK 1941. Studied ceramics at the Royal College of Art, London (before that she had studied harp and piano at the Royal Academy of Music). She has had few solo exhibitions, but each has been important to contemporary British ceramics and excited attention. All her pots are handbuilt and painstakingly painted with coloured slips. Sometimes a piece will be fired three times before she is satisfied with the colour. The pots are made from a grogged stoneware body, fired under oxidation to1260 C, which makes them fully vitrified. Inevitably, since Fritsch's work is highly regarded and in short supply, it is both sought after and expensive; collectors have been quick to see the investment potential. But to this Fritsch responds: 'I insist on museums having the first pick; I make pots for ordinary people.' Public collections with her work include the Crafts Council, London; Victoria and Albert Museum, London; Kunstindustrimuseum, Copenhagen; Boymans-van Beuningen, Rotterdam.

Gebhardt, Johannes b.Germany 1930. He studied at the Kunstakademie, Stuttgart (1948-56), after which he was appointed head of the Ceramic Department at the Muthesius-Werkkunstschule, Kiel (1956–58). He then worked abroad as an advisor to the West Pakistan small-industries corporation in Lahore (1968–70). He established a studio with Christa Gebhardt in 1973 and became Professor of Ceramics at the Fachhochshcule, Kiel, in 1978. He has taken part in numerous solo and international exhibitions in Europe, Japan and the USA. He did an artist's placement at the Europees Keramisch Werkcentrum, Holland, August 1991–January 1992.

Germay, Beatrice de b.France 1946. Studied at the Beaux Arts, Bourges; Beaux Arts, Aix-en-Provence. A somewhat mannered essay by François Pluchart – 'Chère Beatrice', an open letter in the catalogue to the Beatrice de Germay exhibition, Aix-en-Provence 1982 – claims her as a sculptor. Certainly De Germay has added an interesting and important element to the contemporary clay revival in France. Previously she made enclosed boxes and now produces roughly textured clay columns-cum-containers. Public collections with her work include Galerie des Maîtres Contemporains, Aix-en-Provence; Galerie Nane Stern, Paris; Galerie Cupillard, Grenoble.

Gill, Andrea b.USA 1948. Studied at the Rhode Island School of Design; New York State College of Ceramics, Alfred University. Michael McTwigan says of Gill that she retains her connection with the folk potter: 'The almost naive, straightforward way she translates "face" into vase is very familiar to us.' Her decorative work is more figurative now than it used to be – part of the general movement towards content in decoration. Among the group exhibitions to which she has contributed, one of the most important was *Ceramic Echoes*, held at the Nelson-Atkins Museum of Art, Kansas City 1983.

Gilhooly, David b.USA 1943. Studied at the University of California. Gilhooly is a prolific artist, spawning clay frogs by the hundred. His frogs come surrounded by representations in clay of the kitschy debris of the consumer age. Gilhooly is the funk ceramist *par excellence*. Since the middle of the 1960s he has had numerous solo exhibitions and contributed to many group exhibitions. He was one of the six artists represented in the *Ceramic Sculpture* exhibition, Whitney Museum of American Art, New York 1981–82.

Haenen, Babs b.Holland 1948. Studied at the Gerrit Rietveld Academie, Amsterdam, under Jan van der Vaart and worked for a while with Marianne de Trey, potter. Her work is notable for its relative freedom and innovation in a country where studio pottery is for the main part strongly biased towards design. Her method of construction is interesting: she makes different plaster forms to serve as a mould and around the mould places a damp cloth. Next she takes her clay – porcelain body from Limoges – and colours separate portions of it with oxides in different tones. The portions of porcelain are cut up and rejoined into sheets of different patterns, which are then draped around the mould. The foldings of the porcelain form are changed, refolded, shifted and exaggerated. Firing is in a gas kiln to 1260 C. Each pot is part-glazed with a barium-glaze, then burnished. Solo exhibitions include Galerie de Witte Voet, Amsterdam 1982 and 1985; Frans Halsmuseum, Haarlem 1984. She has had three solo exhibitions at the Garth Clark Gallery, New York (1987, 1990, 1992) and contributed to many international group shows in Holland, Germany and the USA. In 1991 the Museum Het Princessehof, Leeuwarden, gave her a retrospective exhibition. A catalogue, with essays by Garth Clark and Ineke Werkman, was published by the museum. Her pots are in all the major public collections in Holland, including the Boymans-van Beuningen, Rotterdam.

Halls, Susan b.UK 1966. Graduated from Medway College of Art and Design, 1988; Royal College of Art, London, 1990. She is one of a new generation of ceramicists to be interested in modelling and sculpting animals and the human figure. A naturally talented draughtswoman, she is a rare example of a young artist with talent, craft knowledge and a certainty about her subject matter.

Hamlyn, Jane b.UK 1940. Studied at Harrow College of Art, London.

She produces salt-glazed domestic ware. Her work is both functional and decorative. She has become one of Europe's leading functional potters because her work is well designed without straying into industrial ware. Hers is an example of a genuine, contemporary craft aesthetic.

Hawkins, Robert b.Australia 1959. Studied at East Sydney Technical College. One of the most interesting young Australian ceramists. An eclectic constructivist, he says: 'In some respects I am an antagonist, I don't particularly mind if my pots sell or not; there is another level I'm working at and that's for myself and for people who can appreciate and not necessarily buy.' He has an interest in tribal art, tribal people, machines and the city. Writer and critic, Peter Emmett, draws attention both to harshness and harmony in his work. Hawkins has exhibited at the annual Mayfair Ceramic Award and other group exhibitions; his work is in the Mayfair Collection.

Heckmann, Hans b.Germany 1935 and **Heckmann, Renate** b.Germany 1937. They work as a team. Both became students of Hubert Griemert after learning their craft in the Heckmann workshop – Hans from 1950 to 1953 and Renate (after studying and training as an interior decorator) from 1959 to 1962. They also both attended the Werkschule für Keramik in Höhr-Grenzhausen (1956–58 and 1963–65, respectively). The Heckmann workshop produces series wares as well as one-off pieces, both types being kept strictly separate. The former are among the finest that have appeared in Germany. The individual pieces (for the most part dishes and vases, but also architectural ceramics) are mainly modelled by hand, but some are thrown.

Heinemann, Steve b.Canada 1957. Studied at the Sheridan College School of Crafts and Design, Mississauga; Kansas City Art Institute; New York State College of Ceramics, Alfred. According to the catalogue *Stone Dragon*, Toronto 1985, Heinemann's work 'explores man's relationships with nature'. His large, semi-sculptural pieces, with their decorated surfaces, encourage easy associations with rocks, boats, lichens and the semi-eroded artefacts of fishing villages or farmyards. He works in earthenware and his methods include press moulding, sandblasting and casting. His work may be seen in the Museum of Fine Arts, Boston; Massey Foundation Collection, Museum of Man, Ottawa.

Henderson, Ewen b.UK 1934. Studied at Goldsmiths' College of Art, London; Camberwell School of Arts and Crafts, London, where he was taught by Lucie Rie and Hans Coper. He combines stoneware and porcelain – a risky combination. In an unpublished essay, British poet, Christopher Reid, writes: 'Henderson finds ways of making clay behave analogously to the processes he has observed in nature. His arm is metaphor. Henderson has never completely relinquished the potter's traditional task of making vessels and containers that keep the imagination under control and oblige it to express itself indirectly.' A major exhibition of his work was held at the British Crafts Centre, London 1986. Both the main London collections – the Victoria and Albert Museum and the Crafts Council – have good examples of his work.

Higby, Wayne b.USA 1943. Studied at the University of Colorado, Boulder; University of Michigan, Ann Arbor. Higby is the opposite of the modern rural-potter-in-retreat figure who has dominated much 20th-century pottery practice. Although he makes pots, lives in the country and draws on landscape as a theme, he is also a traveller, debater, writer, and university professor. He is aware that pottery is as self-conscious an activity as any of the arts or applied arts in this part of the 20th century. He believes the pot can be a vehicle for metaphor – some of his best works demonstrate this. He has done a great deal through example and debate to establish the pot as an object worthy of consideration in its own right – not something that has to be elided with anything which it is not. He has exhibited extensively and he is represented by the Helen Drutt Gallery, Philadelphia.

Jinnai, Yasutoshi b.Japan 1953. Graduated from the ceramics department of Jyoto City University of Arts, 1981; then pursued postgraduate study in Italy and France, 1982–85. In 1983 he won the Gold Prize in the Faenza International Ceramics Exhibition. Several exhibitions followed in Japan and he represented Japan in the International Exchange Pavilion of the Communication Expo in Sapporo, 1992. He completed an artist's residency at the Banff Centre for the Arts, Alberta, Canada in 1993. He uses his installations as metaphors for his interest and sympathy for the natural world, intending the range of subtlety of the surfaces he creates to allude to those in nature.

Kamermans, Klaartje b.Holland 1954. Studied at the Gerrit Rietveld Academie, Amsterdam. Her work is in the following public collections: Stedelijk Museum, Amsterdam; Amsterdamse Arto-teken, Amsterdam; Rijksdienst Beeldende Kunst, the Hague.

Keeler, Wally b.UK 1942. Studied at the Harrow School of Art, London. One of Britain's leading studio potters, producing salt-glazed, wheel-thrown stoneware pots for use. His designs have been described as 'subtly deviant' and they are a mix of the radical with an English vernacular going back a long way – his mugs, jugs and teapots recall medieval leatherware. Keeler has exhibited frequently and widely in Britain, and has shown work elsewhere in Europe, as well as in the USA and Canada. His work is in several important public collections, including the Victoria and Albert Museum, London; Crafts Council collection, London.

Kerstan, Horst b.Germany 1941. Studied at the Keramikstudium of the Werkkunstschule, Offenbach-am-Main; later with the import-ant teacher of ceramics, Professor Richard Bampi, in Kandern, Böscherzenweg. Kerstan is a typical German master of glazes, but he is also an example of another European heavily influenced by Oriental ceramics, especially those of Japan. Clearly what interests Kerstan is the ceramic vessel as an object of contemplation; his work is quietly ritualistic in the agnostic way in which Westerners so often interpret Oriental ware. His work is in the Hetjens Museum, Düsseldorf; Württembergisches Landesmuseum, Stuttgart.

Kippenberg, Heide b.Germany 1941. Since 1968 she has had her own workshop in Buch/Weisendorf. Kippenberg concentrates exclusively on making vessels, both thrown and modelled (some-times both combined), in clear, strictly articulated forms.

Koch, Gaby b. Germany 1948. Studied at the University of Heidelberg (English, history, political science); ceramics at Gold-smiths' College, London. Since graduation from Goldsmiths, she has exhibited in Britain, Germany and Switzerland.

Lap, Geert b.Holland 1951. Studied at the Koninklijke Academie, 's-Hertogenbosch; Gerrit Rietveld Academie, Amsterdam. Lap's reputation is for excellent workmanship; his thrown stoneware pots, with their even colouring, strive for perfection without becoming anonymous, like factory-produced ware. He has shown in the USA, Britain and Holland, and has work in several public collections, including the Boymans-van Beuningen Museum, Rotterdam; Stede-lijk Museum, Amsterdam; Fitzwilliam Museum, Cambridge, UK; Museum Kunst und Gewerbe, Hamburg; Musée des Arts, Montreal.

Mansfield, Janet b.Australia 1934. Studied at East Sydney Technical College. She explains that she has long admired Japanese pottery. Mansfield is one of the potters who believes in a holistic approach to the craft – she uses materials found locally, builds her own kilns and enjoys spending weeks alone concentrating on her work. She throws in stoneware, applies salt glaze, slips and ash glazes, and fires either in gas or wood kilns to 1300°C. She is a regular exhibitor and her work is in many public collections, including Museum of

Applied Arts and Science, Sydney; Queensland Art Gallery Brisbane.

Marks, Graham b.USA 1951. Studied at the New York State College of Ceramics, Alfred; Philadelphia College of Art, Philadelphia. Probably one of the most important of a new generation of American ceramists, and one of the few to combine a sense of the decorative with the monumental without the work being overly expressionistic or formalized and geometrical. The forms are made from hundreds of earthenware coils. Although each 'pot' gives an impression of considerable weight and mass, each is either made up of inner structures which are sometimes like a beehive, or split up with a simpler division of walls made from extruded pieces of clay. The piece is generally created upside-down. The interior structures are built first, then the outer walls are constructed over them. These outer walls are themselves not as massive as they look – being of double-wall construction, supported by coiled arches. The coils are produced by an extruder and then rolled by hand. His work is in a number of public collections, including Rochester Institute of Technology, Rochester, New York; Museum of Art, University of Iowa; American Craft Museum, New York.

McNicoll, Carol b.UK 1948. Studied at Leeds Polytechnic; Royal College of Art, London. Her work is ornamentalist, takes risks, and is frequently elaborate in its construction. McNicoll also produces work for factory or semi-factory production, as well as one-off studio pieces. British sculptor, Richard Deacon, notes that a lot of McNicoll's handbuilt work takes advantage of clay's suitability for imitating other materials and techniques – cloth, fruit, weaving and knitting. Though easily one of the most interesting decorative ceramists in Europe, she has attracted hostility from conservative critics anxious to reinstate the brown-pot tradition to which McNicoll is almost instinctively opposed. She has exhibited widely in Britain and Europe. In 1985 she was given a solo exhibition by the Crafts Council, London, accompanied by an illustrated catalogue. Her work may be seen in several public collections; including the Victoria and Albert Museum, London; Crafts Council collection London; Museum Het Princessehof, Leeuwarden, Holland.

Mincham, Jeffery b.Australia 1950. Studied at Western Teachers' College; South Australia School of Art; Tasmanian School of Art. He works exclusively in raku. Mincham throws pots on the wheel, but embellishes them. He is not interested in production pottery for himself, because his ideas will not fit into classic domestic ware. Like Robert Hawkins, he is one of a generation of Australian potters making quasi-ritualistic vessels for an agnostic age. His work is well composed and gracefully decorated. Mincham has had solo exhibitions each year since 1976, as well as contributing to annual group shows, such as the Mayfair Ceramics Award. He appears to be represented in every public collection in Australia.

Mortensen, Ingrid b.Norway 1941. Studied at the National College of Art and Craft and Industrial Design, Oslo. This was followed by practice in workshops in Norway and Denmark. She has had several solo exhibitions in Norway and has exhibited in Germany and Poland. She works in earthenware, producing mainly handbuilt forms. Mortensen is one of a handful of Norwegian potters, mainly women, who have put Norway back on the 'pottery map'. Her work may be seen in the Museum of Art and Craft and Industrial Design, Oslo.

Nagasawa, Setsuko b.Japan 1949. Teaches ceramics at the Ecole Supérieure d'Art Appliqué, Geneva, and has a studio in Geneva. Her solo exhibitions include Palais de l'Athénée, Geneva, 1985; Gallerie De Witte Voet, Amsterdam, 1992. She has made a number of architectural commissions in various media, including a fountain for the Collège Rousseau, Geneva, 1990. She completed an artist's placement at the Europees Keramisch Werkcentrum, Holland,

August 1991–January 1992. Her work displays an interesting and largely successful synthesis of Japanese material sensibility with the practices of Western art movements, such as minimalism.

Nagle, Ron b.USA 1939. Studied at San Francisco University. As well as being a successful potter, he is also a successful songwriter. His work of the last few years owes a debt to Kenneth Price, though he is a long way from being a Price imitator. Nagle's cups work both in the round and as graphic images – they have strong profiles. The cups are fired in an electric kiln, with up to fifteen china-paint firings. Garth Clark quotes him, in the catalogue to *A Century of Ceramics in the United States*, 1979, comparing his pottery with his music: 'they both have flash and style; but I'm also shooting for content.' Since he is a contemporary potter, that content is partly about pottery itself – Nagle makes cups about cups. Widely exhibited. His work may be seen in various public collections including the Everson Museum of Art, Syracuse; American Craft Museum, New York.

Nakamura, Kimpei b.Japan 1935. Born into a family of ceramicists. Professor of Ceramics at Tama Art University, Tokyo. He has exhibited extensively in Japan, including the International Exhibition of Contemporary Ceramics at the Museum of Contemporary Ceramics, Shigaraki. Nakamura has built on the Anglo–Japanese ceramic revival begun by Bernard Leach sixty years ago. He has evolved a thoroughly contemporary idiom which none the less shows its roots in Japanese traditions of clay craft, philosophy, ceremony and domestic ritual.

Nanning, Barbara b.Holland 1957. Studied at the Gerrit Rietveld Academie, Amsterdam. She has exhibited extensively in Europe and is represented in the Museum Boymans-van Beuningen, Rotterdam; Museum Fodor, Amsterdam; Museum Enschede, Twenthe; Streekmuseum, Schiedam.

Nolen, Matt b.USA 1960. Graduated in architecture from Auburn University, Auburn, Alabama. His work is in the Cooper-Hewitt Museum, New York; Gadsden Museum of Art, Alabama. His most recent solo exhibition was at the Everson Museum of Art, Syracuse, 1994. The published reviews and articles that make reference to his work include 'With Cups Raised To a High Art Form', *New York Times*, 7 January 1993; *American Ceramics*, Spring 1992. He shows with the Archon ceramics gallery, New York.

Notkin, Richard b.USA 1948. Studied at Kansas City Art Institute, Kansas, University of California, Davis. Notkin is a miniaturist. He makes tableaux and figurines that are urban but as lovingly observed in their own style as a Bernard Palissy. Much recent work has taken to commentary about the nuclear bomb, although he delivers his homilies with wit. A teapot with a nuclear mushroom handle is a joke more than a polemic. Notkin appears implicitly to recognize the limitations of pottery's capacity for polemic. Solo exhibitions include Garth Clark Gallery, New York 1985, and he has contributed to many group shows. Work may be seen in the National Collections of Fine Arts, Renwick Gallery, Smithsonian Institution, Washington D.C.; Victoria and Albert Museum, London; Stedelijk Museum, Amsterdam.

Orr, Lisa Kay b.USA. Graduated with a BFA in visual arts from the University of Texas, Austin, 1983; and an MFA in ceramics from New State College of Ceramics, Alfred University, New York, 1992. Her exhibitions include *Soup Tureens*, Helen Drutt Gallery, Philadelphia, 1993; *American Ingenuity*, Swidler Gallery, Detroit,1993. She won a Fulbright Student Scholarship to Bulgaria, 1992–93. Her exuberant work has been welcomed by many for its contribution to a contemporary revival in decoration for the home.

Pearson, Colin b.UK 1923. Studied painting at Goldsmiths' College, London. Later worked with Ray Finch, potter, and David Leach. In 1975 he was awarded the 33rd Prix Faenza. He is interesting because of his architectural use of form and some of his richly allusive pots are like medieval angels. His work is in various British collections, including the Victoria and Albert Museum, London; Crafts Council collection, London.

Poncelet, Jacqui b.UK 1947. Studied at the Royal College of Art, London. Like Alison Britton and Elizabeth Fritsch, she rapidly established a reputation as one of Britain's new generation of talented women potters. In the early 1970s she produced finely carved bone-china bowls, but then startled her followers by moving to an altogether different kind of studio pottery using stoneware; the new style was rougher, more masculine and more American in its approach to the craft than her earlier work. Since then her slab-built containers have developed into sculpture and she has now left the vessel tradition – following an exhibition at the influential Whitechapel Art Gallery, London, she has decided that her natural direction is away from pottery. Her work, even more than that of Carol McNicoll, has attracted hostile criticism. Poncelet's contribution to pottery has been innovative and she continued the tradition of pioneering women potters established by such people as Ruth Duckworth. Her work can be seen in public collections in Britain and Holland, including the Victoria and Albert Museum, London; Museum Het Princessehof, Leeuwarden.

Price, Kenneth b.USA 1935. Studied at Chouinard Art Institute, Los Angeles; University of Southern California, Los Angeles; Otis Art Institute, Los Angeles; New York State College of Ceramics, Alfred. Price has constructed a number of pottery 'environmental' works. One of these, called *Happy's Curios: Town Unit 1*, was a walk-in work, a pottery store that was a celebration of decorated ceramic wares. In an interview with writer Joan Simpson, Price described this work, which engaged him for five years, as his Vietnam: 'I was wiped out in every way when I finished. I did what we did in Vietnam at the end – I called it a victory and got the hell out.' For many people Price's cups are among the most beautiful ceramic pots to have come out of the contemporary ceramics movement in the USA. He says: 'With them the functional side can be metaphorical . . . the cup as a motif . . . I've used the cup form in various ways for over 20 years.' The glazes in Price's work are critical. Price has exhibited throughout the USA and his work is in a variety of public collections, including the Museum of Modern Art, New York; Whitney Museum of American Art, New York; Everson Museum of Art, Syracuse. He had a major retrospective, with an accompanying catalogue, at the Walker Art Center, Minneapolis, 1992.

Rasmussen, Peder b.Denmark 1948. Studied at the Nils and Herman Kahler Workshop, Naestved, Denmark; Accademia di Belle Arte, Florence. After returning from Italy, Rasmussen worked briefly as a designer at Kahler Ceramics. Then he focused on earthenware domestic pottery. This was followed by two years in which he concentrated on painting; the ideas he developed have now been translated into the surfaces of his pottery. Since 1983 Rasmussen has worked with raku. He has exhibited widely in Europe and also shown work in the USA and Japan; a founder member of the Danish group of potters called Multi-Mud, he has work in public collections including the following: Museum of Arts and Crafts, Copenhagen; Malmö Kunstmuseum, Sweden; Museum für Moderne Keramik, Deidesheim, Germany; Museum Het Princessehof, Leeuwarden, Holland; Statens Kunstfond, Copenhagen, Denmark.

Regius, Lene b.Denmark 1940. Studied at the Danish Arts and Crafts School, Copenhagen. In an article in *Ceramics Monthly*, September 1982, she said: 'I've always been obsessed by movements in light and structure. The strong light in the coloured mosaics of Mediterranean towns is accentuated by the blue nuances of the sky and sea.' She has exhibited frequently in Denmark and Germany, as well as Sweden, Holland and Japan.

Public collections with her work include Malmö Kunstmuseum, Sweden; Keramikmuseum, Westerwald, Germany.

Rie, Lucie b.Austria 1902. Studied pottery at the Kunstgewerbe-schule, Vienna. She came to England in 1938. In 1946, Hans Coper joined her in her workshop, which they shared until 1960. Lucie Rie is an important potter in Britain, not because she was an innovator, but because she kept alive a decorative tradition which was constantly under assault from modernists, Anglo-Oriental ruralists, expressionists and clay anarchists. For a while her work faltered because Bernard Leach criticised it. John Houston, critic and editor of the book *Lucie Rie*, 1981, says that it was Hans Coper who gave Rie back her confidence in her own – Viennese – decorative approach. Her work is in collections all over Europe, including the Victoria and Albert; Crafts Council, London; Hetjens Museum, Düsseldorf; Württembergisches Landesmuseum, Stuttgart. Lucie Rie was made a Dame in 1991, the highest honour ever awarded to a potter working in Britain.

Rogers, Mary b.Britain 1929. Trained as a graphic designer and then took up pottery. She is a noted authority on handbuilding and is the author of *On Pottery and Porcelain – a handbuilder's approach*, 1979. Her work may be seen in the Crafts Council collection, London; Museum of Modern Art, New York; Keramion, Frechen, Germany; and many other leading public ceramics collections.

Rothman, Jerry b.USA 1933. Studied at the Otis Art Institute, Los Angeles. He has in the past produced some huge ceramic sculptures, the largest being 20' high. However, his vessel forms are very much a part of the pottery tradition and he has managed to produce objects which have been regarded by many people as downright ugly, but which are also very witty. Their wit comes from the way in which Rothman has conflated two opposed aesthetics – the rich, decorative one of Mannerism and the Baroque, and the formalist aesthetic of the Bauhaus – and then covered the result in a Henry Ford black. Hence the phrase 'Bauhaus Baroque', which has been used in connection with Rothman's work. Rothman's work is in many public collections and his famous Campbell's Soup Tureen is held at the Everson Museum of Art, Syracuse.

Sarri, Alessio b.Italy 1957. Studied at the Istituto d'Arte di Porta Romana, Florence. He collaborated on a collection of ceramics with Matteo Thun and he supervised the production of ceramic work designed by Thun, Ettore Sottsass and other designers linked with the Memphis group. Sarri designs and produces his own work – his personal collection is entitled *Mud Stars* and the works are in batch production.

Saxe, Adrian b.USA 1943. Studied at Chouinard Art Institute, Los Angeles. He says: 'I was one of Modernism's cast-outs. My adherence to high craft, to somewhat decadent visual language, and to the use of imagery, among other things, placed me outside the acceptable academy of modern art. It even placed me outside the ceramic mainstream.' Saxe's imagery is derived in part from 18th- and 19th-century European decorated ceramic and metal ware: the recent history of decorative art is one important part of the content of his work. At Saxe's level of bravura refinement, however, craftsmanship also becomes a part of the subject matter, as it does with all highly skilled and elaborate decoration – Fabergé jewelled objects are an example. Saxe is self-consciously an intellectual craftsman. He has had several solo exhibitions at the American Hand Gallery, Washington D.C., and he shows also with the Garth Clark Gallery, Los Angeles.

Schaffer, Elisabeth b.Austria 1935. After being taught pottery by Leopold Anzengruber in Vienna, Schaffer went to Spain on a study course (1954–55), then to the Akademie für angewandte Kunst in Vienna. She shared a workshop in Vienna from 1961 to 1965 with Iris Brendel and Gerda Spurey. Since 1965 she has lived in or near Munich. In addition to stoneware table services, since 1974 sculptural vessels and sculptures built up from overlapping and interlocking layers of porcelain have become an increasingly important part of Schaffer's artistic output.

Scheid, Karl b.Germany 1929, and **Scheid, Ursula** b.Germany 1932. Attended F. T. Schroeder's ceramics class at the Lehrwerkstätte für bildende Kunst, Darmstadt, at different times, Karl 1949–52, Ursula 1952–54. Since 1956 they have had their own workshop in Büdingen-Düdelsheim. The Scheids are in the modern German tradition of producing finely wrought pots which are subtly glazed. Pieces with relief decoration are by Karl, while the somewhat more rounded, not so sharply angled forms (apart from simple dishes and bowls) are by Ursula. The appeal of their work is to the eye and the hand – they are like attractive fruits. The Scheids are among Germany's most important potters, although the younger generation of potters is showing more interest in sculptural and constructivist forms. Work by Scheids can be seen in all the major public collections in Germany, including the Hetjens Museum, Düsseldorf; Keramion, Frechen; Württembergisches Landesmuseum, Stuttgart.

Shaw, Richard b.USA 1941. Studied at Orange Coast College, Costa Mesa, California; San Francisco Art Institute; New York State College of Ceramics, Alfred. Shaw works in porcelain, employing the craft of assemblage. Fanciful though the comparison might be, Shaw's work could be seen as a modern equivalent of Meissen ware. His work epitomizes several things: first, the versatility and malleability of clay; secondly, the fascination with illusion and Disneyworld replicas that seems to be part of the American psyche. He has had a series of solo exhibitions with the Quay and then the Braunstein galleries, San Francisco. See *A Century of Ceramics* by Garth Clark and Margie Hughto, 1979; *Ceramic Sculpture: Six Artists*, catalogue by Suzanne Foley and Richard Marshall for the Whitney Museum of American Art, New York 1981–82.

Slee, Richard b.Britain 1946. Studied at the Central School of Art and Design, London. Slee works mostly by handbuilding or press moulding. He excels in the use of colour and is fascinated by the idea of excess in decoration. He has few counterparts among contemporary ceramists. Indeed, the most appropriate point of comparison is with a British artist, one-time ceramist, Edward Allington, a *fin-de-siècle* ornamentalist sculptor. Slee works from 18th-, 19th- and 20th-century industrial decorative ceramic precedents, but never directly imitates earlier work. He modifies his historical references to act both as decoration and commentary. The Victoria and Albert Museum and the Crafts Council collection, London, have examples of his work, as do public collections in Holland.

Smith, Martin b.Britain 1950. Studied at Bristol Polytechnic; Royal College of Art, London. He works with red earthenware. Smith is one of the new generation of potters who use the idea of a 'vessel' as a theme for their work; architectural references are also present. He fits well into the contemporary mannerist phase in ceramics or, as curator Antony Wells-Cole has put it: 'Smith's work is calculated, highly sophisticated . . . founded on extreme technical competence.' See exhibition leaflet accompanying Smith's solo exhibition at the British Crafts Centre, London 1985. Since 1989 Smith has been the senior tutor in ceramics at the Royal College of Art. He is one of the very few ceramicists to have taken occupancy of the territory known as abstract tabletop sculpture so cleverly opened up by the sculptor Sir Anthony Caro in the 1970s.

Sperer Scope, Gaby b.Canada. Graduated with a BFA from Concordia University, Montreal, 1991; resident artist at the Banff Centre for the Arts, 1993. Among her solo exhibitions have been *Reflection*, The Other Gallery, Banff; *Timeless Journey*, Barbara

Silverberg, Montreal. Of her work she says, 'I try to convey . . . a sense of journey through ceremony.' Many of her pots take the form of primitive boats and there are always strong allusions to the wild Canadian continent, both through her imagery and through the range of rich textures she has developed in her glazes.

Staffel, Rudy b.USA 1911. Studied painting under various artists, including Hans Hofmann, then studied at the Art Institute of Chicago. In 1940 he joined the staff of the Tyler School of Art, Philadelphia, and taught there for 38 years. He became interested in porcelain in the 1950s. At first his porcelain pieces were decorated with strong colours, but now he is concerned only with white and with light. He is an expressionist in clay, but not like Voulkos or Duckworth: he is a 'watercolourist'. Staffel has been involved with Buddhism and, in response to a question about spontaneity in his work, replied: 'Spontaneity would have to do with the physical mudra or gesture that encompasses Buddhism. That is, the same moment can never happen twice, so be aware of it as it passes.' Staffel has exhibited widely and is represented by the Helen Drutt Gallery, Philadelphia.

Suttie, Angus 1946–92. Studied at the Camberwell School of Art and Craft, London. Suttie's work was eccentric and wayward. He made random shapes from flat slabs of clay and then joined these shapes together in a loose assemblage. He was an idealist, an optimist who wanted his work to give pleasure. In many respects he is one of the most baffling potters in this book – he may have been a sort of Kurt Schwitters, though the objects he found are in his own psyche, which must – for obvious reasons – make it difficult to understand his work. He exhibited quite widely and is represented in several important public collections in Britain and Holland, including the Victoria and Albert, London; Kruithuis Museum, 's-Hertogenbosch, Holland.

Swen, Hiroe b.Japan 1934. Australian resident. Studied at Kyoto Crafts Institute. She has had a series of solo exhibitions, mainly at the Pastoral Gallery, Canberra, and her work is in many public collections in Australia, including the Crafts Board of the Australia Council, Sydney; Queensland Art Gallery, Brisbane.

Tchalenko, Janice b.UK 1942. Studied at the Harrow School of Art, London. At first she worked within the Bernard Leach tradition, but at the end of the 1970s drew away from it by experimenting with high-fire glazes. The results brought an extravagance of colour to British domestic craft pottery and she was the first to revive natural forms – flowers and animals – as a theme for its pattern and decoration. Her work is probably the most popular of the serious craft pottery produced in Britain. Although, naturally, she has exhibited extensively in Britain, her most important solo show was at the Blum Helman Gallery, New York 1985. All her work is in stoneware, much of it wheel-thrown or press moulded. It can be seen in public collections, such as the Victoria and Albert Museum, London; Crafts Council collection, London.

Thun, Matteo b.Italy 1952. Studied at the Academy of Oscar Kokoschka, Salzburg, Austria. Thun is an architect and a designer, not a ceramist as such. However, the designs he has had executed through close involvement with designer-craftsman Alessio Sarri are of great interest and importance to contemporary ceramics, since their radical re-interpretation of 1930s styling is a new look for what is, essentially, craft or studio pottery. The overlap of craft and design could well be one of the more exciting developments for the applied arts generally, as Western applied artists become more engaged with ideas, and designers become more engaged in pushing materials to their limits. Both craftsmen and designers can use batch rather than mass production as a means of satisfying consumer interests – interests which are seldom as uniform as orthodox design training has imagined. Thun was a founding

member of the Memphis design group. Currently he is professor of product design and ceramics at the University of Applied Arts in Vienna.

Turner, Robert b.USA 1913. Studied at Swarthmore College, Pennsylvania; Pennsylvania Academy of Fine Arts; New York State College of Ceramics, Alfred. Turner is regarded as one of the founders of the 'new ceramic presence' in the USA. In 1949 he went to Black Mountain College in Carolina, where a number of artists were working, including John Cage, Franz Kline, and Willem and Elaine de Kooning. By the end of the 1960s Turner felt he was responding to the aesthetic of another time. The reverence he felt for Oriental culture, its forms and glazes, had brought him to a kind of perfection that he perceived as a 'dead end'. He had to face up to one of the challenges confronting the contemporary potter – how to do something new and individual. The history of pottery is full of perfect culs-de-sac. Turner's response to that challenge was good: simple and strong. He is, I believe, a natural heir to Hans Coper and in some respects makes more successful pots. Robert Turner is represented by Exhibit A Gallery, Chicago.

Van Loon, Johan b.Holland 1934. Studied textiles in Amsterdam and Copenhagen. Later studied ceramics with Jan van der Vaart and Lucie Rie. He has worked frequently for the Royal Copenhagen Factory.

Varlan, Claude b.France 1940. Studied applied arts and worked in a variety of other potters' studios before establishing his own. He is a ruralist – a fact amply demonstrated by his pottery.

Verwiel, Jos b.Holland 1954. Studied ceramics and sculpture at the Academies of Tilburg and 's-Hertogenbosch. He was travelled extensively in North America and has acquired for himself an impressive curriculum vitae of exhibitions. His work is essentially sculpture, but he has also produced forms which are clearly centred on the vessel. He uses the vessel as a point of reference, with implied 'function' as a metaphor. The clay is handled skilfully and with a workmanlike roughness which recalls an American rather than European aesthetic.

Vonck, Irene b.Ireland 1952, lives and works in Holland. Studied Falmouth School of Art, UK; Brighton Polytechnic, UK; Gerrit Rietveld Academie, Amsterdam. She has exhibited extensively, but especially in Holland, Britain and the USA. Her work lives up to her own description of it as a 'celebration of colour and movement'. When it succeeds, it is exuberant and baroque; when it fails, it fails totally. She is quite untypical of the prevailing Dutch design orthodoxy in clay work and her natural peers in Holland are very few. Her work is in the following public collections: Stedelijk Museum, Amsterdam; Museum Fodor, Amsterdam; Museum Boymans-van Beuningen, Rotterdam; Museum Het Princessehof, Leeuwarden.

Voulkos, Peter b.USA 1924. Studied painting at Montana State University (graduated 1949) and for a masters degree in ceramics at California College of Arts and Crafts (graduated 1952). In 1951 he began working at the Archie Bray Foundation in Montana with the resident sculptor, Rudy Autio. Voulkos was one of six artists in the *Ceramic Sculpture* exhibition of 1981–82 at the Whitney Museum of American Art; the exhibition catalogue entry declared: 'Peter Voulkos introduced, established, and extended alternatives to the uses of clay for sculptural expression, liberating a new generation of artists from restrictions and traditions imposed by ceramic history and technique.' Much has been made of Voulkos the sculptor by those in the fine-art area, but still Voulkos's most significant contribution has been to the history and living tradition of pottery. He has carried it on a long way – a genuine innovator skilled enough to get his forms established as part of the ceramic craft movement. A press release for an exhibition of his work in 1979 at the Exhibit A

Gallery, Chicago, states: 'In more than thirty years' work, Voulkos has continued to find vitality and validity in the manipulation of basic pottery forms – the jar, the pot, the plate.' His most significant contribution is his sense for volume. Voulkos has been an important teacher and exemplar for younger clay workers, but many have been misguided by the seeming ease with which he works. The followers of Voulkos have often interpreted the generous roughness of his volumes as 'clumsiness'. See *A Century of Ceramics in the United States* by Garth Clark and Margie Hughto, 1979; *American Potters* by Garth Clark, 1981; and the following articles: 'Peter Voulkos: Redemption Through Ceramics' by John Coplans, *Art News*, July 1965; *Peter Voulkos: A Dialogue with Clay* by Rose Slivka, 1978; 'Peter Voulkos: The Clay's the Thing' by Sylvia Brown, *Art in America*, March/April 1979; 'Peter Voulkos in Japan' by Junko Iwabuchi, *Ceramic Monthly*, September 1983; 'Peter Voulkos' by Richard Armstrong, *Artforum*, November 1983. He was awarded an honorary doctorate of fine arts by the San Francisco Art Institute, 1982; a Guggenheim Fellowship, 1984; and a Gold Medal from the American Crafts Council, 1986. In 1993 the Perimeter Gallery, Chicago, gave Voulkos his most important solo exhibition for ten years. The *Chicago Tribune* said of his ceramics: 'They are by one of the finest artists in America and this is an important, highly satisfying show.'

Weigel, Gerald b.Germany 1925, and **Weigel, Gotlind** b.Germany 1935. Since 1961 they have shared a workshop, first in Mainz, then (from 1967) in the Westerwald, and since 1973 in Gabsheim. Gerald has concentrated on the development of glazes, in particular feldspar glazes coloured with cobalt, manganese and rutile oxides. Unlike his wife's thrown works, his are built up and modelled from discs of clay. Since 1969 he has focused on a 'winged' or 'shield' form made from two such discs (similarly shaped and slightly concave) joined together. In 1973 Gotlind developed her 'calyx' vases with their broad, seemingly weightless, undulating rims above hollow cylindrical or oval bodies – forms that were further developed, around 1978, into sculptures. In the mid-1980s her pottery became more concentrated on 'classic' vase shapes.

Winokur, Paula b.USA. Studied at the Tyler School of Art, Philadelphia; New York State College of Ceramics, Alfred. Paula Winokur's recent porcelain still-lifes take some of their quality from Giorgio Morandi's still-life paintings of jars and bottles. Winokur's work is reflective and thoughtful, and one of its themes is secrecy, memories and private musings. She has exhibited extensively and has shown with the Helen Drutt Gallery, Philadelphia; Jackie Chalkley Gallery, Washington D.C.; *The International Symposium Exhibition*, Tolgyfa Gallery, Budapest, Hungary, 1994; the Dorothy McCrae Gallery, Atlanta, Georgia, 1994. Her work has been collected by the Museum of American Art, Renwick Gallery, Smithsonian Institution, Washington, D.C., 1994.

Winokur, Robert b.USA. Studied at New York State College of Ceramics, Alfred; Tyler School of Art, Philadelphia. Originally Winokur was much involved with functional pottery. Although he still retains the vessel form, he is trying to nudge his pottery away to the point where it can be regarded in its own right and not justified in its existence either by function or by reference to some other art form. He has fulfilled a number of public arts commissions, as well as showing in many exhibitions, including the Dorothy McCrae Gallery, Atlanta, and the *Soup Tureén* Exhibition, Helen Drutt Gallery, Philadelphia, both 1993. He completed an artist's residency in the International Ceramic Studio, Kecskemet, Hungary, 1993.

Wood, Beatrice b.USA 1894. Studied in Paris and then went on to the stage. She met Marcel Duchamp and then got to know Francis Picabia, Man Ray and others. She took up ceramics just before the last World War and, when she returned to the USA, she studied with Glen Lukens (a pioneer of American pottery and pottery education) and, briefly, with Gertrude and Otto Natzler. She frequently steers a risky course between high decoration and absolute kitsch; her pottery is generally exciting for its glazing and surface texture even when the forms are wayward. In 1994 she had her 100th birthday.

Woodman, Betty b.USA 1930. Studied at the New York State College of Ceramics, Alfred. One of Woodman's best-known forms is the 'pillow pitcher'; this is frequently decorated very loosely and it gives the sensation that, if you were to jab it, it would deflate. The sensation is heightened by the stiffness of the pitcher's neck compared to its billowing body. Woodman exploits the fact that clay can look soft when it is hard. Her work is not rough-and-ready, but it is broad in its construction – you can trace its manufacture backwards. She works in earthenware and her forms are most often Chinese in origin, whilst the decoration is an amalgam of Mediterranean brightness and post-Pollock deftness. Her work has evolved into more narrative and self-consciously 'art-like' forms, such as her intriguing *Still Life Vase*, made in 1990. She had a major retrospective in Hartford, Connecticut, 1992.

Zimmerman, Arnold b.USA 1954. Studied Kansas City Art Institute, Kansas City; New York State College of Ceramics, Alfred University, New York. Zimmerman carves into his very large clay pots, over 2 metres high. His earlier work, jugs and large drinking vessels, were roughly but not crudely made. Then he hit on the idea of making a large vessel and adding to it smaller vessels as a decoration. He is in the American tradition of strong workmanlike craftsmanship. A collection of his largest pieces is to be seen outside the Everson Museum of Art, Syracuse, New York.

GALLERIES AND MUSEUMS

The following selection of galleries and museums, in which modern ceramics may be seen, is intended as a cross-section – it is not a comprehensive directory of galleries. Many other worthwhile galleries and museums can be discovered through the specialist magazines listed on p. 231. This is especially true of the USA.

Australia

Art Gallery of South Australia, North Terrace, Adelaide 5000, South Australia
Aspect Design, 79 Salamanca Place, Hobart 7000, Tasmania
Australian Craft, 2 Waitomo Plaza, Southport 4215, Queensland
Australian Craftworks, 127 George Street, Sydney, New South Wales
The Australian Design Centre, 70 George Street, The Rocks, Sydney 2000, New South Wales
Australian National Gallery, PO Box 1150, Canberra, ACT 2601
Beaver Galleries, 81B Denison Street, Deakin, ACT 2600
Blackfriars, 172 St Johns Road, Glebe, New South Wales
Cuppacumbalong Craft Centre, Naas Road, Tharwa, ACT 2620
Distelfink Gallery, 43 Burwood Road, Hawthorne 3122, Victoria
Elmswood Fine Craft, 312 Unley Road, Hyde Park, Adelaide, South Australia
Gary Anderson Gallery, 13 McDonald Street, Paddington, New South Wales 2021
Handmark Gallery, 44–6 Hampden Road, Battery Point, Hobart 700, Tasmania
Inner City Clayworkers Gallery, 103 St Johns Road, Glebe 2037, New South Wales
The Jam Factory Craft Centre, 169 Payneham Road, St Peter's Stepney, South Australia
National Gallery of Victoria, Victoria Arts Centre, 180 St Kilda Road, Melbourne 3000, Victoria
The Potters' Gallery, 8 Burton Street, Darlinghurst, Sydney, New South Wales
The Powerhouse, Museum of Applied Arts and Sciences, 500 Harris Street, Ultimo, Sydney, New South Wales 2000
Seasons Gallery, Range Road, North Sydney 2060, New South Wales
Temnoku Gallery, Napoleon Close, Cottisloe, Western Australia
Walker Ceramics Gallery, 826 Glenferrie Road, Hawthorn, Victoria
The Western Australian Art Gallery, Beaufort Street, Perth 6000, Western Australia

Austria

Keramic Studio, Krugerstrasse 18, A 1010 Vienna
Österreichisches Museum für Angewandte Kunst, Stubenring 5, A 1010 Vienna

Belgium

Argile, rue de Neufchâtel 5A, B 1050 Brussels

Atelier 18, rue du Président 18, B 1050 Brussels
Galerie Desko, Hoogledestraat, B 8110 Kostermsark
Galerie La Main, 215 rue de la Victoire, B 1060 Brussels
Galerie Le Volcan, 13 rue Charles Dupret, B 6000 Charleroi
Musées d'Archéolgie et d'Arts Décoratifs, Quai de Maastricht 10, B 54000 Liège

Canada

The Art Gallery at Harbourfront, 235 Queen's Quay West, Toronto, Ontario
Canada National Museum, Ottawa, Ontario
The Canadian Craft Museum, 1411 Cartwright Street, Vancouver, British Columbia V6H 3R7
Musée des Arts Décoratifs de Montréal, 2929 Jeanne d'Arc, Montreal H1W 3W2
Prime Canadian Crafts, 229 Queen Street, W. Toronto, Ontario
Quest Gallery, 105 Banff Avenue, Banff, Alberta
Quest Gallery, 1023 Government Street, Victoria, British Columbia
Royal Ontario Museum, Toronto, Ontario

Denmark

Arhus Kunstmuseum, H. Guldbergsgade 2, DK 8000, Arhus C
Damhuset Kunsthandvaerk, Lyngby Hovedgade 1C, DK 2800, Lyngby
Dansk Kunsthandvaerk, Amagertorv 1, DK 1160, Copenhagen
Galleri Egelund, Ny Ostergade 11, DK 1101, Copenhagen
Gallerie Q, Store Kongens Gade 96, DK 1264, Copenhagen
Holstebro Kunstmuseum, Herngvej 1, Holstebro
Kunstindustrimuseet, Bredgade 68, DK 1260, Copenhagen K
Selskabet Til Handarbejdets Fremme, Tranevej 15, DK 2400, Copenhagen NV
Selskabet Til Handarbejdets Fremme, Lyngby Stottcenter 42, DK 2800, Lyngby
Strandstraede Keramik, Lille Strandstraede 12, DK 1254, Copenhagen K

Eire

H Q Gallery, Powerscourt Townhouse Centre, South William Street, Dublin 2

Finland

Artisaani, Unioninkatu 28, SF 00100, Helsinki
Pot Viapori, Suomenlinna B 45, SF 00190, Helsinki
Suomen Lasimuseo, Tehtaankatu 23, SF 11910, Riihimäki
Taideteollisuus Museo, Korkeavuorenkatu 23, SF 00130, Helsinki

France

Galerie les Couteliers, 27 rue des Couteliers, Nîmes
Galerie Epona, 40 rue Quincampoix, F 75002, Paris

Galerie Noella Gest, 5 rue de la Commume, 13210, Saint-Remy-de-Provence
Galerie le Labyrinthe, 3 place du Duché, 30700, Uzès
Galerie Nestor Perkal, 8 rue des Quatre-Fils, F 75003, Paris
Galerie Sarver, 20 rue St Paul, 75004, Paris
Maison de la Céramique, 25 rue Josué Hofer, F 68200, Mulhouse
Musée des Arts Décoratifs, 107 rue de Rivoli, 75001, Paris
Musée d'Art Moderne du Nord, Allée du Musée, 5650, Villeneuve d'Ascq
Musée Municipal de Céramique, place de la Mairie, F 06220, Vallauris
Musée National de la Céramique, place de la Manufacture, F 92310, Sèvres
Place des Arts, 8 rue Argenterie, 34000, Montpellier

Germany

Badisches Landesmuseum, Schloss, 7500 Karlsruhe 1
Bredeneyer Galerie, Bredeneyer Strasse 19, 4300 Essen 1
Forum Form Clemenswerth, Schloss Clemenswerth, 4475 Sögel
Galerie An Gross St Martin, An Gross St Martin, Nr 6, 5000 Cologne 1
Galerie Art du Feu, Weinhofberg 5, D 7900 Ulm
Galerie b 15, Baaderstrasse 15, D 8000 Munich 5
Galerie Bowig, Am Rathaus, Friedrichstrasse 2A, D 3000 Hanover 1
Galerie Charlotte Hennig, Rheinstrasse 18, 6100 Darmstadt
Galerie der Kunsthandwerker, Danziger Strasse 40, 2000 Hamburg
Galerie für Englische Keramik, Allmenstrasse 31, D 6902 Sanhausen/Heidelberg
Galerie Handwerk, Handwerkspflege in Bayern, Ottostrasse 7, 8000 Munich
Galerie Handwerk, Rizzastrasse 24–26, 5400 Koblenz
Galerie Keramika, Ursula Felzman, Am Wollhaus 18, 7100 Heilbronn
Galerie L, Elbchaussee 31, D 2000 Hamburg 11
Galerie Somers, Ladenburger Strasse 21, 6900 Heidelberg
Galerie Terrakota, Feldstrasse 40, 2300 Kiel
Galerie Dr. Fritz Vehring, Bremer Weg 4, 2800 Syke
Hetjens Museum, Deutsches Keramikmuseum, Palais Nesselröde, Schulstrasse 4, 4000 Düsseldorf
Keramik-Galerie Dr. G & E Schneider, Reidbergstrasse 33, 7800 Freiburg-Günterstal
Keramik-Galerie Wulfter Turm, Sutthauser Strasse 354, 5400 Osnabrück
Keramik-Galerie Böwig, Am Ballhof-Kreuzstrasse 1, 3000 Hanover
Keramikmuseum Westerwald, Lindenstrasse, D 5410 Höhr-Grenzhausen
Keramik-Studio Edith Somerfield, Grenzstrasse 33, 4200 Oberhausen